COMPUTER ALGORITHMS

Introduction to Design and Analysis

COMPUTER ALGORITHMS

Introduction to Design and Analysis

Harish Gupta

ANMOL PUBLICATIONS PVT. LTD.
NEW DELHI-110 002 (INDIA)

ANMOL PUBLICATIONS PVT. LTD.
Regd. Office: 4360/4, Ansari Road, Daryaganj,
New Delhi-110002 (India)
Tel.: 23278000, 23261597, 23286875, 23255577
Fax: 91-11-23280289
Email: anmolpub@gmail.com
Visit us at: www.anmolpublications.com

Branch Office: No. 1015, Ist Main Road, BSK IIIrd Stage
IIIrd Phase, IIIrd Block, Bangalore-560 085 (India)
Tel.: 080-41723429 • Fax: 080-26723604
Email: anmolpublicationsbangalore@gmail.com

Computer Algorithms: Introduction to Design and Analysis

First Edition, 2011

ISBN 978-81-261-4518-8

PRINTED IN INDIA

Printed at Mehra Offset Press, Delhi.

Contents

Preface

This book is intended to survey the most important computer algorithms which are in use today and to teach fundamental techniques to the growing number of people in need of knowing them. The book provides a comprehensive introduction to the modern study of computer algorithms. It presents many algorithms and covers them in considerable depth, yet makes their design and analysis accessible to all levels.

With this text, you gain an understanding of the fundamental concepts of algorithms, the very heart of computer science. It introduces the basic data structures and programming techniques often used in efficient algorithms. Covers use of lists, push-down stacks, queues, trees, and graphs. Later chapters go into sorting, searching and graphing algorithms, the string-matching algorithms, and the Schonhage Strassen integer-multiplication algorithm.

The book is very comprehensive in algorithms, which covers divide-and-conquer, greedy methods, dynamic programming, searching techniques, branch-and-bound, NP-complete, and other important and advanced topics that an algorithm course might have. The book serves as textbook cum reference manual for Computer, Information Technology and Electronics Engineers.

Author

Chapter 1

Introduction

ALGORITHMS

In mathematics, computing, and related subjects, an algorithm is an effective method for solving a problem using a finite sequence of instructions.

Each algorithm is a list of well-defined instructions for completing a task. Starting from an initial state, the instructions describe a computation that proceeds through a well-defined series of successive states, eventually terminating in a final ending state. The transition from one state to the next is not necessarily deterministic; some algorithms, known as randomized algorithms, incorporate randomness.

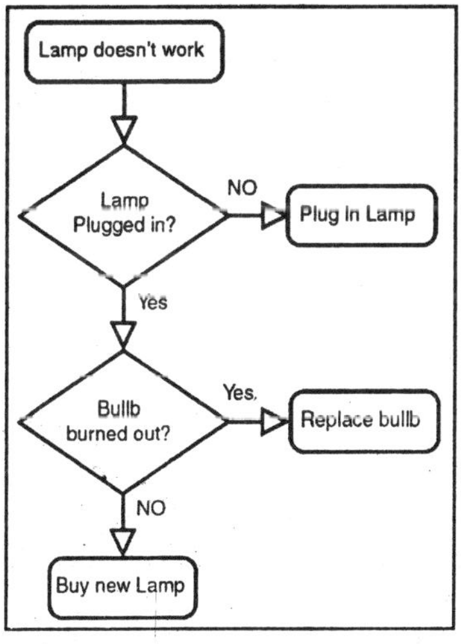

While there is no generally accepted *formal* definition of

"algorithm", an informal definition could be "a process that performs some sequence of operations." For some people, a Programme is only an algorithm if it stops eventually. For others, a Programme is only an algorithm if it stops before a given number of calculation steps.

A prototypical example of an algorithm is Euclid's algorithm to determine the maximum common divisor of two integers. We can derive clues to the issues involved and an informal meaning of the word from the following quotation from Boolos & Jeffrey:

No human being can write fast enough, or long enough, or small enough† (†"smaller and smaller without limit...you'd be trying to write on molecules, on atoms, on electrons") to list all members of an enumerably infinite set by writing out their No human being can write fast enough, or long enough,names, one after another, in some notation.

But humans can do something equally useful, in the case of certain enumerably infinite sets: They can give explicit instructions for determining the *n*th member of the set, for arbitrary finite *n*.

Such instructions are to be given quite explicitly, in a form in which they could be followed by a computing machine, or by a human who is capable of carrying out only very elementary operations on symbols

FORMALIZATION

Algorithms are essential to the way computers process information. Many computer Programmes contain algorithms that specify the specific instructions a computer should perform (in a specific order) to carry out a specified task, such as calculating employees' paychecks or printing students' report cards. Thus, an algorithm can be considered to be any sequence of operations that can be simulated by a Turing-completesystem.

Typically, when an algorithm is associated with processing information, data is read from an input source, written to an output device, and/or stored for further processing. Stored data is regarded as part of the internal state of the entity performing the algorithm. In practice, the state is stored in one or more data structures.

For any such computational process, the algorithm must be rigorously defined: specified in the way it applies in all possible circumstances that could arise. That is, any conditional steps must be systematically dealt with, case-by-case; the criteria for each case must be clear (and computable).

Because an algorithm is a precise list of precise steps, the order of computation will always be critical to the functioning of the algorithm. Instructions are usually assumed to be listed explicitly, and are described as starting "from the top" and going "down to the bottom", an idea that is described more formally by *flow of control.*

So far, this discussion of the formalization of an algorithm has assumed the premises of imperative Programmeming. This is the most common conception, and it attempts to describe a task in discrete, "mechanical" means.

Unique to this conception of formalized algorithms is the assignment, setting the value of a variable. It derives from the intuition of "memory" as a scratchpad. There is an example below of such an assignment.

TERMINATION

But if the length of the process isn't known in advance, then "trying" it may not be decisive, because if the process does go on forever — then at no time will we ever be sure of the answer.

As it happens, no other method can do any better, as was shown by Alan Turing with his celebrated result on the undesirability of the so-called halting. There is no algorithmic procedure for determining of arbitrary algorithms whether or not they terminate from given starting states. The analysis of algorithms for their likelihood of termination is called termination analysis.

The examples of (im-)"proper" subtraction at partial function for more about what can happen when an algorithm fails for certain of its input numbers — e.g.,

- Non-termination,

- Production of "junk" (output in the wrong format to be considered a number) or no number(s) at all (halt ends the computation with no output),
- Wrong number(s),
- A combination of these.

Kleene proposed that the production of "junk" or failure to produce a number is solved by having the algorithm detect these instances and produce e.g., an error message (he suggested "0"), or preferably, force the algorithm into an endless loop.

EXPRESSING ALGORITHMS

Algorithms can be expressed in many kinds of notation, including natural languages, pseudo code, flowcharts, Programmeming languages orcontrol tables (processed by interpreters). Natural language expressions of algorithms tend to be verbose and ambiguous, and are rarely used for complex or technical algorithms. Pseudocode, flowcharts and control tables are structured ways to express algorithms that avoid many of the ambiguities common in natural language statements, while remaining independent of a particular implementation language. Programmeming languages are primarily intended for expressing algorithms in a form that can be executed by a computer, but are often used as a way to define or document algorithms.

There is a wide variety of representations possible and one can express a given Turing machine Programme as a sequence of machine tables (see more at finite state machine and state transition table), as flowcharts (see more at state diagram), or as a form of rudimentary machine code or assembly code called "sets of quadruples"..

Sometimes it is helpful in the description of an algorithm to supplement small "flow charts" (state diagrams) with natural-language and/or arithmetic expressions written inside "block diagrams" to summarize what the "flow charts" are accomplishing.

Representations of algorithms are generally classed into three accepted levels of Turing machine description:

- *High-level description*: "...prose to describe an algorithm, ignoring the implementation details. At this level we do not need to mention how the machine manages its tape or head."
- *Implementation description*: "...prose used to define the way the Turing machine uses its head and the way that it stores data on its tape. At this level we do not give details of states or transition function."
- *Formal description*: Most detailed, "lowest level", gives the Turing machine's "state table".

COMPUTER ALGORITHMS

In computer systems, an algorithm is basically an instance of logic written in software by software developers to be effective for the intended "target" computer(s), in order for the software on the target machines to *do something*. For instance, if a person is writing software that is supposed to print out a PDF document located at the operating system folder "/My Documents" at computer drive "D:" every Friday, they will write an algorithm that specifies the following actions: "If today's date (computer time) is 'Friday,' open the document at 'D:/My Documents' and call the 'print' function".

While this simple algorithm does not look into whether the printer has enough paper or whether the document has been moved into a different location, one can make this algorithm more robust and anticipate these problems by rewriting it as a formal CASE statement or as a (carefully crafted) sequence of IF-THEN-ELSE statements. For example the CASE statement might appear as follows (there are other possibilities):

- *Case* 1: IF today's date is NOT Friday THEN *exit this CASE instruction* ELSE
- *Case* 2: IF today's date is Friday AND the document is located at 'D:/My Documents' AND there is paper in the printer THEN print the document (and *exit this CASE instruction*) ELSE
- *Case* 3: IF today's date is Friday AND the document is NOT located at 'D:/My Documents' THEN display

'document not found' error message (and *exit this CASE instruction*) ELSE

- *Case* 4: IF today's date is Friday AND the document is located at 'D:/My Documents' AND there is NO paper in the printer THEN, (i) display 'out of paper' error message (ii) *exit*. Note that CASE 3 includes two possibilities: (i) the document is NOT located at 'D:/My Documents' AND there's paper in the printer OR (ii) the document is NOT located at 'D:/My Documents' AND there's NO paper in the printer.

The sequence of IF-THEN-ELSE tests might look like this:

- *Test* 1: IF today's date is NOT Friday THEN *done* ELSE TEST 2:
- *Test* 2: IF the document is NOT located at 'D:/My Documents' THEN display 'document not found' error message ELSE TEST 3:
- *Test* 3: IF there is NO paper in the printer THEN display 'out of paper' error message ELSE print the document.

These examples' logic grants precedence to the instance of "NO document at 'D:/My Documents' ".

ANALYSIS OF ALGORITHMS

PROGRAMS

When analyzing a Programme in terms of efficiency, we want to look at questions such as, "How long does it take for the Programme to run?" and "Is there another approach that will get the answer more quickly?" Efficiency will always be less important than correctness; if you don't care whether a Programme works correctly, you can make it run very quickly indeed, but no one will think it's much of an achievement! On the other hand, a Programme that gives a correct answer after ten thousand years isn't very useful either, so efficiency is often an important issue.

The term "efficiency" can refer to efficient use of almost any resource, including time, computer memory, disk space, or network bandwidth. In this section, however, we will deal exclusively with time efficiency, and the major question that we want to ask about a Programme is, how long does it take to perform its task?

It really makes little sense to classify an individual Programme as being "efficient" or "inefficient." It makes more sense to compare two (correct) Programmes that perform the same task and ask which one of the two is "more efficient," that is, which one performs the task more quickly. However, even here there are difficulties.

The running time of a Programme is not well-defined. The run time can be different depending on the number and speed of the processors in the computer on which it is run and, in the case of Java, on the design of the Java Virtual Machine which is used to interpret the Programme.

It can depend on details of the compiler which is used to translate the Programme from high-level language to machine language. Furthermore, the run time of a Programme depends on the size of the problem which the Programme has to solve. It takes a sorting Programme longer to sort 10000 items than it takes it to sort 100 items.

When the run times of two Programmes are compared, it often happens that Programme A solves small problems faster than Programme B, while Programme B solves large problems faster than Programme A, so that it is simply not the case that one Programme is faster than the other in all cases.

In spite of these difficulties, there is a field of computer science dedicated to analyzing the efficiency of Programmes. The field is known as Analysis of Algorithms. The focus is on algorithms, rather than on Programmes as such, to avoid having to deal with multiple implementations of the same algorithm written in different languages, compiled with different compilers, and running on different computers. Analysis of Algorithms is a mathematical field that abstracts away from these down-and-dirty details.

Still, even though it is a theoretical field, every working Programmemer should be aware of some of its techniques and results. This section is a very brief introduction to some of those techniques and results. Because this is not a mathematics book, the treatment will be rather informal. One of the main techniques of analysis of algorithms is asymptotic analysis. The term "asymptotic" here means basically "the tendency in the long run." An asymptotic analysis of an algorithm's run time looks at the question of how the run time depends on the size of the problem.

The analysis is asymptotic because it only considers what happens to the run time as the size of the problem increases without limit; it is not concerned with what happens for problems of small size or, in fact, for problems of any fixed finite size. Only what happens in the long run, as the problem size increases without limit, is important.

Showing that Algorithm A is asymptotically faster than Algorithm B doesn't necessarily mean that Algorithm A will run faster than Algorithm B for problems of size 10 or size 1000 or even size 1000000 – it only means that if you keep increasing the problem size, you will eventually come to a point where Algorithm A is faster than Algorithm B. An asymptotic analysis is only a first approximation, but in practice it often gives important and useful information.

Using this notation, we might say, for example, that an algorithm has a running time that is $O(n^2)$ or $O(n)$ or $O(\log(n))$. These notations are read "Big-Oh of n squared," "Big-Oh of n," and "Big-Oh of log n" (where log is a logarithm function). More generally, we can refer to $O(f(n))$ ("Big-Oh of f of n"), where $f(n)$ is some function that assigns a positive real number to every positive integer n. The "n" in this notation refers to the size of the problem.

Before you can even begin an asymptotic analysis, you need some way to measure problem size. Usually, this is not a big issue. For example, if the problem is to sort a list of items, then the problem size can be taken to be the number of items in the list. When the input to an algorithm is an integer, as in the case of an algorithm that checks whether a given positive integer is prime, the usual measure of the size of a problem is the number of bits in the input integer rather than the integer itself. More generally, the number of bits in the input to a problem is often a good measure of the size of the problem.

To say that the running time of an algorithm is O(f(n)) means that for large values of the problem size, n, the running time of the algorithm is no bigger than some constant times f(n). (More rigorously, there is a number C and a positive integer M such that whenever n is greater than M, the run time is less than or equal to C*f(n).) The constant takes into account details such as the speed of the computer on which the algorithm is run; if you use a slower computer, you might have to use a bigger constant in the formula, but changing the constant won't change the basic fact that the run time is O(f(n)).

The constant also makes it unnecessary to say whether we are measuring time in seconds, years, CPU cycles, or any other unit of measure; a change from one unit of measure to another is just multiplication by a constant. Note also that O(f(n)) doesn't depend at all on what happens for small problem sizes, only on what happens in the long run as the problem size increases without limit.

To look at a simple example, consider the problem of adding up all the numbers in an array. The problem size, n, is the length of the array. Using A as the name of the array, the algorithm can be expressed in Java as:

```
total = 0;
for (int i = 0; i < n; i++)
total = total + A[i];
```

This algorithm performs the same operation, total = total + A[i], n times. The total time spent on this operation is a*n, where a is the time it takes to perform the operation once. Now, this is not the only thing that is done in the algorithm. The value of i is incremented and is compared to n each time through the loop.

This adds an additional time of b*n to the run time, for some constant b. Furthermore, i and total both have to be initialized to zero; this adds some constant amount c to the running time.

The exact running time would then be (a+b)*n+c, where the constants a, b, and c depend on factors such as how the code is compiled and what computer it is run on. Using the fact that c is less than or equal to c*n for any positive integer n, we can say that the run time is less than or equal to (a+b+c)*n. That is, the run time is less than or equal to a constant times n. By definition, this means that the run time for this algorithm is O(n).

If this explanation is too mathematical for you, we can just note that for large values of n, the c in the formula (a+b)*n+c is insignificant compared to the other term, (a+b)*n. We say that c is a "lower order term." When doing asymptotic analysis, lower order terms can be discarded. A rough, but correct, asymptotic analysis of the algorithm would go something like this: Each iteration of the for loop takes a certain constant amount of time. There are n iterations of the loop, so the total run time is a constant times n, plus lower order terms (to account for the initialization). Disregarding lower order terms, we see that the run time is O(n).

Note that to say that an algorithm has run time O(f(n)) is to say that its run time is no bigger than some constant times f(n) (for large values of n). O(f(n)) puts an upper limit on the run time. However, the run time could be smaller, even much smaller. For example, if the run time is O(n), it would also be correct to say that the run time is $O(n^2)$ or even $O(n^{10})$. If the run time is less than a constant times n, then it is certainly less than the same constant times n^2 or n^{10}.

Of course, sometimes it's useful to have a lower limit on the run time. That is, we want to be able to say that the run time is greater than or equal to some constant times f(n) (for large values of n). The notation for this is Ω(f(n)), read "Omega of f of n." "Omega" is the name of a letter in the Greek alphabet, and Ω is the upper case version of that letter. (To be technical, saying that the run time of an algorithm is Ω(f(n)) means that there is a positive number C and a positive integer M such that whenever n is greater than M, the run time is greater than or equal to C*f(n).) O(f(n)) tells you something about the maximum amount of time that you might have to wait for an algorithm to finish; Ω(f(n)) tells you something about the minimum time.

The algorithm for adding up the numbers in an array has a run time that is Ω(n) as well as O(n). When an algorithm has a run time that is both Ω(f(n)) and O(f(n)), its run time is said to be Θ(f(n)), read "Theta of f of n." (Theta is another letter from the Greek alphabet.) To say that the run time of an algorithm is Θ(f(n)) means that for large values of n, the run time is between a*f(n) and b*f(n), where a and b are constants (with b greater than a, and both greater than 0).

Let's look at another example. Consider the algorithm that can be expressed in Java in the following method:

```
/**
* Sorts the n array elements A[0], A[1]...,
A[n-1] into increasing order.
*/
public static simpleBubbleSort(int[] A, int
n) {
 for (int i = 0; i < n; i++) {
// Do n passes through the array...
 for (int j = 0; j < n-1; j++) {
  if (A[j] > A[j+1]) {
// A[j] and A[j+1] are out of order, so swap
them
      int temp = A[j];
      A[j] = A[j+1];
      A[j+1] = temp;
   }
  }
 }
}
```

Here, the parameter n represents the problem size. The outer for loop in the method is executed n times. Each time the outer for loop is executed, the inner for loop is exectued n 1 times, so the if statement is executed n*(n-1) times. This is n^2-n, but since lower order terms are not significant in an asymptotic analysis, it's good enough to say that the if statement is executed about n^2 times.

In particular, the test A[j] > A[j+1] is executed about n^2times, and this fact by itself is enough to say that the run time of the algorithm is W(n^2), that is, the run time is at least some constant times n^2. Furthermore, if we look at other operations — the assignment statements, incrementing i and j, etc. — none of them are executed more than n^2 times, so the run time is also $O(n^2)$, that is, the run time is no more than some constant times n^2. Since it is both $W(n^2)$ and $O(n^2)$, the run time of the simpleBubbleSort algorithm is $Q(n^2)$.

You should be aware that some people use the notation $O(f(n))$ as if it meant $\Theta(f(n))$. That is, when they say that the run time of an algorithm is $O(f(n))$, they mean to say that the run time is about equal to a constant times $f(n)$. For that, they should use $\Theta(f(n))$. Properly speaking, $O(f(n))$ means that the run time is less than a constant times $f(n)$, possibly much less.

So far, the analysis has ignored an important detail. We have looked at how run time depends on the problem size, but in fact the run time usually depends not just on the size of the problem but on the specific data that has to be processed. For example, the run time of a sorting algorithm can depend on the initial order of the items that are to be sorted, and not just on the number of items.

To account for this dependency, we can consider either the worst case run time analysis or the average case run time analysis of an algorithm. For a worst case run time analysis, we consider all possible problems of size n and look at the longest possible run time for all such problems. For an average case analysis, we consider all possible problems of size n and look at the average of the run times for all such problems. Usually, the average case analysis assumes that all problems of size n are equally likely to be encountered, although this is not always realistic — or even possible in the case where there is an infinite number of different problems of a given size.

In many cases, the average and the worst case run times are the same to within a constant multiple. This means that as far as asymptotic analysis is concerned, they are the same. That is, if the average case run time is $O(f(n))$ or $\Theta(f(n))$, then so is the worst case. However, later in the book, we will encounter a few cases where the average and worst case asymptotic analyses differ.

So, what do you really have to know about analysis of algorithms to read the rest of this book? We will not do any rigorous mathematical analysis, but you should be able to follow informal discussion of simple cases such as the examples that we have looked at in this section.

Most important, though, you should have a feeling for exactly what it means to say that the running time of an algorithm is O(f(n)) or Θ(f(n)) for some common functions f(n). The main point is that these notations do not tell you anything about the actual numerical value of the running time of the algorithm for any particular case.

They do not tell you anything at all about the running time for small values of n. What they do tell you is something about the rate of growth of the running time as the size of the problem increases.

Suppose you compare two algorithms that solve the same problem. The run time of one algorithm is $\Theta(n^2)$, while the run time of the second algorithm is $\Theta(n^3)$. What does this tell you? If you want to know which algorithm will be faster for some particular problem of size, say, 100, nothing is certain. As far as you can tell just from the asymptotic analysis, either algorithm could be faster for that particular case — or in any particular case. But what you can say for sure is that if you look at larger and larger problems, you will come to a point where the $\Theta(n^2)$ algorithm is faster than the $\Theta(n^3)$ algorithm. Furthermore, as you continue to increase the problem size, the relative advantage of the $\Theta(n^2)$ algorithm will continue to grow. There will be values of n for which the $\Theta(n^2)$ algorithm is a thousand times faster, a million times faster, a billion times faster, and so on. This is because for any positive constants a and b, the function $a*n^3$ grows faster than the function $b*n^2$ as n gets larger. (Mathematically, the limit of the ratio of $a*n^3$ to $b*n^2$ is infinite as n approaches infinity.)

This means that for "large" problems, a $\Theta(n^2)$ algorithm will definitely be faster than a $\Theta(n^3)$ algorithm. You just don't know — based on the asymptotic analysis alone — exactly how large "large" has to be. In practice, in fact, it is likely that the $\Theta(n^2)$ algorithm will be faster even for fairly small values of n, and absent other information you would generally prefer a $\Theta(n^2)$ algorithm to a $\Theta(n^3)$ algorithm.

So, to understand and apply asymptotic analysis, it is essential to have some idea of the rates of growth of some common functions. For the power functions n, n^2, n^3, n^4..., the larger the exponent, the greater the rate of growth of the function.

Exponential functions such as 2^n and 10^n, where the n is in the exponent, have a growth rate that is faster than that of any power function. In fact, exponential functions grow so quickly that an algorithm whose run time grows exponentially is almost certainly impractical even for relatively modest values of n, because the running time is just too long.

Another function that often turns up in asymptotic analysis is the logarithm function, log(n). There are actually many different logarithm functions, but the one that is usually used in computer science is the so-called logarithm to the base two, which is defined by the fact that $\log(2^x) = x$ for any number x. (Usually, this function is written $\log_2(n)$, but I will leave out the subscript 2, since I will only use the base-two logarithm in this book.)

The logarithm function grows very slowly. The growth rate of log(n) is much smaller than the growth rate of n. The growth rate of n*log(n) is a little larger than the growth rate of n, but much smaller than the growth rate of n^2.

POINTS

- *Introduction*: Analysis of Selection Sort
- *Introduction*: Analysis of Merge Sort
- Asymptotic Notation
- Asymptotic Notation Continued
- Heapsort
- Heapsort Continued
- Priority Queues (more heaps)
- Quicksort
- Bounds on Sorting and Linear Time Sorts
- Stable Sorts and Radix Sort
- Begin Dynamic Programmeming
- More Dynamic Programmeming
- *Begin Greedy Algorithms*: Huffman's Algorithm

- Dÿkstra's Algorithm
- Beyond Asymptotic Analysis: Memory Access Time
- B-Trees
- More B-Trees: Insertion and Splitting
- Union/Find
- Warshall's Algorithm, Floyd's Algorithm
- Large Integer Arithmetic
- RSA Public-Key Cryptosystem
- Begin Algorithms and Structural Complexity Theory
- Continue Algorithms and Structural Complexity Theory
- End Algorithms and Structural Complexity Theory
- Generating Permutations and Combinations
- Exam review with sample questions and solutions

MASTERS THEOREM

INTRODUCTION

In the analysis of algorithms, the master theorem, which is a specific case of the Akra-Bazzi theorem, provides a cookbook solution in asymptotic terms for recurrence relations of types that occur in practice.

It was popularized by the canonical algorithms which introduces and proves Nevertheless, not all recurrence relations can be solved with the use of the master theorem.

Consider a problem that can be solved using recurrence algorithm such as below:

```
  procedure T(n: size of problem)
defined  as:
   ifn<kthen exit
  Do work of amount f(n)
  T(n/b)
  T(n/b)
  repeat for a total of a times...
  T(n/b)
  end procedure
```

In above algorithm we are dividing the problem in to number of sub problems recursively, each sub problem being of size *n*/*b*. This can be visualized as building a call tree with each node of a tree an instance of one recursive call and its child nodes being instance of next calls. In above example, each node would have *a* number of child nodes.

Each node does amount of work that depends on size of sub problem *n* passed to that instance of recursive call and given by *f*(*n*).

For example, if each recursive call is doing sorting then size of work does by each node in the tree would be at least *O*(*nlog*(*n*)). Total size of work done by entire tree is sum of work performed by all the nodes in the tree.

Algorithm such as above can be represented as recurrence relationship,

$$T(n) = aT\left(\frac{n}{b}\right) + f(n).$$

This recursive relationship can be successively substituted in to itself and expanded to obtain expression for total amount of work done[

Original Master theorem allows to easily calculate run time of such a recursive algorithm in Big O notation without doing expansion of above recursive relationship. A generalized form of Master Theorem by Akra and Bazzi introduced in 1998 is more usable, simpler and applicable on wide number of cases that occurs in practice.

The master theorem concerns recurrence relations of the form:

$$T(n) = aT\left(\frac{n}{b}\right) + f(n) \text{Wherea} \geq 1, b > 1.$$

In the application to the analysis of a recursive algorithm, the constants and function take on the following significance:

- *n* is the size of the problem.
- *a* is the number of subproblems in the recursion.
- *n*/*b* is the size of each subproblem. (Here it is assumed that all subproblems are essentially the same size.)
- *f* (*n*) is the cost of the work done outside the recursive calls, which includes the cost of dividing the problem and the cost of merging the solutions to the subproblems.

GENERIC FORM

If it is true that $f(n) = O\left(n^{\log_b(a)-\epsilon}\right)$ for some constant ε > 0 (using Big O notation)

it follows that:

$$T(n) = \Theta\left(n^{\log_b a}\right)$$

Example

$$T(n) = 8T\left(\frac{n}{2}\right) + 1000n^2$$

As one can see in the formula above, the variables get the following values:

$$a = 8, b = 2, f(n) = 1000n^2, \log_b a = \log_2 8 = 3$$

Now we have to check that the following equation holds:

$$f(n) = O\left(n^{\log a-\epsilon}\right)$$

$$1000n^2 = O\left(n^{3-\epsilon}\right)$$

If we choose $\varepsilon = 1$*, we get:*

$$1000n^2 = O\left(n^{3-1}\right) = 0\left(n^2\right)$$

Since this equation holds, the first case of the master theorem applies to the given recurrence relation, thus resulting in the conclusion:

$$T(n) = \Theta\left(n^{\log_b -a}\right)$$

If we insert the values from above, we finally get:

$$T(n) = \Theta\left(n^3\right)$$

Thus the given recurrence relation $T(n)$ was in $\Theta(n^3)$.

CASE 2

Generic form

If it is true, for some constant k e" 0, that:

$$f(n) = \Theta\left(n^{\log_b a} \log^k n\right)$$

it follows that:

$$T(n) = \Theta\left(n^{\log_b a} \log^{k+1} n\right)$$

Example

$$T(n) = 2T\left(\frac{n}{2}\right) + 10n$$

As we can see in the formula above the variables get the following values:

$a = 2$, $b = 2$, $k = 0$, $f(n) = 10n$, $\log_b a = \log_2 2 = 1$

Now we have to check that the following equation holds (in this case k=0):

$$f(n) = \Theta\left(n^{\log_b a}\right)$$

If we insert the values from above, we get:

$$10n = \Theta\left(n^1\right) = \Theta(n)$$

Since this equation holds, the second case of the master theorem applies to the given recurrence relation, thus resulting in the conclusion:

$$T(n) = \Theta(n \log n)$$

If we insert the values from above, we finally get:

$$T(n) = \Theta(n \log n)$$

Thus the given recurrence relation $T(n)$ was in $\Theta(n \log n)$.

DESIGNING OF ALGORITHMS

OVERVIEW

At first glance, the algorithms move-until-out and quick-sort have little in common. One processes structures; the other processes lists. One creates a new structure for the generative step; the other splits up a list into three pieces and recurs on two of them. In short, a comparison of the two examples of generative recursion suggests that the design of algorithms is an ad hoc activity and that it is impossible to come up with a general design recipe. A closer look, however, suggests a different picture.

First, even though we speak of algorithms as processes that solve problems, they are still functions that consume and produce data. In other words, we still choose data to represent a problem, and we must definitely understand the nature of our data if we wish to understand the process. Second, we describe the processes in terms of data, for example, "creating a new structure" or "partitioning a list of numbers."

Third, we always distinguish between input data for which it is trivial to produce a solution and those for which it is not. Fourth, the generation of problems is the key to the design of algorithms. Although the idea of how to generate a new problem might be independent of a data representation, it must certainly be implemented for whatever form of representation we choose for our problem. Finally, once the generated problems have been solved, the solutions must be combined with other values.

Let us examine the six general stages of our structural design recipe in light of our discussion:

Data Analysis and Design

The choice of a data representation for a problem often affects our thinking about the process. Sometimes the description of a process dictates a particular choice of representation. On other occasions, it is possible and worthwhile to explore alternatives. In any case, we must Analyse and define our data collections.

Contract, Purpose, Header

We also need a contract, a definition header, and a purpose statement. Since the generative step has no connection to the structure of the data definition, the purpose statement should not only specify what the function does but should also include a comment that explains in general terms how it works.

Function Examples

In our previous design recipes, the function examples merely specified which output the function should produce for some given input. For algorithms, examples should illustrate how the algorithm proceeds for some given input. This helps us to design, and readers to understand, the algorithm. For functions such as move-until-out the process is trivial and doesn't need more than a few words.

Template

Our discussion suggests a general template for algorithms:

```
(define (generative-recursive-fun problem)
 cond
 [(trivially-solvable? problem)
 (determine-solution problem)]
 [else
 (combine-solutions
 ... problem...
   (generative-recursive-fun (generate-problem-
    1 problem))
    (generative-recursive-fun (generate-
   problem-n problem)))]))
```

Definition

This chapter is only a suggestive blueprint, not a definitive shape. Each function in the template is to remind us that we need to think about the following four questions:

- What is a trivially solvable problem?
- What is a corresponding solution?
- How do we generate new problems that are more easily solvable than the original problem? Is there one new problem that we generate or are there several?
- Is the solution of the given problem the same as the solution of (one of) the new problems? Or, do we need to combine the solutions to create a solution for the original problem? And, if so, do we need anything from the original problem data?

To define the algorithm, we must express the answers to these four questions in terms of our chosen data representation.

Test

Once we have a complete function, we must also test it. As before, the goal of testing is to discover bugs and to eliminate them. Remember that testing cannot validate that the function works correctly for all possible inputs.

Termination

Unfortunately, the standard recipe is not good enough for the design of algorithms. Up to now, a function has always produced an output for any legitimate input. That is, the evaluation has always stopped. After all, by the nature of our recipe, each natural recursion consumes an immediate piece of the input, not the input itself. Because data is constructed in a hierarchical manner, this means that the input shrinks at every stage. Hence the function sooner or later consumes an atomic piece of data and stops.

With functions based on generative recursion, this is no longer true. The internal recursions don't consume an immediate component of the input but some new piece of data, which is generated from the input.

In addition, even the slightest mistake in translating the process description into a function definition may cause an infinite loop. The problem is most easily understood with an example. Consider the following definition of smaller-items, one of the two "problem generators" for quick-sort:

```
;; smaller-items: (listof number) number →
(listof number)
;; to create a list with all those numbers on
alon
;; that are smaller than or equal to threshold
(define (smaller-items alon threshold)
  (cond
    [(empty? alon) empty]
    [else (if (⇐ (first alon) threshold)
           (cons (first alon) (smaller-items (rest
           alon) threshold))
           smaller-items (rest alon)
           threshold))]))
```

Instead of < it employs ⇐ to compare numbers. As a result, this function produces (list 5) when applied to (list 5) and 5.

The lesson from this example is that the design of

algorithms requires one more step in our design recipe: a TERMINATION ARGUMENT, which explains why the process produces an output for every input and how the function implements this idea; or a warning, which explains when the process may not terminate.

For quick-sort, the argument might look like this:

At each step, quick-sort partitions the list into two sublists using smaller-items and larger-items. Each function produces a list that is smaller than the input (the second argument), even if the threshold (the first argument) is an item on the list. Hence each recursive application of quick-sortconsumes a strictly shorter list than the given one. Eventually, quick-sort receives and returns empty.

Without such an argument an algorithm must be considered incomplete. A good termination argument may on occasion also reveal additional termination cases. For example, (smaller-items N (list N)) and (larger-items N(list N)) always produce empty for any N. Therefore we know that quick-sort's answer for (list N) is (list N). To add this knowledge to quick-sort, we simply add a cond-clause:

```
(define (quick-sort alon)
(cond
  [(empty? alon) empty]
  [(empty? (rest alon)) alon]
  [else (append
            (quick-sort  (smaller-items  alon
(first              alon)))
             (list (first alon))
             (quick-sort  (larger-items  alon
(first               alon))))]))
```

The condition (empty? (rest alon)) is one way to ask whether alon contains one item.

Example

Define the function tabulate-div, which accepts a number n and tabulates the list of all of its divisors, starting with 1 and ending in n. A number d is a divisior of a number n if the remainder of dividing n by d is 0, that is, (= (remainder n d) 0) is true. The smallest divisior of any number is 1; the largest one is the number itself.

Exercise

Develop the function merge-sort, which sorts a list of numbers in ascending order, using the following two auxiliary functions:

- The first one, make-singles, constructs a list of one-item lists from the given list of numbers. For example,
- (equal? (make-singles (list 2 5 9 3))
- (list (list 2) (list 5) (list 9) (list 3)))
- The second one, merge-all-Neighbours, merges pairs of Neighbouring lists. More specifically, it consumes a list of lists (of numbers) and merges Neighbours. For example,
- (equal? (merge-all-Neighbours (list (list 2) (list 5) (list 9) (list 3)))
- (list (list 2 5) (list 3 9)))
- (equal? (merge-all-Neighbours (list (list 2 5) (list 3 9)))
- (list (list 2 3 5 9)))

In general, this function yields a list that is approximately half as long as the input. Why is the output not always half as long as the input?

Structural Versus Generative Recursion

The template for algorithms is so general that it even covers functions based on structural recursion. Consider the version with one termination clause and one generation step:

```
(define (generative-recursive-fun problem)
  (cond
   [(trivially-solvable? problem)
   (determine-solution problem)]
  [else
    (combine-solutions
      problem
        (generative-recursive-fun (generate-
         problem problem)))]))
```

If we replace trivially-solvable? with empty? and

generate-problem with rest, the outline is a template for a list-processing function:

```
(define (generative-recursive-fun problem)
  (cond
     [(empty? problem) (determine-solution
     problem)]
     [else
       (combine-solutions
        problem
        (generative-recursive-fun (rest
         problem)))]))
```

MAKING CHOICES

A user cannot distinguish sort and quick-sort. Both consume a list of numbers; both produce a list that consists of the same numbers arranged in ascending order. To an observer, the functions are completely equivalent. This raises the question of which of the two a Programmemer should provide. More generally, if we can develop a function using structural recursion and an equivalent one using generative recursion, what should we do? To understand this choice better, let's discuss another classical example of generative recursion from mathematics: the problem of finding the greatest common divisor of two positive natural numbers.

All such numbers have at least one divisor in common: 1. On occasion, this is also the only common divisor. For example, 2 and 3 have only 1 as common divisor because 2 and 3, respectively, are the only other divisors.

Then again, 6 and 25 are both numbers with several divisors:

- 6 is evenly divisible by 1, 2, 3, and 6;
- 25 is evenly divisible by 1, 5, and 25.

Still, the greatest common divisior of 25 and 6 is 1. In contrast, 18 and 24 have many common divisors:

- 18 is evenly divisible by 1, 2, 3, 6, 9, and 18;
- 24 is evenly divisible by 1, 2, 3, 4, 6, 8, 12, and 24.

The greatest common divisor is 6.

Following the design recipe, we start with a contract, a purpose statement, and a header:

```
;; gcd: N[⇒ 1] N[⇒ 1] → N
;; to find the greatest common divisior of n
and m
(define (gcd n m)
  ...)
```

The contract specifies the precise inputs: natural numbers that are greater or equal to 1 (not 0).

Now we need to make a decision whether we want to pursue a design based on structural or on generative recursion. Since the answer is by no means obvious, we develop both. For the structural version, we must consider which input the function should process: n, m, or both.

A moment's consideration suggests that what we really need is a function that starts with the smaller of the two and outputs the first number smaller or equal to this input that evenly divides both n and m.

```
;; gcd-structural: N[⇒ 1] N[⇒ 1] → N
;; to find the greatest common divisior of n
and m
;; structural recursion using data definition
 of N[⇒ 1] (define (gcd-structural n m) (local
    ((define (first-divisior-⇐ i)
          (cond
            [(= i 1) 1]
            [else (cond
                       [(and (= (remainder n i) 0)
                                (= (remainder m i)
                                     0)) i]
                        [else (first-divisior-⇐ (-
                       i 1))])]))))
                     (first-divisior-⇐ (min m
                        n))))
```

The conditions "evenly divisible" have been encoded as (= (remainder n i) 0) and (=(remainder m i) 0). The two ensure that i divides n and m without a remainder. Testing gcd-structural with the examples shows that it finds the expected answers. Although the design of gcd-structural is rather straightforward, it is also naïve. It simply tests for every number whether it divides both n and m evenly and returns the first such number. For small natural numbers, this process works just fine.

Consider the following example, however:

```
(gcd-structural 101135853 45014640)
```

The result is 177 and to get there gcd-structural had to compare 101135676, that is, 101135853 – 177, numbers. This is a large effort and even reasonably fast computers spend several minutes on this task.

Exercises

Enter the definition of gcd-structural into the Definitions window and evaluate (time (gcd-structural 101135853 45014640)) in the Interactionswindow.

After testing gcd-structural conduct the performance tests in the Full Scheme language (without debugging), which evaluates expressions faster than the lower language levels but with less protection. Add (require-library "core.ss") to the top of the Definitions window. Have some reading handy!

Since mathematicians recognized the inefficiency of the "structural algorithm" a long time ago, they studied the problem of finding divisiors in more depth. The essential insight is that for two natural numbers larger and smaller, their greatest common divisor is equal to the greatest common divisior of smaller and theremainder of larger divided into smaller.

Here is how we can put this insight into equational form:

```
 (gcd larger smaller)
=(gcd smaller (remainder larger smaller))
```

Since (remainder larger smaller) is smaller than both larger and smaller, the right-hand side use of gcd consumes smaller first.

Here is how this insight applies to our small example:

- The given numbers are 18 and 24.
- According to the mathematicians' insight, they have the same greatest common divisor as 18 and 6.
- And these two have the same greatest common divisor as 6 and 0.

And here we seem stuck because 0 is nothing expected. But, 0 can be evenly divided by every number, so we have found our answer: 6.

Working through the example not only explains the idea but also suggests how to discover the case with a trivial solution. When the smaller of the two numbers is 0, the result is the larger number.

Putting everything together, we get the following definition:

```
;; gcd-generative: N[⇒ 1] N[⇒1] → N
;; to find the greatest common divisior of n
and m
;; generative recursion: (gcd n m) = (gcd n
(remainder m n)) if (⇐ m n)
 (define (gcd-generative n m)
  (local ((define (clever-gcd larger smaller)
            (cond
              [(= smaller 0) larger]
              [else (clever-gcd smaller
              (remainder larger smaller))])))
  (clever-gcd (max m n) (min m n))))
```

The local definition introduces the workhorse of the function: clever-gcd, a function based on generative recursion. Its first line discovers the trivially solvable case by comparing smaller to 0 and produces the matching solution.

The generative step uses smaller as the new first argument and (remainder largersmaller) as the new second argument to clever-gcd, exploiting the above equation.

If we now use gcd-generative with our complex example from above:

```
(gcd-generative 101135853 45014640)
```

we see that the response is nearly instantaneous. A hand-evaluation shows that clever-gcd recurs only nine times before it produces the solution: 177. In short, generative recursion has helped find us a much faster solution to our problem.

PROCESS

For the maximum subarray problem, if you didn't know any better, you'd probably implement a solution that Analyses every possible subarray, and returns the one with the maximum sum:

```
  class Array
   def sum
       result = 0
     self.each do |i|
            result+=i
     end
     return result
 end
#test every sub array - brute force!
 def max_sub_array_order_ncubed
       left_index = 0
       right_index = 0
       max_value = self [left_ index.. right_
       index].sum
       for i in (0..self.length)
            for j in (i..self.length
                   this_value = self[i..j].sum
                   if (this_value > max_value)
                   max_value = this_value
                   left_index=i
                   right_index=j
               end
         end
   end
return self[left_index..right_index]
       end
  end
```

If you were a bit more clever, you might notice that self[i..j].sum is equal toself[i..(j–1)].sum + self[j] in the innermost loop (the sum method itself), and use an accumulator there as opposed to calculating it each time. That takes you down from n^3 to n^2 time.

But there are (at least) two other ways to solve this problem:

- A divide and conquer approach that uses recursion and calculates the left and right maximum contiguous subarrays (MCS), along with the MCS that contains the right-most element in the left side and the left-most element in the right side. It compares the three and returns the one with the maximum sum. This gets us to O(n log n) time.

- An approach I'll call "expanding sliding window." If memory serves me correct, this aptly describes it or was the way a professor of mine described it. In any case, the "expanding sliding window" can do it in one pass (O(n) time), at the cost of a few more variables.

SORTING OF ALGORITHMS

INTRODUCTION

It is not always possible to say that one algorithm is better than another, as relative performance can vary depending on the type of data being sorted. In some situations, most of the data are in the correct order, with only a few items needing to be sorted.

In other situations the data are completely mixed up in a random order and in others the data will tend to be in reverse order.

Different algorithms will perform differently according to the data being sorted. Four common algorithms are the exchange or bubble sort, the selection sort, the insertion sort and the quick sort.

The selection sort is a good one to use with students. It is intuitive and very simple to Programme. It offers quite good performance, its particular strength being the small number of exchanges needed.

For a given number of data items, the selection sort always goes through a set number of comparisons and exchanges, so its performance is predictable.

Procedure SelectionSort (d: DataArrayType; n: integer) {n is the number of elements}

```
for k = 1 to n-1 do begin
small = k
for j = k+1 to n do
```

```
if d[j] < d[small] then small = j
{Swap elements k and small}
Swap(d, k, small)
end
```

EXCHANGE (BUBBLE) SORT

Element	1	2	3	4	5	6	7	8
Data	27	63	1	72	64	58	14	9
1st pass	27	1	63	64	58	14	9	72
2nd pass	1	27	63	58	14	9	64	72
3rd pass	1	27	58	14	9	63	64	72...

The first two data items (27 and 63) are compared and the smaller one placed on the left hand side. The second and third items (63 and 1) are then compared and the smaller one placed on the left and so on.

After all the data has been passed through once, the largest data item (72) will have "bubbled" through to the end of the list. At the end of the second pass, the second largest data item (64) will be in the second last position. For n data items, the process continues for n-1 passes, or until no exchanges are made in a single pass.

INSERTION SORT

Element	1	2	3	4	5	6	7	8
Data	27	63	1	72	64	58	14	9
1st pass	27	63	1	72	64	58	9	14
2nd pass	27	63	1	72	64	9	14	58
3rd pass	27	63	1	72	9	14	58	64...

The insertion sort starts with the last two elements and creates a correctly sorted sub-list, which in the example contains 9 and 14. It then looks at the next element (58) and inserts it into the sub-list in its correct position.

It takes the next element (64) and does the same, continuing until the sub-list contains all the data.

SELECTION SORT

Element	1	2	3	4	5	6	7	8
Data	27	63	1	72	64	58	14	9
1st pass	1	63	27	72	64	58	14	9
2nd pass	1	9	27	72	64	58	14	63
3rd pass	1	9	14	72	64	58	27	63...

The selection sort marks the first element (27). It then goes through the remaining data to find the smallest number (1). It swaps this with the first element and the smallest element is now in its correct position. It then marks the second element (63) and looks through the remaining data for the next smallest number (9). These two numbers are then swapped. This process continues until n-1 passes have been made.

QUICK SORT

Element	1	2	3	4	5	6	7	8
Data	27	63	1	72	64	58	14	9
1st pass	1	9	63	72	64	58	14	27
2nd pass	1	9	14	27	64	58	72	63
3rd pass	1	9	14	27	58	63	72	64
4th pass	1	9	14	27	58	63	64	72 sorted!

The quick sort takes the last element (9) and places it such that all the numbers in the left sub-list are smaller and all the numbers in the right sub-list are bigger. It then quick sorts the left sub-list ({1}) and then quick sorts the right sub-list. This is a recursive algorithm, since it is defined in terms of itself. This reduces the complexity of Programmeming it, however it is the least intuitive of the four algorithms.

COMPARING THE ALGORITHMS

There are two important factors when measuring the performance of a sorting algorithm. The algorithms have to compare the magnitude of different elements and they have to move the different elements around. So counting the number of comparisons and the number of exchanges or moves made by an algorithm offer useful performance measures. When sorting large record structures, the number of exchanges made may be the principal performance criterion, since exchanging two records will involve a lot of work. When sorting a simple array of integers, then the number of comparisons will be more important.

It has been said that the only thing going for the bubble (exchange) sort is its catchy name. The logic of the algorithm is simple to understand and it is fairly easy to Programme. It can also be Programmemed to detect when it has finished sorting. The selection sort, by comparison, always goes through the same amount of work regardless of the data and the quick sort performs particularly badly with ordered data. However, in general the bubble sort is a very inefficient algorithm.

The insertion sort is a little better and whilst it cannot detect that it has finished sorting, the logic of the algorithm means that it comes to a rapid conclusion when dealing with sorted data.

The selection sort is a good one to use with students. It is intuitive and very simple to Programme. It offers quite good performance, its particular strength being the small number of exchanges needed. For a given number of data items, the selection sort always goes through a set number of comparisons and exchanges, so its performance is predictable.

The first three algorithms all offer O(n2) performance, that is sorting times increase with the square of the number of elements being sorted. That means that if you double the number of elements being sorted, then there will be a four-fold increase in the time taken. Ten times more elements increases the time taken by a factor of 100! This is not a problem with small data sets, but with hundreds or thousands of elements, this becomes very significant. With most large data sets, the quick sort is a vastly superior algorithm (although as you might expect, it is much more complex), as the table below shows.

RANDOM DATA SET: NUMBER

Sort/Elements	50	100	200	300	400	500
Selection Sort	1225	4950	19900	44850	79800	124750

Exchange Sort	1410	5335	20300	45650	79866	126585
Insertion Sort	1391	5399	20473	44449	78779	123715
Quick Sort	399	990	1954	3384	5066	6256

It should be pointed out that the methods above all belong to one family, they are all internal sorting algorithms. This means that they can only be used when the entire data structure to be sorted can be held in the computer's main memory. There will be situations where this is not possible, for example when sorting a very large transaction file which is stored on, say, magnetic tape or disc.

DESCRIPTION

BUBBLE SORT

Exchange two adjacent elements if they are out of order. Repeat until array is sorted.

This is a slow algorithm:

```
#include <stdlib.h>
#include <stdio.h>
#define uint32 unsigned int
typedef int (*CMPFUN)(int, int);
void ArraySort(int This[], CMPFUN fun_ptr,
uint32 ub)
{
/* bubble sort */
 uint32 indx;
 uint32 indx2;
 int temp;
 int temp2;
 int flipped;
 if (ub ⇐ 1)
 return;
 indx = 1;
 do
 {
  flipped = 0;
  for (indx2 = ub - 1; indx2 ⇒ indx; –
  indx2)
```

```
    {
    temp = This[indx2];
    temp2 = This[indx2 - 1];
    if ((*fun_ptr)(temp2, temp) > 0)
      {
        This[indx2 - 1] = temp;
        This[indx2] = temp2;
        flipped = 1;
        }
      }
    } while ((++indx < ub) && flipped);
  }
#define ARRAY_SIZE 14
int my_array[ARRAY_SIZE];
void fill_array()
{
  int indx;
  for (indx=0; indx < ARRAY_SIZE; ++indx)
  {
  my_array[indx] = rand();
  }
  /* my_array[ARRAY_SIZE - 1] = ARRAY_SIZE/
  3; */
  }
int cmpfun(int a, int b)
{
  if (a > b)
    return 1;
  else if (a < b)
    return -1;
  else
    return 0;
  }
int main()
  {
      int indx;
      int indx2;
      for (indx2 = 0; indx2 < 80000; ++indx2)
```

```
{
  fill_array();
  ArraySort(my_array, cmpfun, ARRAY_SIZE);
  for (indx=1; indx < ARRAY_SIZE; ++indx)
  {
   if (my_array[indx - 1] > my_array[indx])
    {
        printf("bad sort\n");
        return(1);
        }
     }
   }
   return(0);
}
```

SELECTION SORT

Find the largest element in the array, and put it in the proper place. Repeat until array is sorted. This is also slow.

```
#include <stdlib.h>
#include <stdio.h>
#define uint32 unsigned int
typedef int (*CMPFUN)(int, int);
void ArraySort(int This[], CMPFUN fun_ptr,
uint32 the_len)
{
  /* selection sort */
 uint32 indx;
 uint32 indx2;
 uint32 large_pos;
 int temp;
 int large;
 if (the_len <= 1)
 return;
 for (indx = the_len - 1; indx > 0; --indx)
 {
/* find the largest number, then put it at
 the end of the array */
large = This[0];
```

```
  large_pos = 0;
  for (indx2 = 1; indx2 <= indx; ++indx2)
 {
  temp = This[indx2];
  if ((*fun_ptr)(temp,large) > 0)
  {
     large = temp;
     large_pos = indx2;
     }
   }
  This[large_pos] = This[indx];
  This[indx] = large;
  }
}
#define ARRAY_SIZE 14
int my_array[ARRAY_SIZE];
void fill_array()
{
 int indx;
 for (indx=0; indx < ARRAY_SIZE; ++indx)
{
 my_array[indx] = rand();
 }
 /* my_array[ARRAY_SIZE - 1] = ARRAY_SIZE/
 3; */
 }
 int cmpfun(int a, int b)
 {
  if (a > b)
    return 1;
  else if (a < b)
    return -1;
  else
    return 0;
 }
 int main()
 {
   int indx;
```

```
    int indx2;
    for (indx2 = 0; indx2 < 80000; ++indx2)
    {
       fill_array();
       ArraySort(my_array, cmpfun, ARRAY_SIZE);
       for (indx=1; indx < ARRAY_SIZE; ++indx)
       {
         if (my_array[indx - 1] > my_array[indx])
         {
          printf("bad sort\n");
          return(1);
         }
       }
   }
  return(0);
}
```

INSERTION SORT

Scan successive elements for out of order item, then insert the item in the proper place. Sort small array fast, big array very slowly.

```
   #include <stdlib.h>
   #include <stdio.h>
   #define uint32 unsigned int
   typedef int (*CMPFUN)(int, int);
   void ArraySort(int This[], CMPFUN fun_ptr,
   uint32 the_len)
{
   /* insertion sort */
  uint32 indx;
  int cur_val;
  int prev_val;
if (the_len Ü 1)
   return;
prev_val = This[0];
for (indx = 1; indx < the_len; ++indx)
{
 cur_val = This[indx];
```

```
  if ((*fun_ptr)(prev_val, cur_val) > 0)
  {
  /* out of order: array[indx-1] > array[indx]
  */
  uint32 indx2;
  This[indx] = prev_val;/* move up the larger
  item first */
  /* find the insertion point for the smaller
  item */
  for (indx2 = indx - 1; indx2 > 0;)
  {
     int temp_val = This[indx2 - 1];
     if ((*fun_ptr)(temp_val, cur_val) > 0)
     {
        This[indx2—] = temp_val;
        /* still out of order, move up 1 slot to
        make room */
       }
       else
        break;
  }
  This[indx2] = cur_val;/* insert the smaller
  item right here */
}
else
{
  /* in order, advance to next element */
  prev_val = cur_val;
  }
 }
}

#define ARRAY_SIZE 14

int my_array[ARRAY_SIZE];

uint32 fill_array()
{
```

```
int indx;
uint32 checksum = 0;
for (indx=0; indx < ARRAY_SIZE; ++indx)
{
  checksum += my_array[indx] = rand();
 }
 return checksum;
 }
 int cmpfun(int a, int b)
 {
   if (a > b)
      return 1;
   else if (a < b)
    return -1;
   else
      return 0;
 }
 int main()
 {
   int indx;
   int indx2;
   uint32 checksum1;
   uint32 checksum2;
   for (indx2 = 0; indx2 < 80000; ++indx2)
   {
      checksum1 = fill_array();
      ArraySort(my_array, cmpfun, ARRAY_SIZE);
      for (indx=1; indx < ARRAY_SIZE; ++indx)
      {
        if (my_array[indx - 1] > my_array[indx])
        {
         printf("bad sort\n");
         return(1);
       }
   }
   checksum2 = 0;
   for (indx=0; indx < ARRAY_SIZE; ++indx)
   {
```

```
   checksum2 += my_array[indx];
  }
   if (checksum1 != checksum2)
   {
     printf("bad checksum%d%d\n", checksum1,
     checksum2);
   }
 }
  return(0);
 }
```

QUICK SORT

Partition array into two segments. The first segment all elements are less than or equal to the pivot value. The second segment all elements are greater or equal to the pivot value. Sort the two segments recursively. Quicksort is fastest on average, but sometimes unbalanced partitions can lead to very slow sorting.

```
   #include <stdlib.h>
   #include <stdio.h>
   #define INSERTION_SORT_BOUND 16/* boundary
   point to use insertion sort */
   #define uint32 unsigned int
   typedef int (*CMPFUN)(int, int);
   /* explain function
   * Description:
   * fixarray::Qsort() is an internal subroutine
   that implements quick sort.
   *
   * Return Value: none
   */
  void Qsort(int This[], CMPFUN fun_ptr, uint32
  first, uint32 last)
  {
   uint32 stack_pointer = 0;
   int first_stack[32];
   int last_stack[32];
   for (;;)
```

```
{
    if (last - first ⇐ INSERTION_SORT_BOUND)
    {
       /* for small sort, use insertion sort
       */
       uint32 indx;
       int prev_val = This[first];
       int cur_val;
       for (indx = first + 1; indx Ü last;
       ++indx)
      {
       cur_val = This[indx];
       if ((*fun_ptr)(prev_val, cur_val) > 0)
  {
   /* out of order: array[indx-1] > array[indx]
   */
   uint32 indx2;
  This[indx] = prev_val;/* move up the larger
  item first */
  /* find the insertion point for the smaller
  item */
  for (indx2 = indx - 1; indx2 > first;)
  {
     int temp_val = This[indx2 - 1];
     if ((*fun_ptr)(temp_val, cur_val) > 0)
     {
        This[indx2—] = temp_val;
        /* still out of order, move up 1 slot
        to make room */
     }
     else
        break;
   }
   This[indx2] = cur_val;/* insert the smaller
   item right here */
}
else
{
```

```
      /* in order, advance to next element */
       prev_val = cur_val;
     }
   }
}
else
{
   int pivot;
  /* try quick sort */
   {
    int temp;
    uint32 med = (first + last) >> 1;
    /* Choose pivot from first, last, and median
    position. */
    /* Sort the three elements. */
    temp = This[first];
    if ((*fun_ptr)(temp, This[last]) > 0)
    {
       This[first] = This[last]; This[last] =
       temp;
   }
    temp = This[med];
    if ((*fun_ptr)(This[first], temp) > 0)
   {
     This[med] = This[first]; This[first] =
     temp;
   }
   temp = This[last];
   if ((*fun_ptr)(This[med], temp) > 0)
   {
     This[last] = This[med]; This[med] = temp;
   }
    pivot = This[med];
}
{
   uint32 up;
   {
     uint32 down;
```

```
        /* First and last element will be loop
        stopper. */
        /* Split array into two partitions. */
        down = first;
        up = last;
        for (;;)
        {
          do
          {
            ++down;
} while ((*fun_ptr)(pivot, This[down]) > 0);
 do
 {
  —up;
} while ((*fun_ptr)(This[up], pivot) > 0);
 if (up > down)
 {
   int temp;
  /* interchange L[down] and L[up] */
   temp = This[down]; This[down]= This[up];
This[up] = temp;
}
 else
 break;
}
}
 {
   uint32 len1;/* length of first segment */
   uint32 len2;/* length of second segment
   */
   len1 = up - first + 1;
   len2 = last - up;
   /* stack the partition that is larger */
   if (len1 Þ len2)
   {
     first_stack[stack_pointer] = first;
     last_stack[stack_pointer++] = up;
     first = up + 1;
```

```
          /* tail recursion elimination of
          * Qsort(This,fun_ptr,up + 1,last)
          */
       }
       else
      {
         first_stack[stack_pointer] = up + 1;
         last_stack[stack_pointer++] = last;
       last = up;
         /* tail recursion elimination of
         * Qsort(This,fun_ptr,first,up)
         */
       }
   }
     continue;
 }
 /* end of quick sort */
 }
 if (stack_pointer > 0)
 {
   /* Sort segment from stack. */
   first = first_stack[—stack_pointer];
   last = last_stack[stack_pointer];
  }
  else
    break;
  }/* end for */
 }
 void ArraySort(int This[], CMPFUN fun_ptr,
 uint32 the_len)
 {
  Qsort(This, fun_ptr, 0, the_len - 1);
 }
 #define ARRAY_SIZE 250000
 int my_array[ARRAY_SIZE];
 uint32 fill_array()
 {
  int indx;
```

```
 uint32 checksum = 0;
 for (indx=0; indx < ARRAY_SIZE; ++indx)
 {
   checksum += my_array[indx] = rand();
 }
 return checksum;
}
int cmpfun(int a, int b)
{
 if (a > b)
  return 1;
 else if (a < b)
  return -1;
else
 return 0;
}
int main()
{
  int indx;
  uint32 checksum1;
  uint32 checksum2 = 0;
  checksum1 = fill_array();
  ArraySort(my_array, cmpfun, ARRAY_SIZE);
  for (indx=1; indx < ARRAY_SIZE; ++indx)
  {
     if (my_array[indx - 1] > my_array[indx])
       {
         printf("bad sort\n");
         return(1);
        }
  }
  for (indx=0; indx < ARRAY_SIZE; ++indx)
  {
  checksum2 += my_array[indx];
 }
 if (checksum1 != checksum2)
 {
   printf("bad checksum%d%d\n", checksum1,
```

```
    checksum2);
    return(1);
  }
  return(0);
}
```

MERGE SORT

Start from two sorted runs of length 1, merge into a single run of twice the length. Repeat until a single sorted run is left. Mergesort needs N/2 extra buffer. Performance is second place on average, with quite good speed on nearly sorted array. Mergesort is stable in that two elements that are equally ranked in the array will not have their relative positions flipped.

```
#include <stdlib.h>
#include <stdio.h>
#define uint32 unsigned int
typedef int (*CMPFUN)(int, int);
#define INSERTION_SORT_BOUND 8/* boundary
point to use insertion sort */
void ArraySort(int This[], CMPFUN fun_ptr,
uint32 the_len)
{
uint32 span;
uint32 lb;
uint32 ub;
uint32 indx;
uint32 indx2;
if (the_len Ü 1)
 return;
span = INSERTION_SORT_BOUND;
/* insertion sort the first pass */
{
  int prev_val;
  int cur_val;
  int temp_val;
  for (lb = 0; lb < the_len; lb += span)
  {
    if ((ub = lb + span) > the_len) ub =
```

```
        the_len;
        prev_val = This[lb];
      for (indx = lb + 1; indx < ub; ++indx)
      {
        cur_val = This[indx];
        if ((*fun_ptr)(prev_val, cur_val) > 0)
        {
          /* out of order: array[indx-1] >
          array[indx] */
          This[indx] = prev_val;/* move up the
          larger item first */
          /* find the insertion point for the
          smaller item */
         for (indx2 = indx - 1; indx2 > lb;)
       {
         temp_val = This[indx2 - 1];
          if ((*fun_ptr)(temp_val, cur_val) >
           0)
          {
            This[indx2--] = temp_val;
            /* still out of order, move up 1
            slot to make room */
        }
       else
        break;
       }
      This[indx2] = cur_val;/* insert the
      smaller item right here */
      }
      else
      {
    /* in order, advance to next element */
    prev_val = cur_val;
   }
  }
 }
}
 /* second pass merge sort */
```

```
{
 uint32 median;
 int* aux;
 aux = (int*) malloc(sizeof(int) * the_len/
 2);

while (span < the_len)
{
  /* median is the start of second file */
  for (median = span; median < the_len;)
  {
   indx2 = median - 1;
   if ((*fun_ptr)(This[indx2], This[median])
   > 0)
  {
    /* the two files are not yet sorted */
   if ((ub = median + span) > the_len)
   {
     ub = the_len;
   }
   /* skip over the already sorted largest
   elements */
    while ((*fun_ptr)(This[—ub], This[indx2])
   => 0)
 {
 }
 /* copy second file into buffer */
 for (indx = 0; indx2 < ub; ++indx)
 {
   *(aux + indx) = This[++indx2];
 }
  —indx;
 indx2 = median - 1;
 lb = median - span;
 /* merge two files into one */
  for (;;)
 {
   if ((*fun_ptr)(*(aux + indx), This[indx2])
```

```
    ⇒ 0)
    {
       This[ub--] = *(aux + indx);
       if (indx > 0) --indx;
        else
        {
        /* second file exhausted */
         for (;;)
         {
           This[ub--] = This[indx2];
           if (indx2 > lb) --indx2;
           else goto mydone;/* done */
         }
       }
   }
   else
   {
      This[ub--] = This[indx2];
      if (indx2 > lb) --indx2;
      else
      {
         /* first file exhausted */
         for (;;)
         {
           This[ub--] = *(aux + indx);
           if (indx > 0) --indx;
           else goto mydone;/* done */
          }
         }
      }
   }
}
mydone:
median += span + span;
}
 span += span;
}
   free(aux);
```

```
  }
}
#define ARRAY_SIZE 250000
int my_array[ARRAY_SIZE];
uint32 fill_array()
{
  int indx;
  uint32 sum = 0;
  for (indx=0; indx < ARRAY_SIZE; ++indx)
  {
    sum += my_array[indx] = rand();
  }
  return sum;
}

int cmpfun(int a, int b)
{
   if (a > b)
     return 1;
  else if (a < b)
   return -1;
else
   return 0;
}
int main()
{
int indx;
uint32 checksum, checksum2;
checksum = fill_array();
ArraySort(my_array, cmpfun, ARRAY_SIZE);
checksum2 = my_array[0];
for (indx=1; indx < ARRAY_SIZE; ++indx)
{
   checksum2 += my_array[indx];
   if (my_array[indx - 1] > my_array[indx])
   {
      printf("bad sort\n");
       return(1);
```

```
      }
   }
   if (checksum != checksum2)
   {
         printf("bad checksum%d%d\n", checksum,
         checksum2);
          return(1);
    }
    return(0);
    }
```

HEAP SORT

Form a tree with parent of the tree being larger than its children. Remove the parent from the tree successively. On average, Heapsort is third place in speed. Heapsort does not need extra buffer, and performance is not sensitive to initial distributions.

```
   #include <stdlib.h>
   #include <stdio.h>
   #define uint32 unsigned int
   typedef int (*CMPFUN)(int, int);
   void ArraySort(int This[], CMPFUN fun_ptr,
   uint32 the_len)
   {
      /* heap sort */
      uint32 half;
      uint32 parent;
      if (the_len ⇐ 1)
         return;
      half = the_len >> 1;
      for (parent = half; parent Þ 1; –parent)
   {
      int temp;
      int level = 0;
      uint32 child;
      child = parent;
      /* bottom-up downheap */
      /* leaf-search for largest child path */
```

```
    while (child ⇐ half)
    {
        ++level;
        child += child;
        if ((child < the_len) &&
        ((*fun_ptr)(This[child], This[child - 1])
         > 0))
      ++child;
   }
   /* bottom-up-search for rotation point */
   temp = This[parent - 1];
   for (;;)
  {
    if (parent == child)
       break;
    if ((*fun_ptr)(temp, This[child - 1]) ⇐
    0)
        break;
    child >⇒ 1;
    —level;
  }
  /* rotate nodes from parent to rotation point
  */
  for (;level > 0; —level)
  {
    This[(child >> level) - 1] =
        This[(child >> (level - 1)) - 1];
   }
   This[child - 1] = temp;
}
 —the_len;
do
{
   int temp;
   int level = 0;
   uint32 child;
   /* move max element to back of array */
   temp = This[the_len];
```

```
    This[the_len] = This[0];
    This[0] = temp;
    child = parent = 1;
    half = the_len >> 1;
    /* bottom-up downheap */
    /* leaf-search for largest child path */
    while (child ⇐ half)
    {
       ++level;
       child += child;
       if ((child < the_len) &&
          ((*fun_ptr)(This[child], This[child - 1])
           > 0))
    ++child;
  }
  /* bottom-up-search for rotation point */
  for (;;)
  {
   if (parent == child)
     break;
   if ((*fun_ptr)(temp, This[child - 1]) ⇐ 0)
     break;
   child >⇒ 1;
    —level;
   }
   /* rotate nodes from parent to rotation point
   */
   for (;level > 0; —level)
   {
   This[(child >> level) - 1] =
     This[(child >> (level - 1)) - 1];
   }
   This[child - 1] = temp;
   } while (—the_len ⇒ 1);
  }
  #define ARRAY_SIZE 250000
  int my_array[ARRAY_SIZE];
  void fill_array()
```

```
{
   int indx;
   for (indx=0; indx < ARRAY_SIZE; ++indx)
   {
    my_array[indx] = rand();
  }
}

int cmpfun(int a, int b)
{
   if (a > b)
     return 1;
  else if (a < b)
     return -1;
  else
     return 0;
  }
  int main()
{
int indx;
fill_array();
ArraySort(my_array, cmpfun, ARRAY_SIZE);
for (indx=1; indx < ARRAY_SIZE; ++indx)
{
   if (my_array[indx - 1] > my_array[indx])
   {
    printf("bad sort\n");
    return(1);
   }
  }
 return(0);
}
```

SHELL SORT

Sort every Nth element in an array using insertion sort. Repeat using smaller N values, until N = 1. On average, Shellsort is fourth place in speed. Shellsort may sort some distributions slowly.

```
#include <stdlib.h>
#include <stdio.h>
#define uint32 unsigned int
typedef int (*CMPFUN)(int, int);
 /* Calculated from the combinations of 9 *
 (4^n - 2^n) + 1,
* and 4^n - 3 * 2^n + 1
*/
uint32 hop_array[] =
{
1,
5,
19,
41,
109,
209,
505,
929,
2161,
3905,
8929,
16001,
36289,
64769,
146305,
260609,
587521,
1045505,
2354689,
4188161,
9427969,
16764929,
37730305,
67084289,
150958081,
268386305,
603906049,
1073643521,
```

```
2415771649,
0xffffffff};
void ArraySort(int This[], CMPFUN fun_ptr,
uint32 the_len)
{
  /* shell sort */
  int level;
  for (level = 0; the_len > hop_array[level];
  ++level);
  do
  {
      uint32 dist;
      uint32 indx;
      dist = hop_array[-level];
      for (indx = dist; indx < the_len; ++indx)
      {
        int cur_val;
        uint32 indx2;
        cur_val = This[indx];
        indx2 = indx;
        do
        {
          int early_val;
          early_val = This[indx2 - dist];
          if ((*fun_ptr)(early_val, cur_val)
⇐              0)
           break;
         This[indx2] = early_val;
          indx2 -= dist;
         } while (indx2 ⇒ dist);
         This[indx2] = cur_val;
      }
    } while (level Þ 1);
  }
  #define ARRAY_SIZE 250000
  int my_array[ARRAY_SIZE];
  uint32 fill_array()
  {
```

```
        int indx;
        uint32 checksum = 0;
        for (indx=0; indx < ARRAY_SIZE; ++indx)
        {
          checksum += my_array[indx] = rand();
        }
        return checksum;
    }
    int cmpfun(int a, int b)
   {
     if (a > b)
         return 1;
     else if (a < b)
     return -1;
    else
     return 0;
   }
   int main()
   {
   int indx;
   uint32 sum1;
   uint32 sum2;
   sum1 = fill_array();
   ArraySort(my_array, cmpfun, ARRAY_SIZE);
   for (indx=1; indx < ARRAY_SIZE; ++indx)
   {
     if (my_array[indx - 1] > my_array[indx])
   {
     printf("bad sort\n");
     return(1);
    }
  }
  for (indx = 0; indx < ARRAY_SIZE; ++indx)
  {
    sum2 += my_array[indx];
  }
 if (sum1 != sum2)
  {
```

```
    printf("bad checksum\n");
    return(1);
  }
  return(0);
}
```

COMBO SORT

Sorting algorithms can be mixed and matched to yield the desired properties. We want fast average performance, good worst case performance, and no large extra storage requirement. We can achieve the goal by starting with the Quicksort (fastest on average). We modify Quicksort by sorting small partitions by using Insertion Sort (best with small partition). If we detect two partitions are badly balanced, we sort the larger partition by Heapsort (good worst case performance). Of course we cannot undo the bad partitions, but we can stop the possible degenerate case from continuing to generate bad partitions.

```
#include <stdlib.h>
#include <stdio.h>
#define uint32 unsigned int
typedef int (*CMPFUN)(int, int);
void HelperHeapSort(int This[], CMPFUN
fun_ptr, uint32 first, uint32 the_len)
{
    /* heap sort */
    uint32 half;
    uint32 parent;
    if (the_len Ü 1)
        return;
    half = the_len >> 1;
    for (parent = half; parent ⇒ 1; —parent)
    {
        int temp;
        int level = 0;
        uint32 child;
        child = parent;
          /* bottom-up downheap */
```

```
        /* leaf-search for largest child path */
        while (child ⇐ half)
    {
     ++level;
     child += child;
        if ((child < the_len) &&
             ((*fun_ptr)(This[first + child],
              This[first+ child - 1]) > 0))
          ++child;
  }
  /* bottom-up-search for rotation point */
  temp = This[first + parent - 1];
  for (;;)
  {
     if (parent == child)
         break;
      if ((*fun_ptr)(temp, This[first + child -
      1]) ⇐ 0)
         break;
     child >⇒ 1;
     —level;
  }
  /* rotate nodes from parent to rotation point
*/
  for (;level > 0; —level)
  {
     This[first + (child >> level) - 1] =
        This[first + (child >> (level - 1)) -
        1];
   }
     This[first + child - 1] = temp;
  }
  —the_len;
  do
  {
     int temp;
     int level = 0;
     uint32 child;
```

```
   /* move max element to back of array */
   temp = This[first + the_len];
   This[first + the_len] = This[first];
   This[first] = temp;
   child = parent = 1;
   half = the_len >> 1;
   /* bottom-up downheap */
  /* leaf-search for largest child path */
  while (child <= half)
  {
  ++level;
  child += child;
  if ((child < the_len) &&
       ((*fun_ptr)(This[first + child],
     This[first + child - 1]) > 0))
      ++child;
 }
 /* bottom-up-search for rotation point */
 for (;;)
 {
    if (parent == child)
        break;
     if ((*fun_ptr)(temp, This[first + child -
     1]) <= 0)
     break;
    child >>= 1;
     --level;
  }
  /* rotate nodes from parent to rotation point
  */
  for (;level > 0; --level)
  {
   This[first + (child >> level) - 1] =
      This[first + (child >> (level - 1)) - 1];
  }
  This[first + child - 1] = temp;
  } while (--the_len > 1);
 }
```

```
#define INSERTION_SORT_BOUND 16/* boundary
point to use insertion sort */
/* explain function
* Description:
* fixarray::Qsort() is an internal subroutine
that implements quick sort.
*
* Return Value: none
*/
void Qsort(int This[], CMPFUN fun_ptr, uint32
first, uint32 last)
{
  uint32 stack_pointer = 0;
  int first_stack[32];
  int last_stack[32];
  for (;;)
{
  if (last - first Ü INSERTION_SORT_BOUND)
  {
    /* for small sort, use insertion sort */
    uint32 indx;
    int prev_val = This[first];
    int cur_val;
    for (indx = first + 1; indx ⇐ last;
    ++indx)
 {
  cur_val = This[indx];
  if ((*fun_ptr)(prev_val, cur_val) > 0)
{
  uint32 indx2;
  /* out of order */
  This[indx] = prev_val;
  for (indx2 = indx - 1; indx2 > first; –
 indx2)
 {
   int temp_val = This[indx2 - 1];
   if ((*fun_ptr)(temp_val, cur_val) > 0)
 {
```

```
    This[indx2] = temp_val;
  }
  else
    break;
  }
    This[indx2] = cur_val;
  }
   else
 {
   /* in order, advance to next element */
   prev_val = cur_val;
   }
  }
 }
  else
  {
    int pivot;
   /* try quick sort */
 {
   int temp;
   uint32 med = (first + last) >> 1;
   /* Choose pivot from first, last, and median
   position. */
   /* Sort the three elements. */
   temp = This[first];
   if ((*fun_ptr)(temp, This[last]) > 0)
 {
   This[first] = This[last]; This[last] = temp;
 }
 temp = This[med];
 if ((*fun_ptr)(This[first], temp) > 0)
 {
   This[med] = This[first]; This[first] = temp;
 }
 temp = This[last];
 if ((*fun_ptr)(This[med], temp) > 0)
 {
  This[last] = This[med]; This[med] = temp;
```

```
}
 pivot = This[med];
}
{
  uint32 up;
  {
    uint32 down;
    /* First and last element will be loop
    stopper. */
   /* Split array into two partitions. */
   down = first;
   up = last;
   for (;;)
 {
    do
    {
       ++down;
     } while ((*fun_ptr)(pivot, This[down]) >
    0);

    do
     {
        --up;
     } while ((*fun_ptr)(This[up], pivot) >
     0);

       if (up > down)
       {
         int temp;
         /* interchange L[down] and L[up] */
          temp = This[down]; This[down]=
           This[up]; This[up] = temp;
        }
         else
           break;
        }
   }
        {
```

```
        uint32 len1;/* length of first
        segment */
        uint32 len2;/* length of second
        segment */
        len1 = up - first + 1;
        len2 = last - up;
        if (len1 => len2)
        {
           if ((len1 >> 5) > len2)
            {
           /* badly balanced partitions, heap
           sort first segment */
            HelperHeapSort(This, fun_ptr,
            first,len1);
       }
       else
       {
           first_stack[stack_pointer] =
first;             /* stack first segment */
            last_stack[stack_pointer++] = up;
         }
         first = up + 1;
           /* tail recursion elimination of
            * Qsort(This,fun_ptr,up + 1,last)
            */
       }
        else
       {
         if ((len2 >> 5) > len1)
         {
            /* badly balanced partitions,
heap              sort second segment */
            HelperHeapSort(This, fun_ptr, up
            + 1, len2);
       }
       else
       {
         first_stack[stack_pointer] = up +1;
```

```
            /* stack second segment */
            last_stack[stack_pointer++] = last;
        }
         last = up;
          /* tail recursion elimination of
           * Qsort(This,fun_ptr,first,up)
           */
        }
      }
    continue;
  }
  /* end of quick sort */
 }
 if (stack_pointer > 0)
 {
   /* Sort segment from stack. */
   first = first_stack[-stack_pointer];
   last = last_stack[stack_pointer];
 }
 else
   break;
 }/* end for */
}
void ArraySort(int This[], CMPFUN fun_ptr,
uint32 the_len)
{
 Qsort(This, fun_ptr, 0, the_len - 1);
}
#define ARRAY_SIZE 250000
int my_array[ARRAY_SIZE];
void fill_array()
{
int indx;
for (indx=0; indx < ARRAY_SIZE; ++indx)
{
  my_array[indx] = rand();
 }
}
```

```
int cmpfun(int a, int b)
{
   if (a > b)
      return 1;
   else if (a < b)
      return -1;
   else
      return 0;
}
int main()
{
 int indx;
 fill_array();
 ArraySort(my_array, cmpfun, ARRAY_SIZE);
 for (indx=1; indx < ARRAY_SIZE; ++indx)
 {
    if (my_array[indx - 1] > my_array[indx])
    {
       printf("bad sort\n");
       return(1);
    }
 }
  return(0);
  }
```

Chapter 2

Advance Data Structure

INTRODUCTION

THE STACK

The art of Programmeming beyond this simple beginning depends on inventing, or should reinventing, sophisticated data structures. The problem is where to begin and the general consensus is that the stack is where it's at.

A stack is exactly what it sounds like. Make a stack of cards, say, on a table and you have everything you need to know about a stack. What are the basic stack operations – you can put a new card on the top of the stack and you can take a card off the top of the stack. As long are you aren't cheating and dealing from the bottom (that would make it a data structure called a deque) putting something on the top and taking something off the top are the only two stack operations allowed.

Usually these two operations are called "push" and "pull" or "push" and "pop" but what you call them doesn't really matter as long as you understand what is going on.

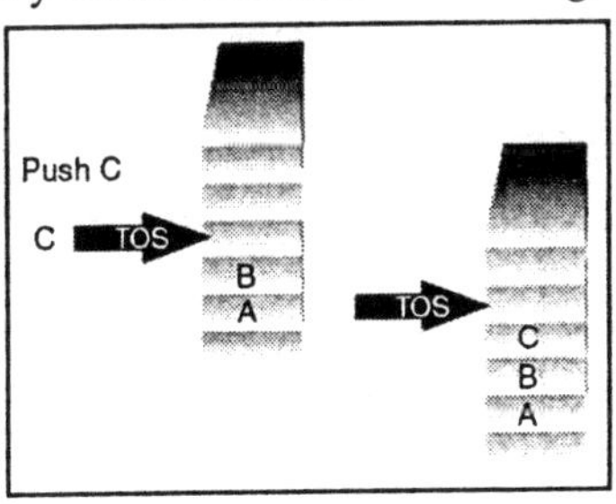

Pushing C onto a stack stores it where the TOS pointer indicates

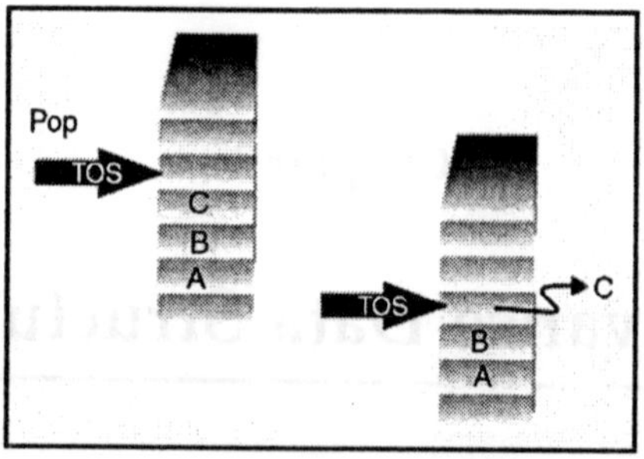

Popping the stack retrieves the top data item and moves the TOS down one

If we have a stack and we do Push A, Push B and Push C what do you think you get if we next do a Pop? If your answer is C you understand how a stack works.

Stacks are interesting because they can be used to alter the order of things. You stack A, B and C and you get back C, B and then A. It reverses the order without you having to do anything and this is very useful.

This accounts for the other name for a stack – a Last In First Out stack or LIFO stack. In fact this order changing ability is such a powerful property that you can build computers that have no other memory than a stack and no other storage operations than push and pop.

You can even create Programmeming languages that have nothing but a stack as their single data structure and all of their commands refer to the stack.

Even though you can have stack-oriented languages there are few popular or common languages that have stacks as standard – you have to create your own using whatever they provide. If you know how fine, if not then you have to use something less appropriate.

So, how is it done? All you need is an array and a variable to act as a pointer to the top of stack or TOS as it is usually known.

The array simply has to be big enough to hold the maximum number of items. The pointer is simply set initially to the start of the array. You might set up the stack as:

```
Dim Stack(10)
Pointer=1
```

To push something on to the stack the operation is:

```
Stack(Pointer)=something
Pointer=Pointer+1
```

To pop something off the stack the operation is:

```
Pointer=Pointer-1
Something=Stack(Pointer)
```

If you want to get picky about stacks you can argue the point of whether the pointer should point to the item on the top of the stack or to the next free space on the stack. Experts prefer to have the pointer to the item on the top of stack rather than the next free space. About the only thing that can go wrong with a stack is that it runs out of space i.e. the stack pointer goes beyond the end of the array or that it under runs, i.e. the user of the stack attempts to pop something off the stack when there isn't anything to pop.

OBJECTS

Of course the modern view isn't that the stack is a data structure – it's an object. That is, something with methods, i.e. pop and push, and an existence that goes beyond mere data. If "CStack" is a class based implementation of a stack then in an object-oriented language we can create as many stacks as we like:

```
Dim MyStack1 As CStack
Dim MyStack2 As CStack
```

These would be used something like:

```
MyStack1.push "A"
```

or

```
Data=MyStack2.pop
```

where it is assumed that the methods are push and pop.

Notice that the object-based implementation has the advantage that you don't need to ask how the stack works, what's inside the object if you like. This means that the Programmemer can implement the internal working any way that they want and they can even change things without the outside world being any the wiser. Objects are good...

Queue & the Deque

Once you have seen a stack you can invent all of the stack-like objects that have ever been thought of, and some. For example, a queue or a First In First Out (FIFO) stack is simply an array with two pointers – one to the start and one to end of the queue. Anything added to the queue goes to the end anything taken from the queue comes from the front.

In object-oriented terms the queue has two methods, Join and Leave. A queue doesn't change the order that things are stored in and it's mostly useful to slow things down so that they can be processed when the Programme is ready. (Hardware people often call queues "buffers".)

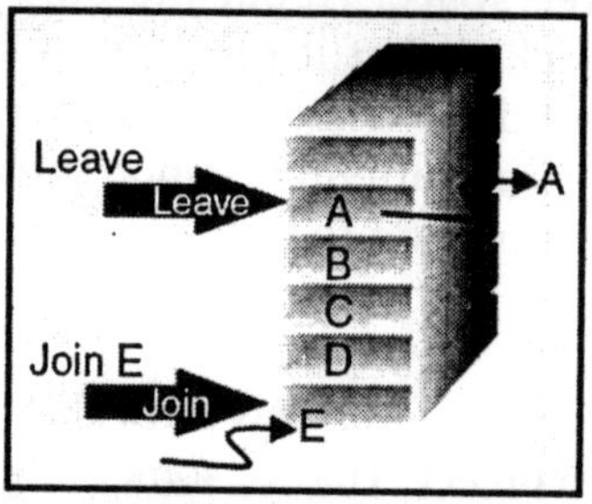

A queue has two pointers – one to the start of the queue and one to the end A deque is a queue that you can join and leave from the front or the back and it has four methods, JoinFront, JoinEnd, LeaveFront and LeaveEnd. You are probably getting the idea by now.

This sort of data structure simply has methods that adds new things and methods that retrieve new things according to when they were added.

Trees

The tree is probably the most important of the really advanced data structures and in many ways it's the most complicated and sophisticated.

To be abstract for the moment, a tree consists of a set of nodes – the places where the branches do their branching – and the branches that connect the nodes. The idea, or rather the picture, that you should have in your head of a branching tree-like structure is simple enough, actually implementing it in computer terms is not quite as straightforward.

To start with the nodes are the things that we work with. A node has space to store the data in the tree, a person's name for example, and it also stores "pointers" to the nodes that are connected to its child nodes.

The big problem is how many pointers? In general a tree can have nodes with as many child nodes as you care to imagine and this is difficult to implement.

As a result we like trees that have a fixed number of child nodes – 2 say gives us the binary tree. In this case, i.e. a binary tree, we can refer to the "right child node" and the "left child node" or just the "right" and "left" nodes. A tree also has a first or "root node" that everything else grows from.

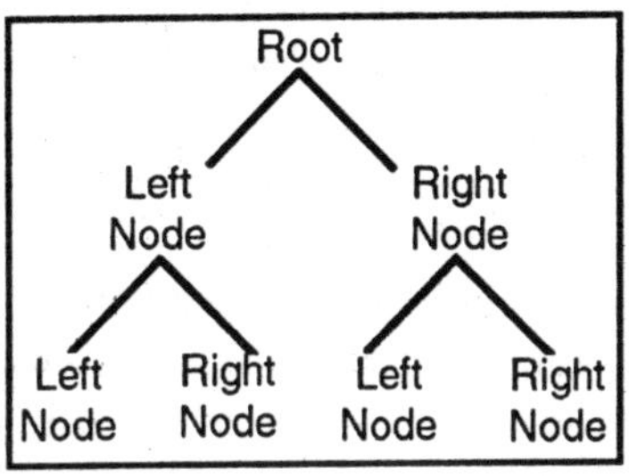

In a binary tree each node has two child nodes – one left and one right.

Now we can invent an object that behaves like a node in a binary tree, i.e. an object with two properties - left and right child nodes, and a single data property, which stores the value at the node.

We can now build a tree by creating a root node:

```
Dim root As New Node
```

and then add extra nodes as required:

```
Root.LeftNode=New Node
Root.RightNode=New Node
```

How do we get at these nodes so that we can grow the tree another level? Easy we just continue the same notation:

```
Root.LeftNode.LeftNode=New Node
Root.LeftNode.RightNode=New Node
```

and so on.

Of course we are also assuming that nodes have a data property which can be used to store whatever you want at each node. For example,

```
Root.LeftNode.data= "john"
```

would store the indicated name at the first left child node from the root. You should be able to see how to build up a data structure that corresponds to a family tree in which each "node" gives rise to just two offspring.

If you want more, or even a variable number of, offspring at each node then it works in the same sort of way but you need a collection of pointers to the child nodes and this is awkward to write down.

There is also the small problem of working with trees. Clearly you can keep on writing out Left Node.Right Node.Right Node. Left Node type names to specify a node of your choice – it's too clumsy. What actually happens in practice is that a pointer to a node is used as the "current" node and this moves its way down the tree by being set to the current nodes left or right child:

```
CurrentNode=CurrentNode.LeftNode
```

And so on. You can generalise this to more than two child nodes and even work out ways of writing Programmes that do standard tasks such as visiting every node in a tree.

This is again another area where things can seem complicated because you can ask that every node is visited in a particular order.

For example going down each branch as far as possible before starting again to go down the next branch is called"depth first", while visiting all nodes at the same depth before going deeper, is called"breadth first".

The jargon also gets more impressive - we talk of"traversing the tree" and eventually you will encounter the fact that trees and"recursion" go together.

Recursion is a whole topic in its own right and the source of the only good computer science joke I know - dictionary definition of recursion"Recursion - see recursion".

What are trees used for? Well, everything from keeping track of where files are stored on a disk drive to analysing natural language and applications in artificial intelligence. It's worth point out that XML is a data language that can only describe tree structures so the idea must be powerful. You can't Programme for long without meeting trees.

RED-BLACK TREES

DEFINITION

So, we've built up some pretty nifty binary trees - we can use the binary tree both as the basis of an implementation of a set, or as an implementation of a dictionary.

But our implementation has had one major problem: it's got absolutely no way to maintain balance. What that means is that depending on the order in which things are inserted to the tree, we might have excellent performance, or we might be no better than a linear list.

For example, look at these trees. As you can see, a tree with the same values can wind up quite different. In a good insert order, you can wind up with a nicely balanced tree: the minimum distance from root to leaf is 3; the maximum is 4. On the other hand, take the same values, and insert them in a different order and you get a rotten tree; the minimum distance from root to leaf is 1, and the maximum is 7.

So depending on luck, you can get a tree that gives you good performance, or one that ends up giving you no better than a plain old list.

Playing with a bit of randomization can often give you reasonably good performance on average - but if you're using a tree, it's probably because O(n) complexity is just too high. You want the O(lg n) complexity that you'll get from a binary tree - and not just sometimes.

To fix that, you need to change the structure a bit, so that as you insert things, the tree stays balanced. There are several different approaches to how you can do this. The one that we're going to look at is based on labeling nodes in ways that allow you to very easily detect when a serious imbalance is developing, and then re-arrange the tree to re-balance it. There are two major version of this, called the AVL tree, and the red-black tree. We're going to look at the red-black. Building a red-black tree is as much a lesson in data structures as it is in Haskell, but along with learning about the structure, we'll see a lot about how to write code in Haskell, and particularly about how to use pattern-matching for complex structures.

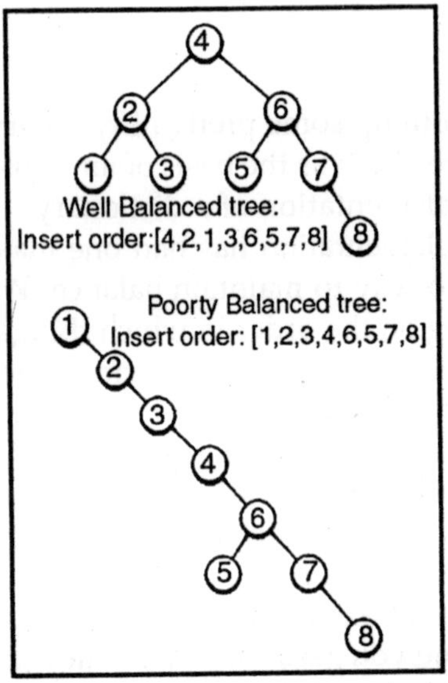

We'll start with a basic definition. A red-black tree is a normal binary search tree, except that each node is assigned a *Colour,* which is either red or black, and there are several invariant properties that must hold about the Colouring of the tree:

- The root of the tree is always black.
- All branches of a tree end in a null which is *black.*
- All children of red nodes are black.
- For all nodes in the tree, all downward paths from the node to a leaf contain the same number of *black* nodes.

If these invariants are maintained, they guarantee that tree is *almost* balanced: for the entire tree, and every subtree of it, the *longest* path from the root to a leaf is no more than twice the *shortest* path from the root to a leaf.

We'll start by writing the Haskell type declaration for a

red/black tree. We'll just do it as a tree of ordered values to keep things simple.

```
>data Colour = Red | Black deriving (Eq, Show)
>
>data (Ord a) ⇒ RedBlackTree a = RBTNode a
Colour (RedBlackTree a) (RedBlackTree a)
> | RBTEmpty deriving (Eq,Show)
```

Also, for convenience, we'll write a couple of accessor functions that we'll use later on. Something interesting to note about these accessors is that they use *non-exhaustive patterns*: there are values of type RedBlackTree a for which these functions are undefined. If you call any of these accessors on a tree whose value is RBTEmpty, you'll get a runtime error.

It is, at the very least, considered bad style to write non-exhaustive functions. It's actually a way of cheating the type system. You're claiming that you're writing a function from type T to type U, but in fact, there are values of T for which the function won't work: the real type of the function is T′ → U, where T′ is a subset of T.

But you can't say that in Haskell - so you're cheating. To be more concrete, you're writing functions like rbtLeftChildwhich *claims* that for any red-black tree passed to it, it will return a valid red-black tree. But in fact, that's only true for the subset of red-black trees that were built with theRBTNode constructor; for other values, the function will fail.

The best solution to make it exhaustive would be to use the Maybe type to allow you to return a valid value for all trees passed as inputs. But that would make the code *much* more complex, unless we used monads - and we're not ready for monads yet.

```
>
>rbtLeftChild:: (Ord a) ⇒ RedBlackTree a →
RedBlackTree a
>rbtLeftChild (RBTNode _ _ l _) = l
>
>rbtRightChild:: (Ord a) ⇒ RedBlackTree a →
RedBlackTree a
```

```
>rbtRightChild (RBTNode _ _ _ r) = r
>
>rbtValue:: (Ord a) ⇒ RedBlackTree a → a
>rbtValue (RBTNode v _ _ _) = v
>
>rbtColour:: (Ord a) ⇒ RedBlackTree a →
Colour
>rbtColour (RBTNode _ c _ _) = c
>rbtColour RBTEmpty = Black
```

Inserting data into the tree is where things get interesting. It starts off the same as how you insert into a typical BST: search for the correct position, and then insert the value as a new leaf node. But in a red-black tree, the new node needs a Colour. New nodes are always red - so you're inserting a red node. Now you need to check to make sure that you're not violating any of the tree invariants. If you are, then you need to fix it.

To keep things reasonably clean and separate, we'll use the tail-calling version of tree insert, and then tail-call a rebalance function when the basic insert is complete. Rebalance will fix the balance of the tree, and do the tree re-assembly as it climbs up the tree.

```
>rbtInsert:: (Ord a) Þ RedBlackTree a → a
→ RedBlackTree a
>rbtRebalance:: (Ord a) Þ RedBlackTree a →
[RedBlackTree a] → RedBlackTree a
>—rbtRebalance      focus
 ancestors
>
>rbtInsert node v =
> rbtInsertTailCall node v []
>
>rbtInsertTailCall node@(RBTNode v Colour left
right) newval path
> | v > newval = rbtInsertTailCall left newval
(node:path)
> | otherwise = rbtInsertTailCall right newval
```

```
(node:path)
>rbtInsertTailCall RBTEmpty v path =
>rbtRebalance (RBTNode v Red RBTEmpty RBTEmpty)
path
```

All over the place as we rebalance the tree, we'll have places where we want to "rebuild" nodes to patch in the insertion change; as usual, we separate that into its own function.

```
>- Reconstruct takes a child node and a parent
node, and creates a replacement
>- for the parent node with the child in the
appropriate position. It allows
>- the Colour of the new node to be specified.
>reconstructNode node@(RBTNode v c l r)
parent@(RBTNode pv pc pl pr) Colour =
> if (pv > v)
> then (RBTNode pv Colour node pr)
> else (RBTNode pv Colour pl node)
```

Now, we need to think about what we're going to do to keep the tree balanced as we walk back up the insertion path fixing the tree. There are two things we can do to make the tree respect the invariants: we can re-Colour nodes, or we can *pivot* subtrees.

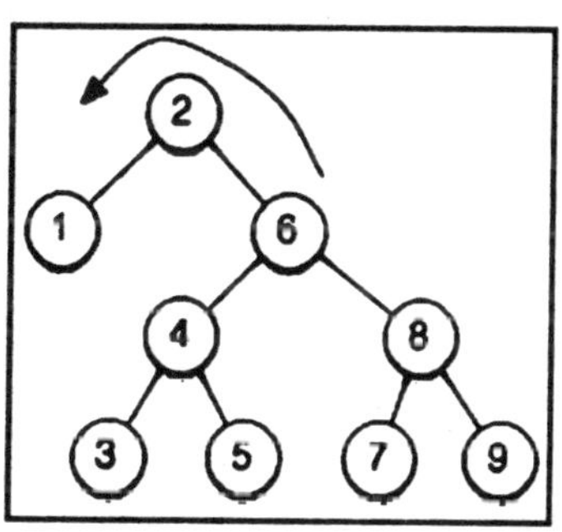

Pivoting a tree is an interesting operation - it's a process of swapping a node and one of its children to rotate a section of the tree. Suppose we have a binary search tree like the one in the diagram to the side. It's poorly balanced; it's got only one node to its left, but 7 nodes to its right. To correct this by pivoting, what we'll do is take node 6 - currently a child of the root, and rotate the tree counterclockwise around it, so that 6 becomes the root, the old root (2) becomes the left child of 6, and the old left child of 6 (node 4) becomes the*right* child of the old root.

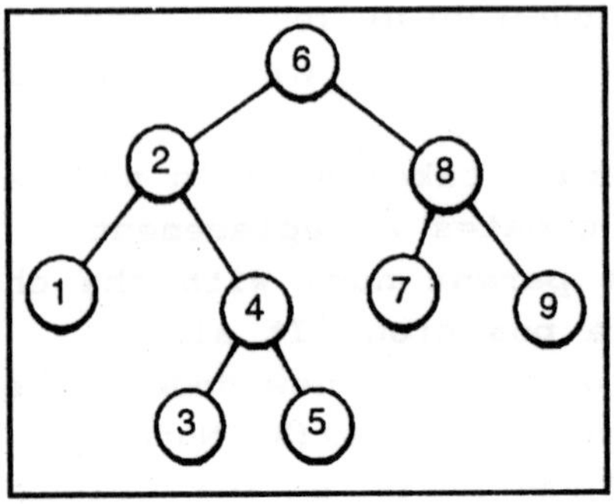

So after the pivot, our tree looks like this. This operation was a *left* pivot; a right pivot does the same kind of thing, but rotating the tree clockwise instead of counterclockwise.

So let's go ahead and write the pivot operations. We'll write two pivot functions: one for each direction. We'll pass the pivot operation a subtree whose root and child in the appropriate direction are to be rotated. In addition, we'll also add a parameter for managing the Colour of the new root node. In some cases, we'll want to swap the Colours of the nodes being moved; in other cases, we won't. So we'll put a boolean parameter in to specify whether or not to swap the Colours.

```
> – pivot left tree at root; second parent
indicates whether or not to swap
> – Colours of the nodes that are being moved.
>rbtPivotLeft:: (Ord a) ⇒ RedBlackTree a →
Bool → RedBlackTree a
>rbtPivotLeft (RBTNode rootval rootColour sib
(RBTNode focval focColour focleft focright))
swap =
> (RBTNode focval newrootColour oldroot focright)
where
> newrootColour = if swap then rootColour else
focColour
```

```
> oldrootColour = if swap then focColour else
rootColour
> oldroot = RBTNode rootval oldrootColour sib
focleft
>
>
>rbtPivotRight (RBTNode rootval rootColour
(RBTNode focval focColour focleft focright) sib)
swap =
> (RBTNode focval newrootColour focleft oldroot)
where
> newrootColour = if swap then rootColour else
focColour
> oldrootColour = if swap then focColour else
rootColour
> oldroot = RBTNode rootval oldrootColour
focright sib
>
```

So, let's try taking a look at how the pivots work. First, we need to construct some trees to rebalance. We'll just do it manually, since the insert code isn't properly finished yet.

```
>twentyseven = RBTNode 27 Black RBTEmpty
RBTEmpty
>twentytwo = RBTNode 22 Black RBTEmpty RBTEmpty
>twentyfive = RBTNode 25 Black twentytwo
twentyseven
>sixteen = RBTNode 16 Black RBTEmpty RBTEmpty
>twenty = RBTNode 20 Black sixteen twentyfive
>twelve = RBTNode 12 Black RBTEmpty RBTEmpty
>fifteen = RBTNode 15 Black twelve twenty
>two = RBTNode 2 Black RBTEmpty RBTEmpty
>seven = RBTNode 7 Black RBTEmpty RBTEmpty
>five = RBTNode 5 Black two seven
>ten = RBTNode 10 Black five fifteen
```

That produces a unbalanced binary tree that looks like this:

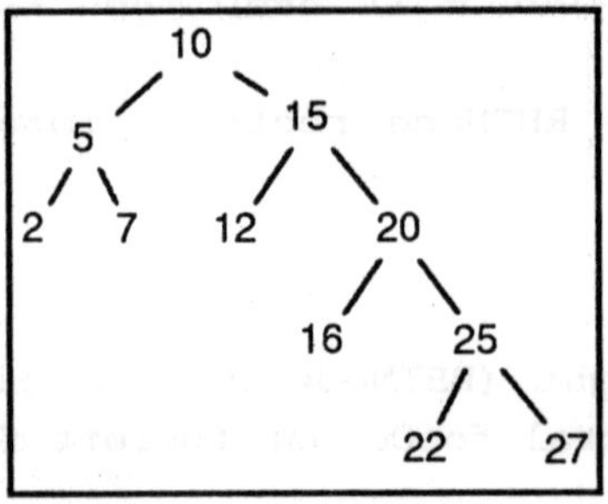


```
RBTNode 10 Black
  (RBTNode 5 Black – 10left
    (RBTNode 2 Black RBTEmpty RBTEmpty) –
   5 left
    (RBTNode 7 Black RBTEmpty RBTEmpty)) – 5
    right
(RBTNode 15 Black – 10 right
   (RBTNode 12 Black RBTEmpty RBTEmpty) – 15
   left
   (RBTNode 20 Black – 15 right
   (RBTNode 16 Black RBTEmpty RBTEmpty) – 20
   left
(RBTNode 25 Black – 20 right
(RBTNode 22 Black RBTEmpty RBTEmpty) – 25 left
(RBTNode 27 Black RBTEmpty RBTEmpty)))) – 25
right
```

Let's do a quick test, and try doing a left pivot on the root.

```
*Main> rbtPivotLeft ten False
RBTNode 15 Black (RBTNode 10 Black (RBTNode 5
Black (RBTNode 2 Black RBTEmpty RBTEmpty)
(RBTNode 7 Black RBTEmpty RBTEmpty)) (RBTNode
12 Black RBTEmpty RBTEmpty)) (RBTNode 20 Black
(RBTNode 16 Black RBTEmpty RBTEmpty) (RBTNode
25 Black (RBTNode 22 Black RBTEmpty RBTEmpty)
(RBTNode 27 Black RBTEmpty RBTEmpty)))
*Main>
```

Cleaned up, that looks like this:

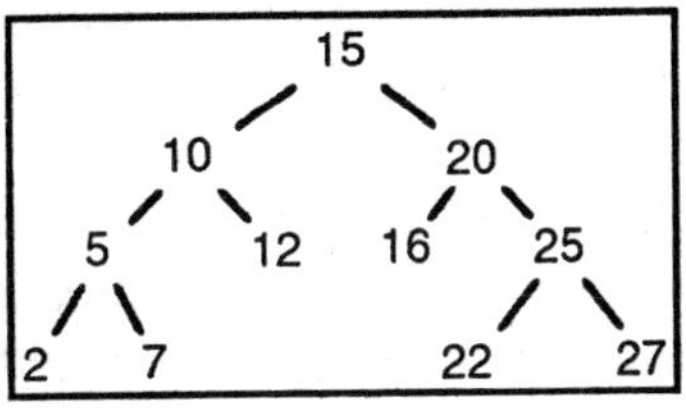


```
RBTNode 15 Black
  (RBTNode 10 Black
     (RBTNode 5 Black
          (RBTNode 2 Black RBTEmpty RBTEmpty)
          (RBTNode 7 Black RBTEmpty RBTEmpty))
     (RBTNode 12 Black RBTEmpty RBTEmpty))
(RBTNode 20 Black
     (RBTNode 16 Black RBTEmpty RBTEmpty)
     (RBTNode 25 Black
          (RBTNode 22 Black RBTEmpty RBTEmpty)
          (RBTNode 27 Black RBTEmpty RBTEmpty)))
```

Much better - that's much closer to a balanced tree! So now that we know how to do the pivot, and we've seen that it works correctly, we can look at building the rebalance code.

With pivots out of the way, we can start looking at how to decide what operations to do to rebalance the tree. When we're doing an insert, we end up inserting a red node on the bottom of the tree. It's got two children, both null, which are considered black. If the parent of our new node is black, then everything is fine; we haven't altered the number of black nodes on any path from a node to a leaf. So we're done. But if the parent is red, then we've got a red child of a red node, so we need to do some fixing.

Fixing an imbalance in a red-black tree can (and in fact often will) trigger a cascade of changes. But part of what makes the structure so elegant is that we only need to look at the *local* structure immediately around the new insert; and then when we've corrected that, there's only *one* place where the next problem could be. In every case where we're rebalancing, we can look at a specific problem, and fix it, and then immediately move to where the next potential problem is. To code this, we'll look at in terms of a *focal node,* which is the node causing the immediate problem we're fixing; and we'll fix the problem by looking at the local context of the focus.

The potential cases we can encounter are:

- The focal node is the root of the tree. In that case, we make it black. That adds one black node to every path in the tree, which leaves us with a valid tree, so we're done.
- The focal node is red, but has a black parent. Again, that's fine. No problem.
- The focal node is red; it's parent is also red. Then we need to look at its *uncle*; that is, the node that is the sibling of its parent. If both the new node, the parent and the uncle are all red, then we change the Colour of the parent and uncle to black, and the grandparent to red. After this, the grandparent becomes the focal node, and we continue to do our tree-fixing with the new focus.
- Here's where it gets a bit messy. If the focal node and its parent are both red, but the uncle is black, then we're going to need to pivot. Getting the pivot right is tricky. There are four cases:
  - The focal node is the *right* child of its parent, and the parent is the *left* node of the grandparent, then we do a *left* pivot of the focal node and its parent, and the former parent becomes the new focal node.
  - The focal node is the *left* child of its parent, and the parent is the *right* child of the grandparent, then we do a *right* pivot of the focal node and its parent, and the former parent becomes the new focus.
  - The focal node is the left child of its parent, and the parent is the left child of the grandparent. Then we do a *right* pivot of the parent and the grandparent and swap the Colours of the parent and grandparent. The parent becomes the focus.
  - The focal node is the right child of its parent, and

the parent is the right child of the grandparent. Then we do a *left* pivot of the parent and the grandparent and swap the Colours of the parent and grandparent. The parent becomes the focus.

AUGMENTING DATA STRUCTURES

There are some Programmeming situations that can be perfectly solved with standard data structures such as a linked lists, hash tables, or binary search trees. Many others require a dash of creativity. Only in rare situations will you need to create an entirely new type of data structure, though. More often, it will suffice to augment (to modify) an existing data structure by storing additional information in it. You can then Programme new operations for the data structure to support the desired application. Augmenting a data structure is not always straightforward, however, since the added information must be updated and maintained by the ordinary operations on the data structure.

This lecture discusses two data structures that are constructed by augmenting red-black trees (see the previous post on red-black trees).

The first part of the lecture describes a data structure that supports general order-statistic operations on a dynamic set. It's called dynamic order statistics. The notion of order statistics was introduced in lecture six. In lecture six it was shown that any order statistic could be retrieved in O(n) time from an unordered set. In this lecture it is shown how red-black trees can be modified so that any order statistic can be determined in O(lg(n)) time. It presents two algorithms OS-Select(i), which returns i-th smallest item in a dynamic set, and OS-Rank(x), which returns rank (position) of element x in sorted order.

The lecture continues with general methodology of how to augment a data structure.

Augmenting a data structure can be broken into four steps:

- Choosing an underlying data structure.
- Determining additional information to be maintained in the underlying data structure.

- Verifying that the additional information can be maintained for the basic modifying operations (insert, delete, rotate, etc.) on the underlying data structure.
- Developing new operations.

The second part of the lecture applies this methodology to construct a data structure called interval trees. This data structure maintains a dynamic set of elements, with each element x containing an interval. Interval is simply pair of numbers (low, high). For example, a time interval from 3 o'clock to 7 o'clock is a pair (3, 7).

Lecture gives an algorithm called Interval-Search(x), which given a query interval x, quickly finds an interval in the set that overlaps it. Time complexity of this algorithm is O(lg(n)).

ABOUT LUCTURE

The lecture is motivated by two things:

- The implementation of ADTs that extend standard ADTs by one or more additional operations;
- Application in which data "live in" various data structures simultaneously.

Augmentation is a process by which one adds fields to the nodes as necessary.

Augmenting a data structure can be broken into four steps:

- choosing an underlying data structure
- determining additional information to be maintained in the underlying data structure
- verifying that the additional information can be efficiently maintained for the basic modifying operations on the underlying data structure
- developing new operations

DYNAMIC ORDER-STATISTIC TREES

ADT: set S; Dictionary operations (*Insert, Delete, Search*) + two additional operations:

- *Rank(S,x)*: Returns rank of node x (smallest rank is 1)
- *Select(S, i)*: Select ith smallest element from set S

Implementation

An *order-statistic tree* T is simply a red-black tree with additional information stored at each node. Besides the usual red-black tree fields *key*[x], *left*[x], *right*[x],*p*[x] and *Colour*[x] in a node *x*, we have another field *size*[*x*]. This field contains the number of internal nodes in the subtree rooted at *x* (including x itself), that is, the size of the subtree.

$$size[x] = size[left[x]] + size[right[x]] + 1$$

The node of the *order-statistic tree* will now look as follows: figure

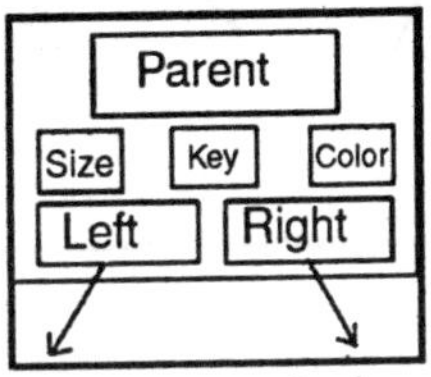

There are couple of things though that we have to worry about:

1. Can *size* be updated in $O(\log_2 n)$ time per operation?
2. *Rank*(x) and *select*(S, i) to be done in $O(\log_2 n)$ time.

Operations on Order-statistic trees

Insert

As we know, insertion into a red-black tree consists of two phases. Phase 1 goes down the path from the root inserting the new node as a child of the existing node. To maintain the subtree sizes we simply increment *size*[x] for each node *x* on the path traversed from the root down toward the leaves. The new node added gets size 1. Figure illustrates Phase 1.

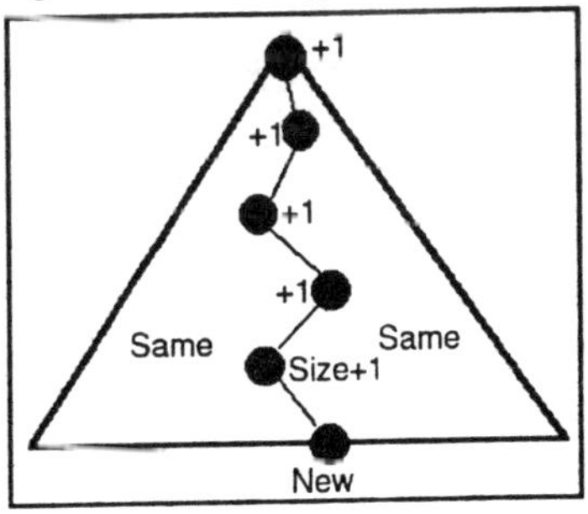

In the Phase 2, the only structural changes to the underlying red-black tree are caused by *rotations*, of which there are at most two.

Rotation is a local operation and it invalidates only the two *size* fields in the nodes incident on the link around which the rotation is performed. Figure shows *Left* and *Right*rotations.

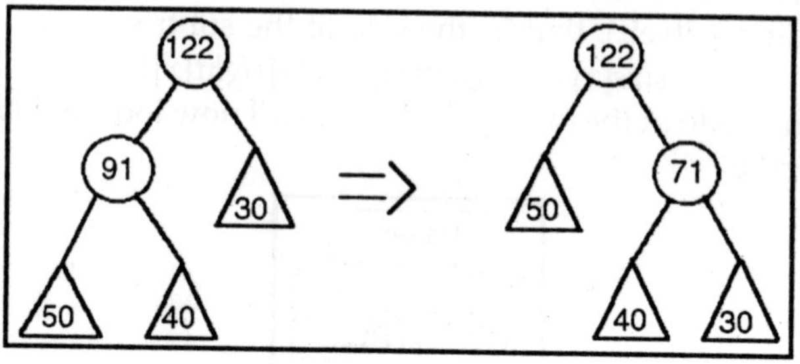

Delete

Phase 1 splices out the node we wish to delete. To update subtree sizes we simply traverse a path from node we wish to delete up to the root, decrementing*size* field for each node on the path.

Figure illustrates this process.

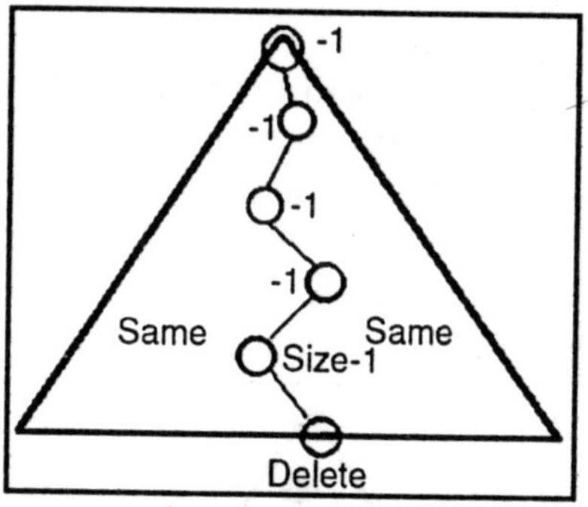

The rotations in the Phase 2 are handled in the same manner as for insertion.

Running time: To maintain tree sizes in the Phase 1 of insertion or deletion we have to increment or decrement *size*[x] for each node x on the path from the root down toward the leaves. Since there are O($\log_2 n$) nodes on the traversed path, the additional cost of maintaining the *size* fields is $O(\log_2 n)$. Moreover, rotation is a local operation and hence only O(1) additional time is spent updating *size* fields in the Phase 2. Thus, both insertion and deletion take $O(\log_2 n)$ time.

Select

The procedure *Select(x, i)* returns a pointer to the node containing the ith smallest key in the subtree rooted at *x*.

```
Select(x, i)
r (rank of root) = size[left[x]] + 1
case r = i: return x
case r > i: return Select(left[x], i)
case r < i: return Select(right[x], i)
```

Because each recursive call goes down one level in the order-statistic tree, the total time for *Select* is at worst proportional to the height of the tree. Since the tree is the red-black tree, its height is $O(\log_2 n)$. Thus, the running time of *Select* is $O(\log_2 n)$.

Rank

The procedure *Rank(T, x)* returns the position of *x* in the linear order determined by an inorder tree walk of *T*. Let *x* is a pointer to the node in the tree.

```
Rank(T, x)
r = size[left[x]] + 1
y = x
while y <> root do
if right[parent[y]] = y
then r += size[left[parent[y]]] + 1
y = parent[y]
return r
```

Since each iteration of the while loop takes O(1) time and *y* goes up one level in the tree with each iteration, the running time of *Rank* is at worst proportional to the height of the tree: $O(\log_2 n)$.

Figure illustrates the *Rank* procedure.

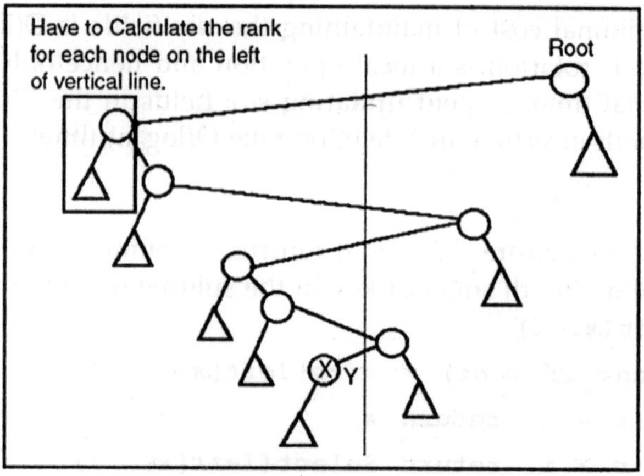

Fig. Link to our Java Applet

BINARY SEARCH TREES FOR BROWSING ADT

Dictionary + Browsing operations:

- MIN
- MAX
- Predecessor
- Successor

Implementation

The underlying data structure is a red-black tree where besides usual red-black tree fields each node is augmented with *Min*[*x*], *Max*[*x*], *Predecessor*[*x*] and*Successor*[*x*]. Figure 6 shows the augmented Red-Black tree on the input {1 2 3 4 5 6 7 8 9 10 11}.

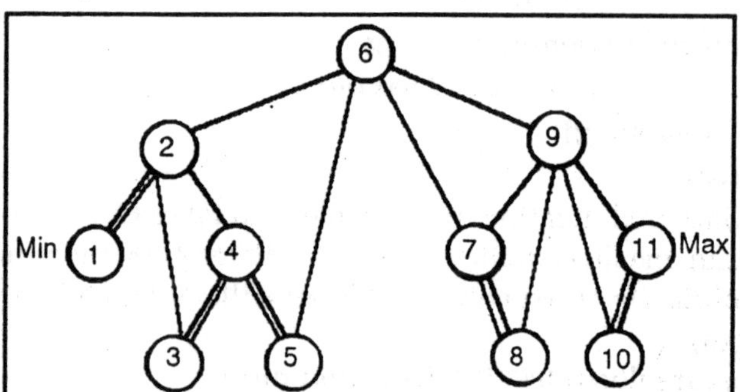

The data structure in Figure 6 can be looked at as a binary search tree or a sorted linked list as shown in Figure 7. In fact, according to Prof. Devroye, it is a smooth "marriage" of both data structures.

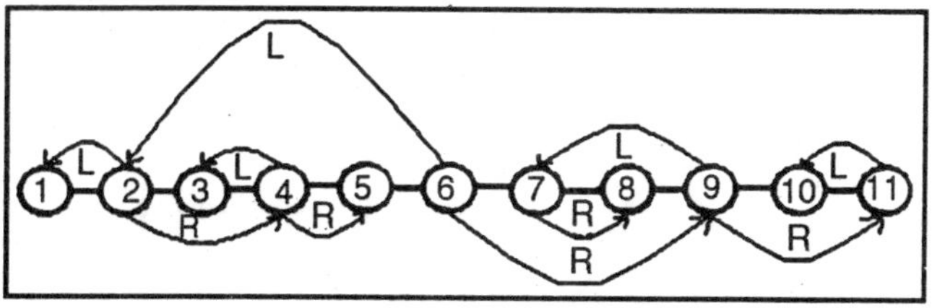

When we insert or delete a node we always have to update *predecessor* and *successor* pointers. In the Figure 8 we have deleted a new node with a *key*value 8. Accordingly we have to update *successor* and *predecessor* pointers. The time it takes to update pointers is equal to $O(\log_2 n)$, since we either follow a path up the tree or down the tree. Rotation operations take as usual O(1) time, so the running time for insertion or deletion is $O(\log_2 n)$. In figure the updated pointer.

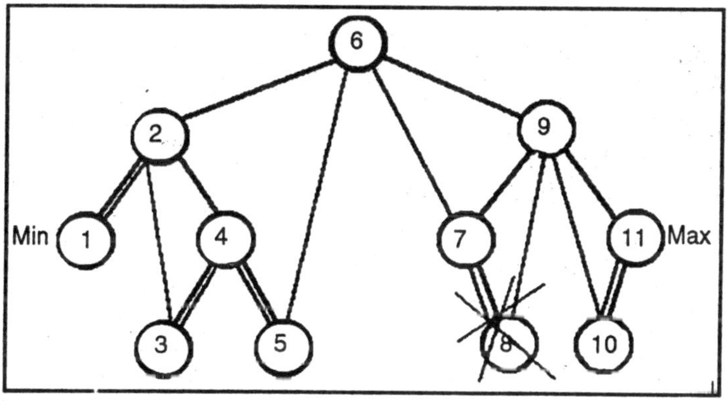

INTERVAL TREES

Interval tree is a binary search tree for intervals which are efficient for the dictionary operations and overlap. *Overlap(x, i)* for interval *i* and a tree rooted at *x*, returns a pointer to an interval in the collection that overlaps the given interval *i* or returns NIL otherwise.

The underlying data structure is a red-black tree in which each node x contains an interval $int[x]$ and the key of x is a low endpoint of interval, $low[int[x]].high[x]$ is the high endpoint of interval. In addition, each node x contains a value $max[x]$ which is the maximum value of any interval endpoint stored in the subtree rooted at x.

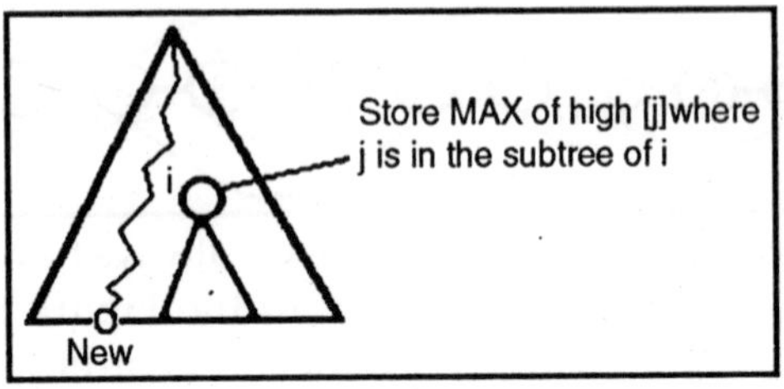

Operations

- Determine overlap with some interval in the tree: return Yes or No
- Dictionary operations (Insert, Delete, Search)

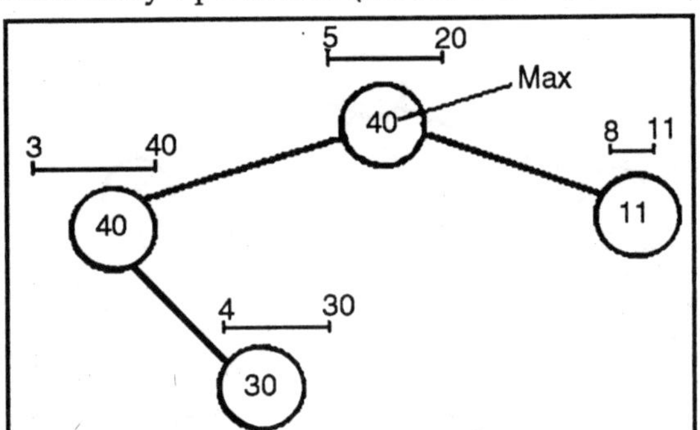

Given interval i and pointer to the root x Overlap(x, i) returns NIL if no overlap occured or pointer to the node if there is an overlap.

```
Overlap(x, i)
if x = NIL then return NIL
while x <> NIL and i doesn't overlap int[x] do
if left[x] <> NIL and low[i] Ü max[left[x]]
then x = left[x]
else x = right[x]
```

Running Time

The search for the inteval that overlaps *i* starts with *x* at the root of the tree and proceeds downward. It terminates when either overlapping interval is found or *x* becomes NIL. Since each iteration of the basic loop takes O(1) time, and since the height or the red-black tree is $O(\log_2 n)$ *Overlap*takes $O(\log_2 n)$ time.

Insertion of a node *x* into a tree consists of *two* phases. During the first phase *x* is inserted as a child of an existing node. The value of *max*[*x*] can be computed in O(1) time since it depends only on information in the other fields of *x* itself and *x*'s children, but *x*'s children are both NIL. Once *max*[*x*] is computed, the change propagates up the tree. Thus, total time for the first phase is $O(\log_2 n)$. During second phase the only structural changes are caused by rotations. Since only *two* nodes change in rotation, the total time for updating the *max* fields is $O(\log_2 n)$ per rotation. Since the number of rotations during insertion is at most *two,* the total time for insertion is $O(\log_2 n)$.

In the first phase of deletion, changes occur if the deleted node is replaced by its successor, and then again when either the deleted node or its successor is spliced out. Propagating the updates to *max* caused by these changes costs at most $O(\log_2 n)$ since the changes modify the tree locally. Fixing up the red-black tree during the second phase requires at most *three* rotations, and each rotation requires at most $O(\log_2 n)$ time to propagate the updates to *max*. Thus, like insertion, the total time for deletion is $O(\log_2 n)$.

Problem: Layout of VSLI chips

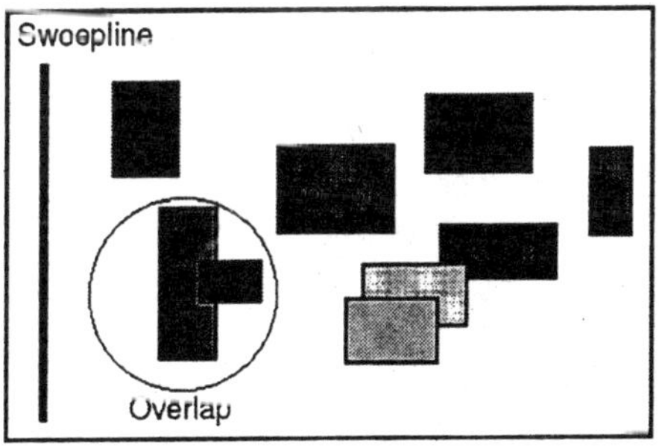

In this section we present a problem which is motivated by automated chip design. The problem is how can we place many printed circuits on one chip without overlapping?

To make the problem more amenable to analysis, we assume that all n rectangles to be aligned with horizontal axis. We also assume that we are given a configuration of the rectangles, and our task is merely to check whether there is any overlap between rectangles.

In the naive solution we try to remove overlapped rectangles and place them randomly again. It takes time of Θ (n^2). The more efficient algorithm, which takes $O(n\log_2 n)$ time, uses a technique known as *sweeping*.

In sweeping an imaginary vertical sweep line passes through a given set of geometric objects (rectangles), usually from left to right. Sweeping provides a method for ordering geometric objects, usualy by placing them into dynamic data structure.

We sort the rectangles' endpoints by increasing x-coordinate and proceed from left to right. We insert y-direction intervals into an interval tree when its left endpoint is encountered and we delete it from interval tree when its right endpoint is encountered. Whether two segments first become consecutive in the total order, we check if they overlap.

Sweepline (Turning 2-d into 1-d)

- Sort x coordinates of rectangles
- Interval tree for y direction intervals
- for i = 1 to 2n do

If ith point is start then if (a, ß) overlap some interval in interval tree - STOP: Insert((*a*, ß), interval tree) *endpoint* then Delete((*a*, ß), interval tree) *a* is a segment immediately above segment *i* and ß is a segment immediately below segment *i*. Sorting takes $O(n\log_2 n)$ time using mergesort or heapsort.

Since there are $2n$ points the *for* loop iterates at most $2n$ times. Each iteration takes $O(\log_2 n)$ time, since each red-black tree operation takes $O(\log_2 n)$ time. To check if there is an overlap takes $O(1)$ time. Thus the total running time is $O(\log_2 n)$.

B-TREES

INTRODUCTION

B-Tree is an indexing technique most commonly used in databases and file systems where pointers to data are placed in a balance tree structure so that all references to any data can be accessed in an equal time frame. It is also a tree data structure which keeps data sorted so that searching, inserting and deleting can be done in logarithmic amortized time.

Compared to a real tree, the B-Tree has roots at the top and leaves and nodes at the bottom. The B-Tree belongs to a group of techniques in computer science known as self-balancing search trees which attempts to automatically keep the number of levels of nodes under the root small at all times. It is the most preferred way to implement sets, associative arrays and other data structures that are used in computer Programmeming languages, relationaldatabase management systems and low level data manipulations.

In the B-Tree, the records are stored in the leaves. This is the location where there is nothing more beyond it. The order of the tree determines the maximum number of children per node. Depth refers to the number of required disk access. A B-Tree can have up to millions and billions of records although it is not all the time that leaves necessarily contain a record but more than half certainly do.

When decision points on the tree, which are called nodes, are on the hard disk instead of on random access memory (RAM), B-Tree is the preferred technique as hard disks could work a thousand times slower compared to RAM because processes on hard disks requires mechanical parts. On RAM, processes are done purely in electronic media.

The nodes in a B-Tree can have a variable number of child nodes within a range pre-defined by the system. When a data is inserted or removed from a node, the number ofchild nodes also changes but the pre-defined ranged should be maintained so internal nodes may either be split or joined.

B-trees do not need frequent re-balancing as both the upper and lower bounds on the number of child nodes are typically fixed. As an example, a 2-3 B-Tree implementation has internal nodes that can only have 2 or 3 child nodes.

To keep the B-tree well balanced, all leaf nodes are required to be of the same depth. The depth only increases very slowly and infrequently.

Searching in a B-Tree structure starts from the root and traversed from top to bottom. Insertion is done by looking for a node where a new leaf or element should be. If there is still room or the maximum legal number of elements is not exceeded, insertion takes place. Otherwise, the leaf node splits into another tow nodes. Deletion in a B-Tree has two strategies. The first involves locating the item to be deleted and immediately doing the action then restructuring the tree. The second involves doing a traversing down the tree and laying out the restructure before deleting.

In a file system, a file may contain any number of B-Trees and each B-Tree must have a unique name composed of any string of characters. Each B-Tree names is saved in the file an item containing the number of the rood node of the B-Tree. Searching, inserting and deleting through the B-Tree starts from the root node.

The B-Tree was created by Rudolf Bayer and Ed McCreight. The B in the B-Tree has ambiguous meaning. Some say it stands for Bayer while others say it stands for Balanced and still there are other who consider it to stand for Boeing where both men were working for Boeing Scientific Research Labs at the time they created the B-tree.

B-Tree structures support various basic dynamic set operations including *Search, Predecessor, Successor, Minimum, Maximum, Insert,* and *Delete* in time proportional to the height of the tree. Ideally, a tree will be balanced and the height will be *log n* where *n* is the number of nodes in the tree. To ensure that the height of the tree is as small as possible and therefore provide the best running time, a balanced tree structure like a red-black tree, AVL tree, or b-tree must be used.

When working with large sets of data, it is often not possible or desirable to maintain the entire structure in primary storage (RAM). Instead, a relatively small portion of the data structure is maintained in primary storage, and additional data is read from secondary storage as needed. Unfortunately, a magnetic disk, the most common form of secondary storage, is significantly slower than random access memory (RAM). In fact, the system often spends more time retrieving data than actually processing data.

B-trees are balanced trees that are optimized for situations when part or all of the tree must be maintained in secondary storage such as a magnetic disk. Since disk accesses are expensive (time consuming) operations, a b-tree tries to minimize the number of disk accesses. For example, a b-tree with a height of 2 and a branching factor of 1001 can store over one billion keys but requires at most two disk accesses to search for any node.

STRUCTURE OF B-TREES

Unlike a binary-tree, each node of a b-tree may have a variable number of keys and children. The keys are stored in non-decreasing order. Each key has an associated child that is the root of a subtree containing all nodes with keys less than or equal to the key but greater than the preceeding key. A node also has an additional rightmost child that is the root for a subtree containing all keys greater than any keys in the node.

A b-tree has a minumum number of allowable children for each node known as the *minimization factor*. If t is this *minimization factor*, every node must have at least t - 1 keys. Under certain circumstances, the root node is allowed to violate this property by having fewer than t - 1 keys. Every node may have at most $2t$ - 1keys or, equivalently, $2t$ children.

Since each node tends to have a large branching factor (a large number of children), it is typically neccessary to traverse relatively few nodes before locating the desired key. If access to each node requires a disk access, then a b-tree will minimize the number of disk accesses required. The minimzation factor is usually chosen so that the total size of each node corresponds to a multiple of the block size of the underlying storage device. This choice simplifies and optimizes disk access. Consequently, a b-tree is an ideal data structure for situations where all data cannot reside in primary storage and accesses to secondary storage are comparatively expensive (or time consuming).

Height of B-Trees

For *n* greater than or equal to one, the height of an *n*-key b-tree T of height *h* with a minimum degree *t* greater than or equal to 2,

$$H \leq \log_t \frac{n+1}{2}$$

For a proof of the above inequality, refer to Cormen, Leiserson, and Rivest pages 383-384.

The worst case height is *O(log n)*. Since the "branchiness" of a b-tree can be large compared to many other balanced tree structures, the base of the logarithm tends to be large; therefore, the number of nodes visited during a search tends to be smaller than required by other tree structures. Although this does not affect the asymptotic worst case height, b-trees tend to have smaller heights than other trees with the same asymptotic height.

OPERATIONS ON B-TREES

The algorithms for the *search, create,* and *insert* operations are shown below. Note that these algorithms are single pass; in other words, they do not traverse back up the tree. Since b-trees strive to minimize disk accesses and the nodes are usually stored on disk, this single-pass approach will reduce the number of node visits and thus the number of disk accesses. Simpler double-pass approaches that move back up the tree to fix violations are possible.

Since all nodes are assumed to be stored in secondary storage (disk) rather than primary storage (memory), all references to a given node be be preceeded by a read operation denoted by *Disk-Read*. Similarly, once a node is modified and it is no longer needed, it must be written out to secondary storage with a write operation denoted by *Disk-Write*. The algorithms below assume that all nodes referenced in parameters have already had a corresponding *Disk-Read* operation. New nodes are created and assigned storage with the *Allocate-Node* call. The implementation details of the *Disk-Read, Disk-Write,* and *Allocate-Node* functions are operating system and implementation dependent.

B-Tree-Search(x, k)

```
 i ← 1
 while i ⇐ n[x] and k > key_i[x]
   do i ← i + 1
 if i ⇐ n[x] and k = key_i[x]
      then return (x, i)
if leaf[x]
      then return NIL
      else Disk-Read(c_i[x])
              return B-Tree-Search(c_i[x], k)
```

The search operation on a b-tree is analogous to a search on a binary tree. Instead of choosing between a left and a right child as in a binary tree, a b-tree search must make an n-way choice.

The correct child is chosen by performing a linear search of the values in the node. After finding the value greater than or equal to the desired value, the child pointer to the immediate left of that value is followed. If all values are less than the desired value, the rightmost child pointer is followed. Of course, the search can be terminated as soon as the desired node is found. Since the running time of the search operation depends upon the height of the tree, *B-Tree-Search* is $O(\log_t n)$.

B-Tree-Create(T)

```
 x ¬ Allocate-Node()
 leaf[x] ¬ TRUE
 n[x] ¬ 0
 Disk-Write(x)
 root[T] ← x
```

The *B-Tree-Create* operation creates an empty b-tree by allocating a new root node that has no keys and is a leaf node. Only the root node is permitted to have these properties; all other nodes must meet the criteria outlined previously. The *B-Tree-Create* operation runs in time $O(1)$.

B-Tree-Split-Child(x, i, y)

```
z ¬ Allocate-Node()
leaf[z] ¬ leaf[y]
n[z] ¬ t - 1
for j ¬ 1 to t - 1
    do key_j[z] ¬ key_j+t[y]
if not leaf[y]
    then for j ¬ 1 to t
        do c_j[z] ¬ c_j+t[y]
n[y] ¬ t - 1
for j ¬ n[x] + 1 downto i + 1
        do c_j+1[x] ¬ c_j[x]
c_i+1 ¬ z
for j ¬ n[x] downto i
      do key_j+1[x] ¬ key_j[x]
key_i[x] ¬ key_t[y]
n[x] ¬ n[x] + 1
Disk-Write(y)
Disk-Write(z)
Disk-Write(x)
```

If is node becomes "too full," it is necessary to perform a split operation. The split operation moves the median key of node x into its parent y where x is the ith child of y.

A new node, z, is allocated, and all keys in x right of the median key are moved to z. The keys left of the median key remain in the original node x. The new node, z, becomes the child immediately to the right of the median key that was moved to the parent y, and the original node, x, becomes the child immediately to the left of the median key that was moved into the parent y.

The split operation transforms a full node with $2t - 1$ keys into two nodes with $t - 1$ keys each. Note that one key is moved into the parent node. The *B-Tree-Split-Child* algorithm will run in time $O(t)$ where t is constant.

B-Tree-Insert(T, k)

```
r ← root[T]
```

```
if n[r] = 2t - 1
    then s ← Allocate-Node()
          root[T] ← s
          leaf[s] ← FALSE
          n[s] ← 0
          c1 ← r
          B-Tree-Split-Child(s, 1, r)
          B-Tree-Insert-Nonfull(s, k)
else B-Tree-Insert-Nonfull(r, k)
```

B-Tree-Insert-Nonfull(x, k)

```
i ¬ n[x]
if leaf[x]
then while i Þ 1 and k < keyi[x]
do keyi+1[x] ¬ keyi[x]
 i ¬ i - 1
keyi+1[x] ¬ k
 n[x] ¬ n[x] + 1
 Disk-Write(x)
else while i Þ and k < keyi[x]
do i ¬ i - 1
 i ¬ i + 1
 Disk-Read(ci[x])
 if n[ci[x]] = 2t - 1
 then B-Tree-Split-Child(x, i, ci[x])
 if k > keyi[x]
  then i ¬ i + 1
B-Tree-Insert-Nonfull(ci[x], k)
```

To perform an inscrtion on a b-tree, the appropriate node for the key must be located using an algorithm similiar to *B-Tree-Search*.

Next, the key must be inserted into the node. If the node is not full prior to the insertion, no special action is required; however, if the node is full, the node must be split to make room for the new key.

Since splitting the node results in moving one key to the parent node, the parent node must not be full or another split operation is required. This process may repeat all the way up to the root and may require splitting the root node. This approach requires two passes.

The first pass locates the node where the key should be inserted; the second pass performs any required splits on the ancestor nodes.

Since each access to a node may correspond to a costly disk access, it is desirable to avoid the second pass by ensuring that the parent node is never full. To accomplish this, the presented algorithm splits any full nodes encountered while descending the tree. Although this approach may result in unecessary split operations, it guarantees that the parent never needs to be split and eliminates the need for a second pass up the tree.

Since a split runs in linear time, it has little effect on the $O(t \log_t n)$ running time of *B-Tree-Insert*.

Splitting the root node is handled as a special case since a new root must be created to contain the median key of the old root. Observe that a b-tree will grow from the top.

B-Tree-Delete

Deletion of a key from a b-tree is possible; however, special care must be taken to ensure that the properties of a b-tree are maintained. Several cases must be considered. If the deletion reduces the number of keys in a node below the minimum degree of the tree, this violation must be corrected by combining several nodes and possibly reducing the height of the tree. If the key has children, the children must be rearranged.

EXAMPLES

Sample B-Tree

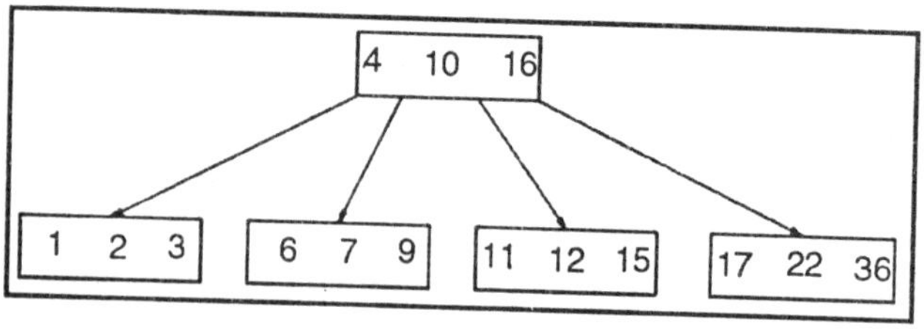

Searching a B-Tree for Key 21

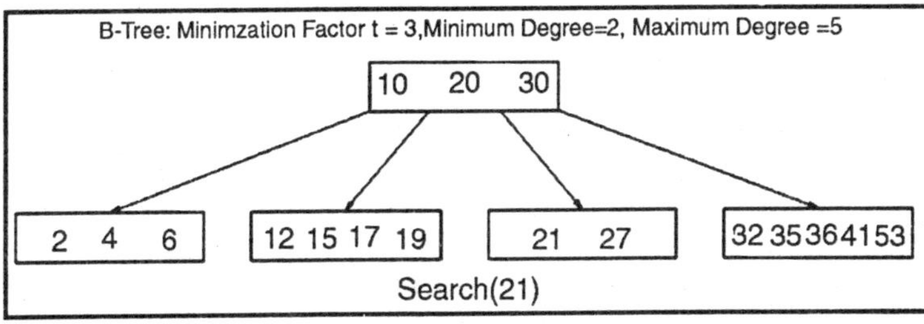

Inserting Key 33 into a B-Tree (w/ Split)

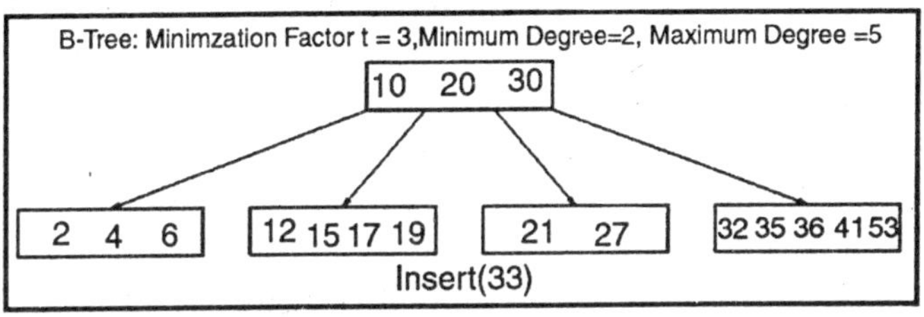

APPLICATIONS

Databases

A database is a collection of data organized in a fashion that facilitates updating, retrieving, and managing the data. The data can consist of anything, including, but not limited to names, addresses, pictures, and numbers. Databases are commonplace and are used everyday. For example, an airline reservation system might maintain a database of available flights, customers, and tickets issued. A teacher might maintain a database of student names and grades.

Because computers excel at quickly and accurately manipulating, storing, and retrieving data, databases are often maintained electronically using a database management system. Database management systems are essential components of many everyday business operations. Database products like Microsoft SQL Server, Sybase Adaptive Server, IBM DB2, and Oracle serve as a foundation for accounting systems, inventory systems, medical recordkeeping sytems, airline reservation systems, and countless other important aspects of modern businesses.

It is not uncommon for a database to contain millions of records requiring many gigabytes of storage. For examples, TELSTRA, an Australian telecommunications company, maintains a customer billing database with 51 billion rows (yes, billion) and 4.2 terabytes of data. In order for a database to be useful and usable, it must support the desired operations, such as retrieval and storage, quickly.

Because databases cannot typically be maintained entirely in memory, b-trees are often used to index the data and to provide fast access.

For example, searching an unindexed and unsorted database containing n key values will have a worst case running time ofO(n); if the same data is indexed with a b-tree, the same search operation will run in O(log n).

To perform a search for a single key on a set of one million keys (1,000,000), a linear search will require at most 1,000,000 comparisons. If the same data is indexed with a b-tree of minimum degree 10, 114 comparisons will be required in the worst case. Clearly, indexing large amounts of data can significantly improve search performance. Although other balanced tree structures can be used, a b-tree also optimizes costly disk accesses that are of concern when dealing with large data sets.

Concurrent Access to B-Trees

Databases typically run in multiuser environments where many users can concurrently perform operations on the database. Unfortunately, this common scenario introduces complications. For example, imagine a database storing bank account balances. Now assume that someone attempts to withdraw $40 from an account containing $60. First, the current balance is checked to ensure sufficent funds.

After funds are disbursed, the balance of the account is reduced. This approach works flawlessly until concurrent transactions are considered. Suppose that another person simultaneously attempts to withdraw $30 from the same account. At the same time the account balance is checked by the first person, the account balance is also retrieved for the second person.

Since neither person is requesting more funds than are currently available, both requests are satisfied for a total of $70. After the first person's transaction, $20 should remain ($60 - $40), so the new balance is recorded as $20. Next, the account balance after the second person's transaction, $30 ($60 - $30), is recorded overwriting the $20 balance. Unfortunately, $70 have been disbursed, but the account balance has only been decreased by $30. Clearly, this Behaviour is undesirable, and special precautions must be taken.

A b-tree suffers from similar problems in a multiuser environment. If two or more processes are manipulating the same tree, it is possible for the tree to become corrupt and result in data loss or errors.

The simplest solution is to serialize access to the data structure. In other words, if another process is using the tree, all other processes must wait. Although this is feasible in many cases, it can place an unecessary and costly limit on performance because many operations actually can be performed concurrently without risk.Locking, introduced by Gray and refined by many others, provides a mechanism for controlling concurrent operations on data structures in order to prevent undesirable side effects and to ensure consistency. For a detailed discussion of this and other concurrency control mechanisms

BINOMIAL

WHAT IS A BINOMIAL EXPERIMENT

A binomial experiment has the following characteristics:

- The experiment involves repeated trials.
- Each trial has only two possible outcomes - a success or a failure.
- The probability that a particular outcome will occur on any given trial is constant.

- All of the trials in the experiment are independent.

A series of coin tosses is a perfect example of a binomial experiment. Suppose we toss a coin three times. Each coin flip represents a trial, so this experiment would have 3 trials.

Each coin flip also has only two possible outcomes - a Head or a Tail. We could call a Head a success; and a Tail, a failure. The probability of a success on any given coin flip would be constant (i.e., 50%). And finally, the outcome on any coin flip is not affected by previous or succeeding coin flips; so the trials in the experiment are independent.

BINOMIAL DISTRIBUTION

A binomial distribution is a probability distribution. It refers to the probabilities associated with the number of successes in a binomial experiment.

For example, suppose we toss a coin three times and suppose we define Heads as a success. This binomial experiment has four possible outcomes: 0 Heads, 1 Head, 2 Heads, or 3 Heads. The probabilities associated with each possible outcome are an example of a binomial distribution, as shown below.

Outcome,x	Binomial probability, P(X = x)	Cumulative probability, P(X < x)
0 Heads	0.125	0.125
1 Head	0.375	0.500
2 Heads	0.375	0.875
3 Heads	0.125	1.000

NUMBER OF TRIALS

The number of trials refers to the number of attempts in a binomial experiment. The number of trials is equal to the number of successes plus the number of failures.

Suppose that we conduct the following binomial experiment. We flip a coin and count the number of Heads. In this experiment, Heads would be classified as success; tails, as failure. If we flip the coin 3 times, then 3 is the number of trials. If we flip it 20 times, then 20 is the number of trials.

NUMBER OF SUCCESSES

Each trial in a binomial experiment can have one of two outcomes. The experimenter classifies one outcome as a success; and the other, as a failure. The number of successes in a binomial experient is the number of trials that result in an outcome classified as a success.

PROBABILITY OF SUCCESS ON SINGLE TRIAL

In a binomial experiment, the probability of success on any individual trial is constant. For example, the probability of getting Heads on a single coin flip is always 0.50. If "getting Heads" is defined as success, the probability of success on a single trial would be 0.50.

BINOMIAL PROBABILITY

A binomial probability refers to the probability of getting EXACTLY n successes in a specific number of trials. For instance, we might ask: What is the probability of getting EXACTLY 2 Heads in 3 coin tosses. That probability (0.375) would be an example of a binomial probability.

CUMULATIVE BINOMIAL PROBABILITY

Cumulative binomial probability refers to the probability that the value of a binomial random variable falls within a specified range.

The probability of getting AT MOST 2 Heads in 3 coin tosses is an example of a cumulative probability. It is equal to the probability of getting 0 heads (0.125) plus the probability of getting 1 head (0.375) plus the probability of getting 2 heads (0.375). Thus, the cumulative probability of getting AT MOST 2 Heads in 3 coin tosses is equal to 0.875.

Notation associated with cumulative binomial probability is best explained through illustration. The probability of getting FEWER THAN 2 successes is indicated by $P(X < 2)$; the probability of getting AT MOST 2 successes is indicated by $P(X < 2)$; the probability of getting AT LEAST 2 successes is indicated by $P(X > 2)$; the probability of getting MORE THAN 2 successes is indicated by $P(X > 2)$.

RELATION BETWEEN BINOMIAL AND NORMAL DISTRIBUTIONS

When the number of trials is large and when the probability of success is not extreme (i.e., neither close to 0 nor close to 1), then the normal distribution may be used to very closely approximate results from the binomial distribution.

Note: When the number of trials is greater than 20,000, the Binomial Calculator uses a normal distribution to estimate the cumulative binomial probability.

In most cases, this yields very good results - often accurate to the third decimal place.

BINOMIAL DISTRIBUTION: PROBLEMS

Question

- Suppose you toss a fair coin 12 times. What is the probability of getting exactly 7 Heads.

Solution

We know the following:

- The number of trials is 12.
- The number of success is 7 (since we define getting a Head as success).
- The probability of success (i.e., getting a Head) on any single trial is 0.5.

Therefore, we plug those numbers into the Binomial Calculator and hit the Calculate button. The calculator reports that the binomial probability is 0.193.

That is the probability of getting EXACTLY 7 Heads in 12 coin tosses. (The calculator also reports the cumulative probability - the probability of getting AT MOST 7 heads in 12 coin tosses. The cumulative probability is 0.806.)

Question

- Suppose the probability that a college freshman will graduate is 0.6 Three sisters (triplets) enter college at the same time. What is the probability that at most 2 sisters will graduate?

Solution

We know the following:

- The number of trials is 3 (because we have 3 sisters).
- The number of successes is 2.
- The probability of success for any individual sister is 0.6.

Therefore, we plug those numbers into the Binomial Calculator and hit the Calculate button. The calculator reports that the cumulative binomial probability is 0.784. That is the probability that 2 or fewer sisters will graduate is 0.784. (Note that the calculator also displays the binomial probability - the probability that EXACTLY 2 sisters graduate. The binomial probability is 0.432.)

INSTRUCTIONS

A "Begin" button will appear on the left when the applet is finished loading. This may take a minute or two depending on the speed of your internet connection and computer. Please be patient. If no begin button appears, it is probably because your browser does not support Java 1.1.

SETTING UP CONDITIONS

Press the "Begin" button to start the applet in another window.

This Java applet shows how the binomial distribution can be approximated by the normal distribution. The initial values are for a binomial distribution with the parameters N = 8 and p = 0.5 where N is the number of trials and p is the probability of success on each trial. You can change the values of N and p and see the result (Hit the enter or tab key after changing a value).

You can use this applet to calculate the probability of obtaining a given number of successes. For example, to calculate the probability of exactly 6 successes out of 8 trials with p = 0.50, enter 6 in both the "from" and "to" fields and hit the "Enter" key. The actual binomial probability is 0.1094 and the approximation based on the normal distribution is 0.1059.

Note that the normal approximation computes the area between 5.5 and 6.5 since the probability of getting a value of exactly 6 in a continuous distribution is nil.

Similarly, to approximate the probability of from 0 to 6 successes, you enter 0 in the "from" field and 6 in the "to" field. The area from below 6.5 is computed.

BINOMIAL PROBABILITIES

- Exact binomial probabilities
- Approximation via the normal distribution
- Approximation via the Poisson Distribution

The logic and computational details of binomial probabilities are described earlier.

This will calculate and/or estimate binomial probabilities for situations of the general"k out of n" type, where k is the number of times a binomial outcome is observed or stipulated to occur, p is the probability that the outcome will occur on any particular occasion,q is the complementary probability (1-p) that the outcome will not occur on any particular occasion, and n is the number of occasions.

For example: In 100 tosses of a coin, with 60 "heads" outcomes observed or stipulated to occur among the 100 tosses,

n = 100 [the number of opportunities for a head to occur]

k = 60 [the stipulated number of heads]

p =.5 [the probability that a head will occur on any particular toss]

q =.5 [the probability that a head will not occur on any particular toss]

Method 1

If n ≤ 1000, exact binomial probabilities will be calculated through repeated applications of the standard binomial formula$_Q$

$$P_{(k \text{ out of } n)} = \frac{n!}{k!(n-k)!}\left(p^k\right)\left(q^{n-k}\right)$$

In principle, Method 1 is preferable in all cases, since it involves direct calculation of exact binomial probabilities. Its limitation is that it is not computationally feasible with very large samples. The Programmeming on this page is capable of performing the calculation up through n=1000.

Method 2

If np ≥ 5 and nq ≥ 5, binomial probabilities will be estimated by way of the binomial approximation of the normal distribution, according to the formula$_Q$

$$z = \frac{(k-m) \pm 5}{\sigma}$$

where:

- M = np [the mean of the binomial sampling distribution]
- σ = sqrt[npq] [the standard deviation of the binomial sampling distribution]

Method 3

If ne"150 and the mean (np) and variance (npq) of the binomial sampling distribution are within 10% of each other, binomial probabilities will be estimated through repeated applications of the Poisson probability function

where:

e = the base of the natural logarithms; and

M = np [the mean of the binomial sampling distribution]

The defining characteristic of a Poisson distribution is that its mean and variance are identical. In a binomial sampling distribution, this condition is approximated as p becomes very small, providing that n is relatively large. The Programmeming on this page permits the Poisson procedure to be performed whenever np and npq are within 10% of each other, providing that ne"150. Do keep in mind, however, that the results of the Poisson procedure are only approximations of the true binomial probabilities, valid only in the degree that the binomial mean and variance are very close.

HEAPS

A heap is a complete tree with an ordering-relation R holding between each node and its descendant. *Examples for R*: smaller-than, bigger-than

ASSUMPTION

In what follows, *R* is the relation 'bigger-than', and the trees have degree 2.

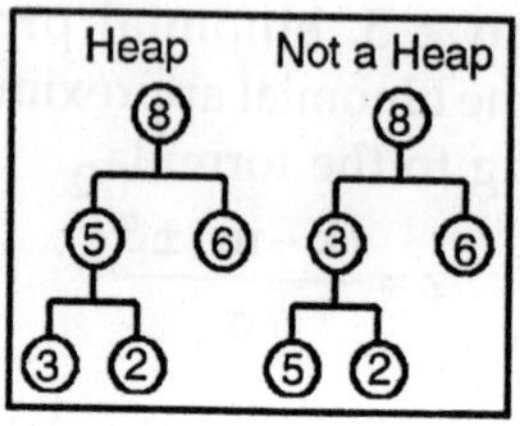

ADDING AN ELEMENT

- Add a node to the tree

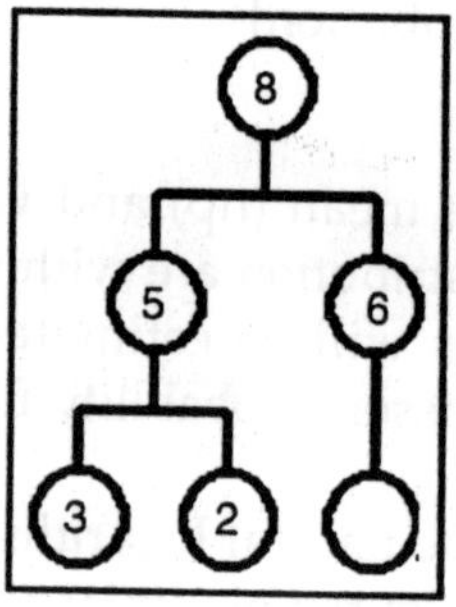

- Move the elements in the path from the root to the new node one position down, if they are smaller than the new element

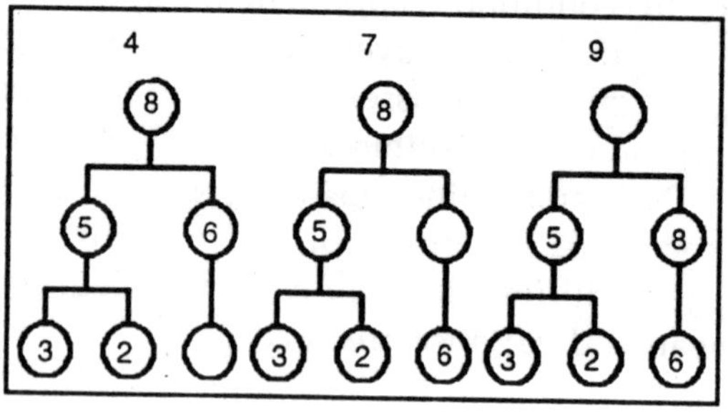

- Insert the new element to the vacant node

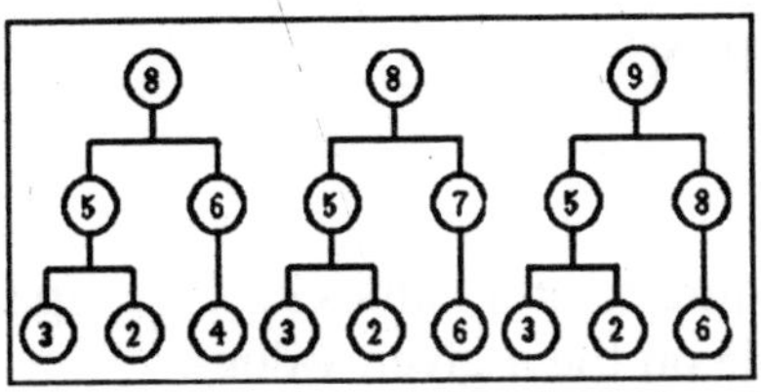

- A complete tree of n nodes has depth $\lceil \log n \rceil \log n$ O(log), hence the time complexity is $O(\log n)$

DELETING AN ELEMENT

- Delete the value from the root node, and delete the last node while saving its value.

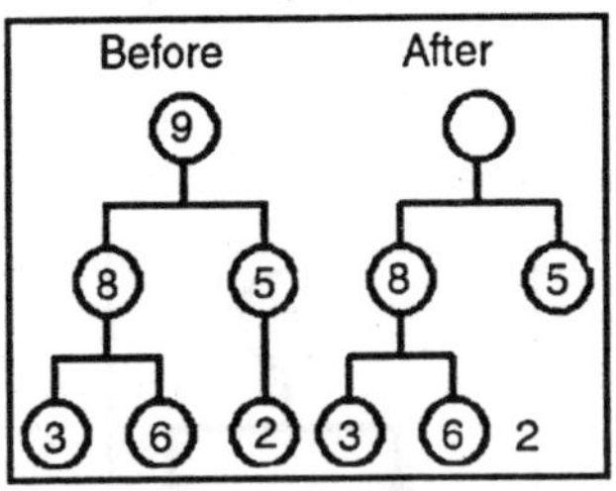

- As long as the saved value is smaller than a child of the vacant node, move up into the vacant node the largest value of the children.

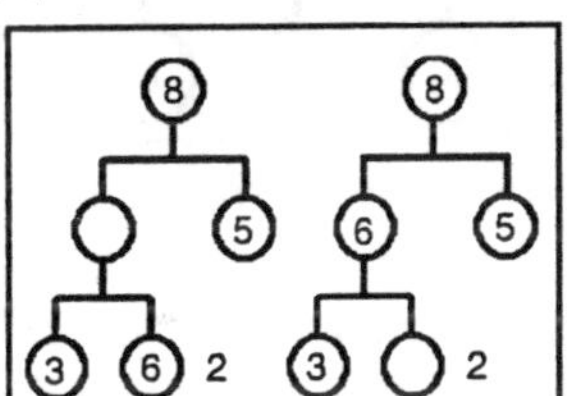

- Insert the saved value into the vacant node

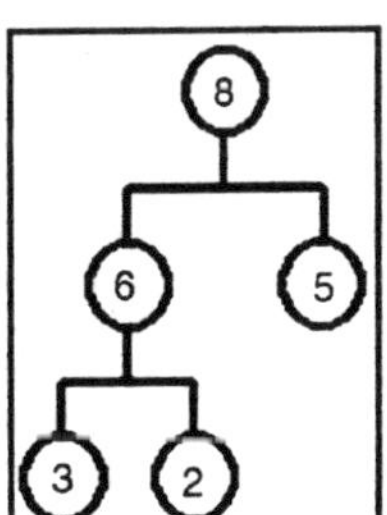

- The time complexity is $O(\log n)$

INITIALIZATION

Brute Force

Given a sequence of n values $e_1 \ldots, e_n$, repeatedly use the insertion module on the n given values.

- Level h in a complete tree has at most $2^{h-1} = O(2^n)$ elements
- Levels $1 \ldots, h - 1$ have $2^0 + 2^1 + \ldots + 2^{h-2} = O(2^h)$ elements
- Each element requires $O(\log n)$ time. Hence, brute force initialization requires $O(n \log n)$ time.

Efficient

- Insert the n elements $e_1 \ldots, e_n$ into a complete tree

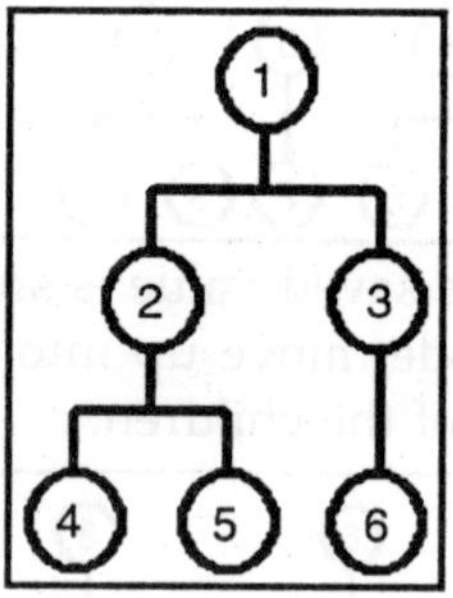

- For each node, starting from the last one and ending at the root, reorganize into a heap the subtree whose root node is given. The reorganization is performed by interchanging the new element with the child of greater value, until the new element is greater than its children.

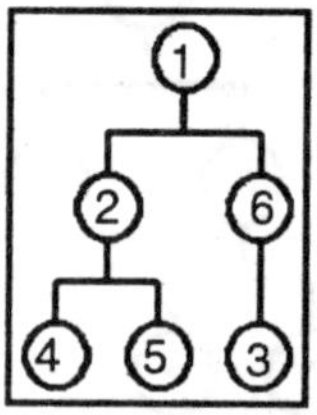

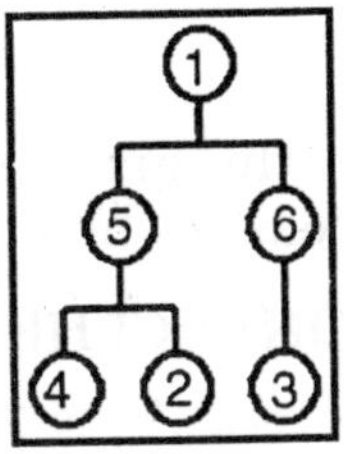

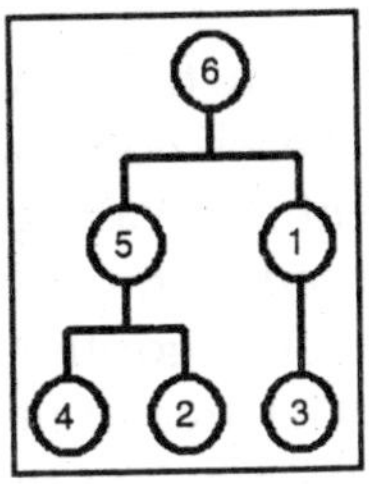

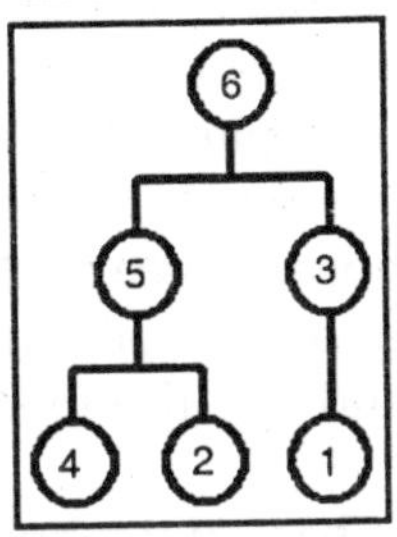

- The time complexity is $O(0 * (n/2) + 1 * (n/4) + 2 * (n/8) + ... + (\log n) * 1) = O(n(0.\ 2^{-1} + 1...\ 2^{-2} + 2.\ 2^{-3} + ... + (\log n).2^{-\log n})) = O(n)$
since the following equalities holds.

$$\sum_{k=1} \infty (k-1)2-k = 2\left[\sum_{k=1} \infty (k-1)2-k\right] -$$
$$\left[\sum_{k=1} \infty (k-1)2-k\right] = \left[\sum_{k=1} \infty k2 \quad k\right] -$$
$$\left[\sum_{k=1} \infty (k-1)2-k\right] \sum_{k-1} \infty [k-(k-1)]2-k =$$
$$\sum_{k=1} \infty 2-k = 1$$

APPLICATIONS

Priority Queue

A dynamic set in which elements are deleted according to a given ordering-relation.

Heap Sort

Build a heap from the given set ($O(n)$) time, then repeatedly remove the elements from the heap ($O(n \log n)$).

FIBONACCI HEAP

DEFINITION

A heap is a data structure that is a special case of abinary tree. In which the value of each node is greater than the values of its leaves. Thus a parent is always greater in value than it's children. A heap is a used inimplementation of a priority queue, as well as a heapsort algorithm.

A heap is also a special area of memory. Its complement is the stack. It is used to store data that isinitialized, created while a Programme is executing.

A Fibonacci heap is a particular type of data structure (specifically, a type of heap) that consists of a collection of heap-ordered trees. Fibonacci heaps are a desirable way to store data if the number of "extract minimum" and "delete" operations are small and the number of "decrease value" operations are large.

A Fibonacci heap is basically a normal heap with only a few changes specifically to speed up the ability to decrease a certain key in a tree. A Fibonacci heap consists of a collection of heap-ordered trees, where a heap-ordered tree is a tree in which each child node is greater in value than its parent (and, alternately, each parent is lesser in value than its child). These trees are collected together in a doubly-linked list constructed in a circular fashion, so that there is no beginning nor end; traversing one way along the list will eventually bring you back to the start.

Let's take a look at a sample Fibonacci heap:

```
/---------->----------->---------->---------->----------\
|                                                       |
\----(23)---<----(7) ----<----(3)----<----(17)---<----(24)---/
                              /|\          |          /\
                             / | \         |         /  \
                  /-->---/--|--\-->--\     |     /->--/-->-\--->--\
                  |     /   |   \    |     |     |   /       \    |
                  \--(18)--(52)-(38)-/   (30)    \-(26)--<--(46)--/
                      |          |                  |
                     (39)       (41)               (35)
```

You can see that the basic heap is linked together by a circular linked list, and each set of children of these are linked together in a similar list. Also note that each child has a greater value than his or her parent. The reason for the particular ordering (and large number of root nodes) is that the nodes were added in an order such that whenever a new "minimum" node for the whole heap is added, it is added to the base of the heap itself and a new tree is started, with all future nodes with higher value being added only to that tree.

This tree is most effective when you have to reduce the value of a particular node, because it operates in O(1), or linear time on average; this is because a particular node, when its value is reduced in a Fibonacci heap, rarely is required to move when the heap covers a reasonable set of values. This tree is very slow, however, at deleting operations, because there is no efficient way to re-insert the children of the node other than one at a time.

Fibonacci heaps are good for solving mazes, simply because most of the operations in finding the best solution to a maze revolve around building a tree (comparable to similar data structures in speed) and then reducing the values in the tree when improved paths are found (faster than similar data structures). In essence, this data structure is very useful when attempting to solveminimum spanning tree problems and single-source shortest pathproblems.

However, most algorithms that use heaps for data storage require speedy extraction of specific pieces of data from that heap, and for that, the Fibonacci heap is a very poor choice, indeed. In summary, Fibonacci trees are useful data structures for solving certain types of problems, but are quite poor at aiding in the solution of other problems.

Credit for development of the fibonacci heap goes to Ronald Rivest, Thomas Cormen, and Charles Leiserson.

DATA STRUCTURES DISJOINT SETS

INTRODUCTION

Many times the efficiency of an algorithm depends on the

data structures used in the algorithm. A wise choice in the structure you use in solving a problem can reduce the time of execution, the time to implement the algorithm and the amount of memory used. During SRM competitions we are limited to a time limit of 2 seconds and 64 MB of memory, so the right data structure can help you remain in competition. While some Data Structures have been covered before, in this article we'll focus on data structures for disjoint sets.

THE PROBLEM

Let's consider the following problem: In a room are N persons, and we will define two persons are friends if they are directly or indirectly friends. If A is a friend with B, and B is a friend with C, then A is a friend of C too. A group of friends is a group of persons where any two persons in the group are friends. Given the list of persons that are directly friends find the number of groups of friends and the number of persons in each group. For example N = 5 and the list of friends is: 1-2, 5-4, and 5-1. Here is the figure of the graph that represents the groups of friends. 1 and 2 are friends, then 5 and 4 are friends, and then 5 and 1 are friends, but 1 is friend with 2; therefore 5 and 2 are friends, etc.

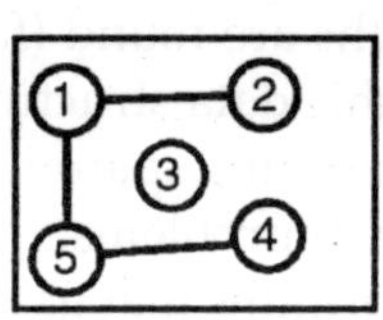

In the end there are 2 groups of friends: one group is {1, 2, 4, 5}, the other is {3}.

The Solution

This problem can be solved using BFS, but let's see how to solve this kind of problem using data structures for disjoint sets. First of all: a disjoint-set data structure is a structure that maintains a collection $S_1, S_2, S_3, \ldots, S_n$ of dynamic disjoint sets. Two sets are disjoint if their intersection is null. For example set {1, 2, 3} and set {1, 5, 6} aren't disjoint because they have in common {1}, but the sets {1, 2, 3} and {5, 6} are disjoint because their intersection is null. In a data structure of disjoint sets every set contains a representative, which is one member of the set.

Let's see how things will work with sets for the example of the problem. The groups will be represented by sets, and the representative of each group is the person with the biggest index. At the beginning there are 5 groups (sets): {1}, {2}, {3}, {4}, {5}. Nobody is anybody's friend and everyone is the representative of his or her own group.

The next step is that 1 and 2 become friends, this means the group containing 1 and the group with 2 will become one group. This will give us these groups: {1, 2}, {3}, {4}, {5}, and the representative of the first group will become 2. Next, 5 and 4 become friends. The groups will be {1,2}, {3}, {4, 5}. And in the last step 5 and 1 become friends and the groups will be {1, 2, 4, 5}, {3}. The representative of the first group will be 5 and the representative for second group will be 3. (We will see why we need representatives later). At the end we have 2 sets, the first set with 4 elements and the second with one, and this is the answer for the problem example: 2 groups, 1 group of 4 and one group of one.

Perhaps now you are wondering how you can check if 2 persons are in the same group. This is where the use of the representative elements comes in. Let's say we want to check if 3 and 2 are in the same group, we will know this if the representative of the set that contains 3 is the same as the representative of the set that contains 2. One representative is 5 and the other one is 3; therefore 3 and 2 aren't in same groups of friends.

SOME OPERATIONS

Let's define the following operations:

- *Create-set(x)*: Creates a new set with one element {x}.
- *Merge-sets(x, y)*: Merge into one set the set that contains element x and the set that contains element y (x and y are in different sets). The original sets will be destroyed.
- *Find set(x)*: Returns the representative or a pointer to the representative of the set that contains element x.

Solution Using these Operations

Let's see the solution for our problem using these operations:

```
Read N;
for (each person x from 1 to N) CREATE-SET(x)
for (each pair of friends (x y)) if (FIND-
SET(x) != FIND-SET(y)) MERGE-SETS(x, y)
```

Now if we want to see if 2 persons (x, y) are in same group we check if FIND-SET(x) == FIND-SET(y).

We will Analyse the running time of the disjoint-set data structure in terms of N and M, where N is the number of times that CREATE-SET(x) is called and M is the total number of times that CREATE-SET(x), MERGE-SETS(x, y) and FIND-SET(x) are called.

Since the sets are disjoint, each time MERGE-SETS(x, y) is called one set will be created and two will be destroyed, giving us one less set.

If there are n sets after n-1 calls of MERGE-SETS(x,y) there will remain only one set. That's why the number of MERGE-SETS(x,y) calls is less than or equal to the number of CREATE-SET(x) operations.

IMPLEMENTATION WITH LINKED LISTS

One way to implement disjoint set data structures is to represent each set by a linked list. Each element (object) will be in a linked list and will contain a pointer to the next element in the set and another pointer to the representative of the set.

Here is a figure of how the example of the problem will look like after all operations are made. The blue arrows are the pointers to the representatives and the black arrows are the pointers to the next element in the sets.

Representing sets with linked lists we will obtain a complexity of O(1) for CREATE-SET(x) and FIND-SET(x). CREATE-SET(x) will just create a new linked list whose only element (object) is x, the operation FIND-SET(x) just returns the pointer to the representative of the set that contains element (object) x.

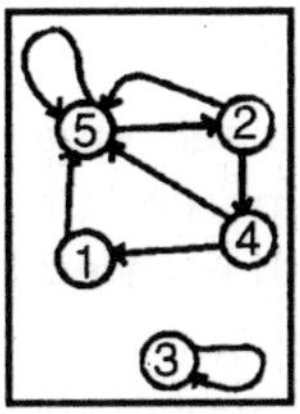

Now let's see how to implement the MERGE-SETS(x, y) operations. The easy way is to append x's list onto the end of y's list. The representative of the new set is the representative of the original set that contained y. We must update the pointer to the representative for each element (object) originally on x's list, which takes linear time in terms of the length of x's list. It's easy to prove that, in the worst case, the complexity of the algorithm will be O(M^2) where M is the number of operations MERGE-SETS(x, y). With this implementation the complexity will average O(N) per operation where N represents the number of elements in all sets.

WEIGHTED UNION HEURISTIC

Let's see how a heuristic will make the algorithm more efficient. The heuristic is called "a weighted-union heuristic." In this case, let's say that the representative of a set contains information about how many objects (elements) are in that set as well.

The optimization is to always append the smaller list onto the longer and, in case of ties, append arbitrarily. This will bring the complexity of the algorithm to O(M + NlogN) where M is the number of operations (FIND-SET, MERGE-SETS, CREATE-SETS) and N is the number of operations CREATE-SETS. I will not prove why the complexity is this, but if you are interested you can find the proof in the resources mentioned at the end of the article..

So far we reach an algorithm to solve the problem in O(M + NlogN) where N is the number of persons and M is the number of friendships and a memory of O(N). Still the BFS will solve the problem in O(M + N) and memory of O(N + M). We can see that we have optimized the memory but not the execution time.

Next Step: Root Trees

The next step is to see what we can do for a faster implementation of disjoint set data structures. Let's represent sets by rooted trees, with each node containing one element and each tree representing one set. Each element will point only to its parent and the root of each tree is the representative of that set and its own parent. Let's see, in steps, how the trees will look for the example from the problem above.

Step 1: Nobody is anybody friend

We have 5 trees and each tree has a single element, which is the root and the representative of that tree.

Step 2: 1 and 2 are friends, MERGE-SETS(1, 2):

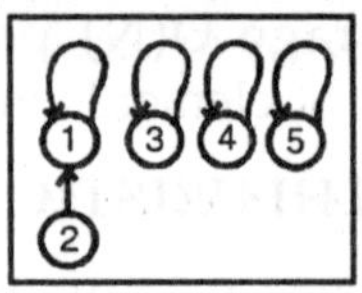

The operation made is MERGE-SETS(1, 2). We have 4 trees one tree contain 2 elements and have the root 1. The other trees have a single element.

Step 3: 5 and 4 are friends, MERGE-SETS(5, 4)

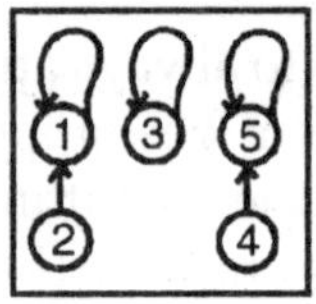

The operation made is MERGE-SETS(5, 4). Now we have 3 trees, 2 trees with 2 elements and one tree with one element.

Step 4: 5 and 1 are friends, MERGE-SETS(5, 1)

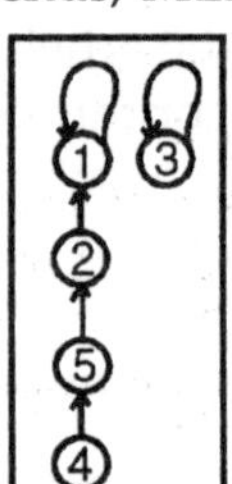

The operation made is MERGE-SETS(5, 1). Now we have 2 trees, one tree has 4 elements and the other one has only one element. As we see so far the algorithm using rooted trees is no faster than the algorithm using linked lists.

Two Heburistics

Next we will see how, by using two heuristics, we will achieve the asymptotically fastest disjoint set data structure known so far, which is almost linear in terms of the number of operations made. These two heuristics are called "union by rank" and "path compression." The idea in the first heuristic "union by rank" is to make the root of the tree with fewer nodes point to the root of the tree with more nodes. For each node, we maintain a rankthat approximates the logarithm of the sub-tree size and is also an upper bound on the height of the node. When MERGE-SETS(x, y) is called, the root with smaller rank is made to point to the root with larger rank. The idea in the second heuristic "path compression," which is used for operation FIND-SET(x), is to make each node on the find path point directly to the root. This will not change any ranks.

To implement a disjoint set forest with these heuristics, we must keep track of ranks. With each node x, we keep the integer value *rank[x],* which is bigger than or equal to the number of edges in the longest path between node x and a sub-leaf. When CREATE-SET(x) is called the initial rank[x] will be 0. When a MERGE-SETS(x, y) operation is made then the root of higher rank will become the parent of the root of lower rank – or, in case of tie, we arbitrarily choose one of the roots as the parent and increment its rank.

Let's see how the algorithm will look

```
Let P[x] = the parent of node x.
CREATE-SET(x)
   P[x] = x
   rank[x] = 0
   MERGE-SETS(x, y)
   PX = FIND-SET(X)
   PY =FIND-SET(Y)
   If (rank[PX] > rank[PY]) P[PY] = PX
```

```
    Else P[PX] = PY
    If (rank[PX] == rank[PY]) rank[PY] =
  rank[PY] + 1
```

And the last operation looks like:

```
FIND-SET(x)
    If (x != P[x]) p[x] = FIND-SET(P[X])
Return P[X]
```

Now let's see how the heuristics helped the running time. If we use only the first heuristic "union by rank" then we will get the same running time we achieved with the weighted union heuristic when we used lists for representation. When we use both "union by rank" and "path compression," the worst running time is O(m α(m,n)), where α(m,n) is the very slowly growing inverse of Ackermann function. In application α(m,n) ⇐ 4 that why we can say that the running time is linear in terms of m, in practical situations. (For more details on Ackermann's function or complexity see the references below.)

Back to the Problem

The problem from the beginning of the article is solvable in O(N + M) and O(N) for memory using disjoint-set data structure. The difference for time execution is not big if the problem is solved with BFS, but we don't need to keep in memory the vertices of the graph. Let's see if the problem was like: In a room are N persons and you had to handle Q queries. A query is of the form "x y 1," meaning that x is friends with y, or "x y 2" meaning that we are asked to output if x and y are in same group of friends at that moment in time. In this case the solution with disjoint-set data structure is the fastest, giving a complexity of O(N + Q).

Practice

Disjoint-set data structures are a helpful tool for use in different algorithms, or even for solving problems in an SRM. They are efficient and use small amount of memory. They are useful in applications like "Computing the shorelines of a terrain," "Classifying a set of atoms into molecules or fragments," "Connected component labeling in image analysis," and others.

To practice what you've learned, try to solve GrafixMask – the Division 1 500 from SRM211. The idea is to keep track of all the blocks and consider each grid point as a node. Next, take all the nodes that aren't blocked and let (x, y) be the coordinate of the left, right, down or up node, and if (x, y) is not blocked then you do the operation MERGE-SETS(node, node2). You should also try to determine how disjoint-set data structures can be used in the solution of RoadReconstruction from SRM 356. Disjoint-set data structures can also be used inTopographicalImage from SRM 210 and PathFinding, from SRM 156.

OPERATIONS ON SETS

Let x be an object. We wish to support the following operations:

- MAKE-SET(x) creates a new set whose only member is pointed by x; Note that x is not in the other sets.
- UNION(x,y) unites two dynamic sets containing objects x and y, say Sx and Sy, into a new set that Sx *" Sy, assuming that Sx)" Sy =";
- FIND-SET(x) returns a pointer to the representative of the set containing x.
- INSERT(a,S) inserts an object a to S, and returns S*"{a}.
- DELETE(a,S) deletes an object a from S, and returns S-{a}.
- SPLIT(a,S) partitions the objects of S into two sets S1 and S2 such that S1 ={bbd"a&b"S}, and S2 =S- S1.
- MINIMUM(S) returns the minimum object in S.

DISJOINT-SET DATA STRUCTURES

Here we show two application examples:

- Connected components (CCs)
- Minimum Spanning Trees (MSTs)

Algorithm for Connected Components

Connected components (G)

```
for each v"V
   do MAKE-SET (v)
for every edge (u,v)"E
    do if FIND-SET (u) '" FIND-SET (v)
         then UNION (u,v)
Same-Components (u,v)
if FIND-SET (u) = FIND-SET (v)
       then return TRUE
return FALSE
```

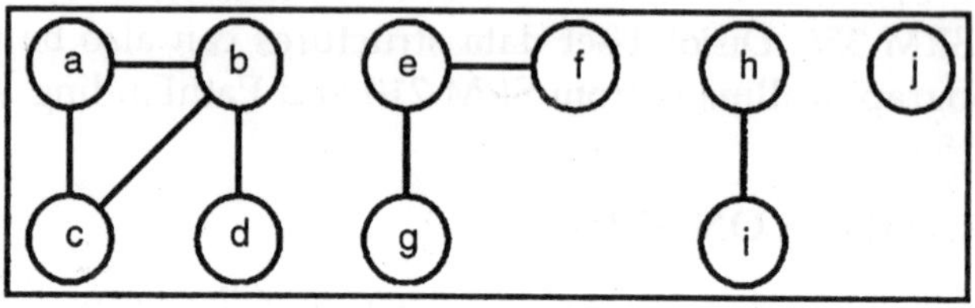

Fig: A Graph with four Connected Components: {a,b,c,d}, {e,f,g}, {h,i}, and {j}.

Table. This Table Shows the State of the Collection of Disjoint Sets as Each Edge is Processed. The Processed Edge is Listed on the Left and the Rest of the Columns show the State of the Collection.

Edge processed	Collection of disjoint sets									
Initial sets	{a}	{b}	{c}	{d}	{e}	{f}	{g}	{h}	{i}	{j}
(b,d)	{a}		{c}		{e}	{f}	{g}	{h}	{i}	{j}
(e,g)	{a}	{b,d}	{c}		{e,g}	{f}		{h}	{i}	{j}
(a,c)	{a,c}	{b,d}			{e,g}	{f}		{h}	{i}	{j}
(h,i)	{a,c}	{b,d}			{e,g}	{f}		{h,i}		{j}
(a,b)	{a,b,c,d}				{e,g}	{f}		{h,i}		{j}
(e,f)	{a,b,c,d}				{e,f,g}			{h,i}		{j}
(b,c)	{a,b,c,d}				{e,f,g}			{h,i}		{j}

DISJOINT SET REPRESENTATION

The Linked-list Representation

A set can be represented by a linked list. In this representation, each node has a pointer to the next node and a pointer to the first node.

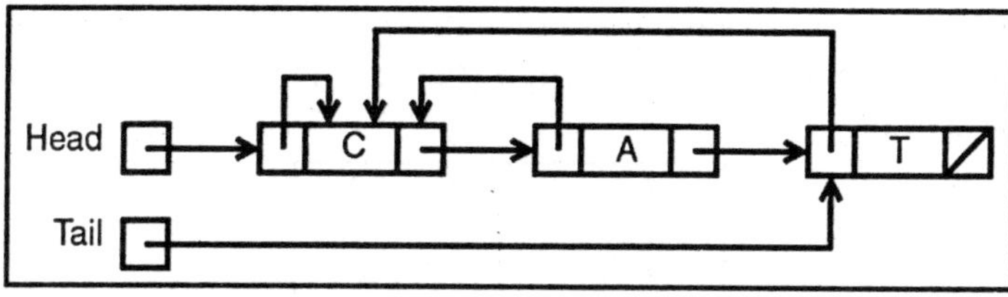

Fig. Linked-list Representation.

Each disjoint set can be represented by a linked-list. Each node has a pointer to the head node and a pointer to the next node.

Consider the following operation sequence:

```
MAKE-SET (x1),
MAKE-SET (x2),
:,
MAKE-SET (xn-1),
MAKE-SET (xn),
UNION (x1, x2),
UNION (x2, x3),:,
UNION (xn-1, xn).
```

What's the total time complexity of the above operations?

A Weighted-union Heuristic

Assume that the representative of each set maintains the number of objects in the set, and always merge the smaller list to the larger list, then

Theorem

Using the linked list representation of disjoint sets and the weighted-union heuristic, a sequence of m MAKE-SET, Union, and Find_Set operations, n of which are MAKE-SET, takes O(m+nlogn) time.

Hint: observe that for any kd"n, after x's representative pointer has been updated #logk# times, the resulting set containing x must have at least k members.

DISJOINT SET FORESTS

A faster implementation of disjoint sets is through the

rooted trees, with each node containing one member and each tree representing one set. Each member in the tree has only one parent.

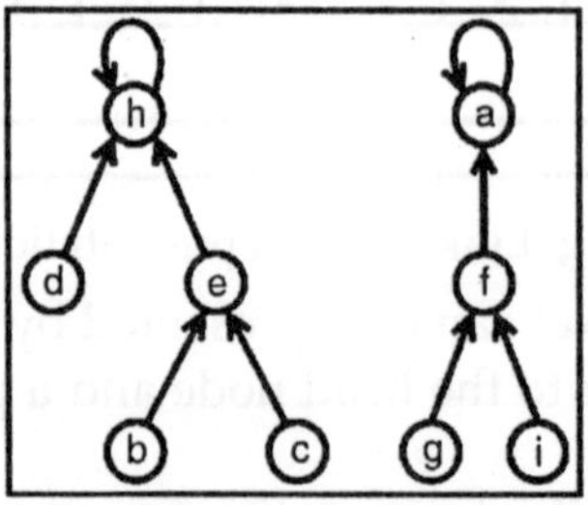

Fig. Rooted Tree Representation of Disjoint Sets.

Each tree has a "representative" h for the left tree and a for the right tree.

Heuristics for Disjoint Set Operations

- Union by rank.
- Path compression

The idea of union by rank is to make the root of the tree with fewer nodes point to the root of the tree with more nodes. Rather than explicitly keeping track of the size of the subtree rooted at each node, for each node we maintain a *rank* that approximates the logarithm of the subtree size and is also an upper bound on the height of the node.

Time complexity: O(mlogn), assuming that there are m union operations. Path compression is quite simple and very effective. We use this approach during FIND-SET operations to make each node on the path point directly to the root. Path compression does not change any ranks.

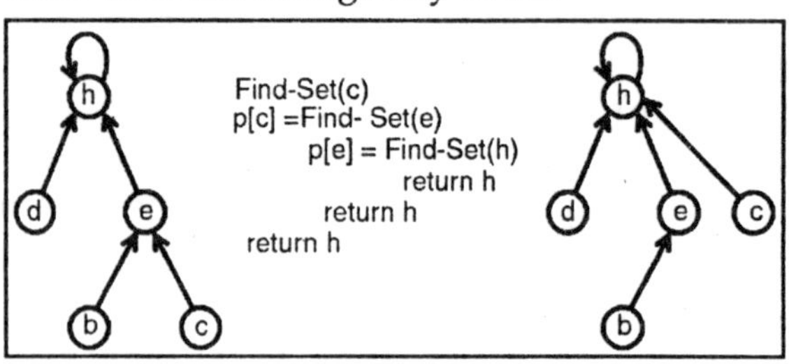

Fig. Path Compression Takes Place During the FIND-SET Operation.

This works by recursing from the given input node up to the root of the tree, forming a *path*. Then the root is returned and assigned as the parent for each node in *path*. The parent of c after FIND-SET (c) is h.

Time complexity: Θ(f log1+f/n) n) if fe"n and Θ(n+flogn) otherwise, assume that there are n MAKE-SET operations and f FIND-SET operations.

```
MAKE-SET (x)
p[x] ← x
rank[x] ← 0
FIND-SET (x)
if x'"p[x]
     then p[x] ← FIND-SET (p[x])
return p[x]
UNION (x,y)
LINK(FIND-SET (x), FIND-SET (y))
LINK (x,y)
if rank[x]>rank[y]
     then p[y] ← x
     else p[x] ← y
          if rank[x]=rank[y]
             then rank[y] ← rank[y]+1
```

where rank[x] is the height of x in the tree. If both of the above methods are used together, the time complexity is O(mα(m,n)).

The Rank Properties

- rank[x] ≤ rank[p[x]]
- for any tree root x, size(x) ≥ 2rank[x] (Link operation)
- for any integer r, there are at most n/ 2r nodes of rank r
- each node has rank at most $\lfloor \log n \rfloor$, assuming there are at n objects involved.

Chapter 3

Design and Analysis Techniques

OVERVIEW

Advanced distribution design and analysis software solutions streamline the design of overhead and underground transmission and distribution lines, optimize designs for project cost, building standards and system reliability, and integrate seamlessly with existing utility business systems for improved data accuracy and reliability throughout the utility.

LD-PRO

A powerful design solution for overhead and underground electric distribution lines, gas distribution lines and joint use applications. Capable of saving energy providers 15 to 20 Per cent on materials and Labour, this application covers the entire design process.

LD-Pro is a powerful tool for designing overhead and underground electric distribution lines, gas distribution lines and joint-use applications. LD-Pro integrates design data from multiple sources and produces detailed, compliant designs.

Features & Benefits

Using LD-Pro for distribution line design is as easy as loading your design criteria into the system, hit optimize, and watch the system produce high-quality, consistent designs that are standards- and code-compliant. Whether working in the field or in the office, LD-Pro identifies the least-cost route and materials, sends an order to your work management application, updates GIS systems, estimates building costs, and produces detailed construction packets on the spot.

Ease of use and the ability to automate design tasks can save you about 15 or 20 Per cent on materials and Labour.

When you use LD-Pro, you can:

- Design systems according to the standards you define and ensure enterprise-wide compliance.
- Get more capacity out of existing infrastructure.
- Tackle overhead transmission lines, overhead and underground distribution lines, and gas distribution and transmission lines with one tool.
- Interface with CAD, work management, materials management, reporting, and other systems.
- Consider alternate design scenarios quickly and easily.
- Eliminate redundant data entry.

LD-TRACK

Know where you're at in the LD-Pro design process with work order tracking. Compare actuals to estimates and track projects with this optional LD-Pro software tool.

LD-Track provides interactive and proactive feedback to LD-Pro designers, enabling them to compare designs to utility-set benchmarks and/or targets. Use LD-Track to compare costs, track material usage, and flag discrepancies to improve quality control.

Features & Benefits

LD-Track performs the necessary "checks and balances" function that allows a utility to track and measure how they are doing in their design and cost control process using LD Pro. Use LD-Track to generate reports that track cost reductions, standard material usage, comparison costs, design project status and company-wide savings using LD-Pro.

DESIGN AND ANALYSIS TECHNOLOGIES

The Design and Analysis Technologies critical technology area includes technologies or processes that are pervasive within the aerospace and defence sector. The technology elements within the Design Technologies critical technology area are depicted in the figure below and described in subsequent paragraphs:

Multidisciplinary Design and Optimization

Multidisciplinary design and optimization is as the name implies, the process of combining a full set of computational design tools to create an optimum design. The process is necessarily iterative in nature and all of the disciplines normally utilized in an aircraft design are computationally intensive.

An MDO approach for an aircraft could include aerodynamics, structures, and systems Computer Aided Engineering (CAE) tools. Initial design assumptions would be input to each CAE toolset and the constraints and parameters to be optimized defined. Each CAE suite would then compute design parameters that would be utilized by the other CAE tools as a subset of their required inputs.

The ultimate design would theoretically be structurally sounder, lighter and more cost effective to fabricate. The design timeframe would be also very much shortened. The challenges to this process are in the exchange of data between the CAE applications and the tuning of the entire process to achieve convergence on the final solution set in an efficient manner.

Structural Analysis

The optimization of analytical design tools is a process that will lead to shortened design time frames, lighter and more efficient designs, with reduced production and life cycle costs of the final design.

The many analytical tools now available have been typically developed for specific applications and are often not readily applicable outside of their original design target arena. An example lies in the structural analysis field where tools developed for metallics will be much different from those developed for composite materials where material properties may vary according to axis.

The ability to rapidly define an optimized aircraft structure having light weight, and improved fatigue and damage tolerance capabilities, is a critical technology to maintain competitive leadership in the development and supply of future new aircraft. This will be achieved by the extensive use of computerized methods for structural analysis and design optimization, and the analysis of failure and fracture mechanics. The methods must be integrated with the in-house design and manufacturing data bases, the 3-D CAD/ CAMsystems, and also be easy to use. Suppliers and partners will have access to the resulting design information via Technical Data Interchange (TDI). This will ensure consistency with an up-to-date knowledge of the requirements for loads, interfaces and the space envelopes available for their products. The immediate dissemination to suppliers of information on design changes will help diminish subsequent redesign activity and the time and cost penalties incurred for rework.

The preliminary structural design will often use detailed Finite Element Methods (FEM) for analysis, coupled with constrained optimization, and the process must be highly automated for rapid creation of FEM meshing for models. In order to achieve shortened design cycle time, the loads and dynamics stiffness requirements must become available much sooner than at present. This will require early development of MDO models for overall aerodynamic and structural optimization that will define the static and dynamic loads for flight and ground operations. Trade-off studies must rapidly search for the best designs and arrive at realistic structural sizes, providing space envelopes and accurate weights to minimize subsequent redesign.

Structural Design, Analysis and Optimization

Shortened design cycle times are necessary for achieving market advantage in the aerospace and defence sector. Improvements in the structural analysis, design and optimization of gas turbine engines is necessary to achieve these goals while also meeting the overall objectives of increased durability and efficiency at lower costs.

A Multi-disciplinary Design Optimization (MDO) approach that combines finite element analysis and aerodynamic design techniques is employed. MDO is necessary to rapidly determine the structure of the engine and identify critical areas requiring further or more detailed analysis.

Many of the structural and aerodynamic codes developed by companies are proprietary in nature and the integration and refinement of these codes is an on-going challenge.

Computational Fluid Dynamics

Computational Development and Validation

Computational Fluid Dynamics (CFD) has had the greatest effect on both aircraft and engine design of any single design tool over the past twenty-five years. Computational power and cost have enabled widespread application and development of CFD techniques. Computational fluid dynamics is basically the use of computers to numerically model flows of interest. Nodes in the flowpath are identified and equations of motion solved at these locations to identify flow parameters.

In essence a grid or mesh is defined over the surface of the object that extends outwards into the flowfield containing the object. Flow equations are then calculated at each node in the grid, and iteratively re-calculated until all results for each node are within an acceptable variance. The equations used are either Euler based which do not include viscous effects (boundary layers) directly, or Navier-Stokes equations which include viscous effects and which produce more accurate but computationally more demanding solutions. Such methods can be used for external flows about an aircraft or for internal flows in a gas turbine including combustion. The Euler based analyses are typically less computationally demanding but are less precise for modeling separated flows on wings and bodies, or for internal reversed flows. It should be noted that Navier first developed his equations in 1823 and that Stokes refined them in 1845. The development of solutions to these equations was not feasible until the latter part of this century. Today much R&D effort on NS methods is expended on improving modeling of the turbulent flow terms for specific problems.

Numerous forms of Euler and Navier-Stokes solutions have been developed to address particular design problems. Solutions to these equations are dependent on experimentation for both coefficients and for validation.

Mesh selection and node placement is critical to the solution of the flowfield. The automated generation of meshes is now in wide spread use and can often be linked to Computer Aided Engineering and Design tools. The form of the equation used, the density of the mesh or grid and convergence requirements determine computational demands. Complete aircraft solutions require huge computer resources and much R&D is aimed at improving the speed of the solution.

Computational Fluid Dynamics - Gas Turbines

CFD is perhaps the single most critical technology for gas turbine engines. Gas turbineCFD needs have typically posed the greatest challenges to engine designers, and computational power and code developers. While CFD is of utmost importance to the engine designer it is a very specific disciplinary design requirement and competence is held by a very small number of engine design firms worldwide.

Computation techniques for gas turbine engines also tend to be very module specific — compressor, transition duct, combustor, turbine and exhaust duct/military afterburner are examples. Computational techniques are often also specific to engine size class and thus Canada, focusing on small gas turbines, has a specific set of technology requirements.

Advanced 3D CFD codes have been used to generate the following design improvements:

- In the compressor to develop advanced swept airfoils capable of high compression ratios that in turn yield higher efficiency at less weight and with a smaller parts count (significant life cycle cost factor);
- In the combustor for higher intensity (smaller volumes with much higher energy density)

combustors that approach stoichiometric conditions to yield higher efficiency with lower weight; and
- In the turbine to produce higher stage loading with reduced turbine cooling air requirements that again reduces weight and cost while reducing fuel burn.

Combustion Systems Computation

The combustor of a gas turbine engine is that part of the engine that receives the compressed air from the compressor. Energy is added to the airflow in the combustor in the form of chemical energy derived from fuel. The combustor discharge air is expanded across a turbine or turbines where energy is extracted to drive the compressor and gearbox of a turboshaft/turboprop engine, or to provide jet thrust via a turbofan and core nozzle in a thrust engine.

Small gas turbines, of the size that have typically been designed and built in Canada pose significant design challenges because of their size. Pratt and Whitney Canada combustors are the highest intensity combustors in the world, where intensity can be thought of as the amount of energy converted per unit volume within the combustor. The design objectives for gas turbine engines, including small ones, are to increase both overall pressure ratios and cycle temperatures, which lead to increased efficiency and smaller size and weight, while simultaneously producing reduced noise and noxious emissions levels.

Combustor technology development challenges for Canadian engine manufacturers include.

Computational fluid dynamics: CFD analyses are complicated by the reverse flow designs typically selected to maintain short combustors within small volumes. Cooling flow and chemical additions to the CFD design further complicate the process as the temperatures of gases at the core of the flows are well above the melting temperatures of the combustor materials. Pressure losses and cooling flow requirements must be minimized to improve performance.

Materials: Increasing compressor ratios result in increased compressor discharge temperatures and decreased cooling capability. These increased temperatures also push for higher fuel to air ratios and higher temperatures within the combustor. Stoichiometric ratio is that ratio when all oxygen is consumed in the combustion process leaving less air for cooling. Materials challenges in this environment are the most demanding. Fuel injection and mixing: CFD and injector specific techniques are required.

Emissions: While not legislated and not contributing significantly in absolute terms, there is a drive for lower emissions that drives designs often in the opposite direction to those factors identified above.

Aerodynamics and Flight Mechanics

Aerodynamics is the study of forces on wing bodies and controls due to air pressure and viscous (drag) effects. Flight mechanics is the study of the resulting motion of objects through the air and includes the stability and control Behaviour. The laws of motion and aerodynamics are combined to ensure that an aircraft flies in the intended manner. Much of the aerodynamics and flight mechanics work that is pursued for the purposes of aircraft designed and built in Canada will pertain to such issues as the design of improved wings, the integration of various components onto an aircraft or issues such as flight in adverse conditions where the handling qualities of an aircraft will be adversely influenced by the build up of ice on the surface of the wing. Advanced technology development in this field will be directed towards supersonic transports and eventually hypersonic flight. There are considerable differences between fixed wing and rotary wing aircraft aerodynamics and flight mechanics and both areas are of considerable interest to the Canadian aerospace and defence industry.

Technologies relevant to Aerodynamics and Flight Mechanics are described below:

Advanced Aerodynamics and Handling

Included here are technologies that will enable the Canadian Aerospace industry to contribute to the design of advanced concept aircraft technologies or components or be the lead design integrator.

These enabling technologies should be pursued dependent on their links to, and pre-positioning for potential application to specific aircraft platforms or types as follows:

- *Future Transport Aircraft*: Future transport aircraft will have to demonstrate increased speed and load carrying capabilities over greatly extended ranges. Specific targets have been set by the U.S. for next generation transport aircraft although no new advanced concept transport aircraft are currently well advanced. Wing loading factors will double over that of existing aircraft with the development of materials new to the transport aircraft envelope. For shorter-range aircraft, a key enabling technology will be that of high efficiency turboprop engines with cruise speeds above the M.72 range. Propulsion technology and propulsion integration issues, aircraft design optimization, CFD, and materials technology development and insertion will be key to the success of the future transport aircraft.
- *Hypersonic Aircraft*: Hypersonic aircraft are in exploratory or advanced development model stage at this time and will be used initially for low cost space launch and delivery platforms and subsequently for commercial transport. Propulsion technologies are significant to hypersonic vehicle feasibility and are now the limiting factor. Variable cycle engines, advanced materials, endothermic fuels and fuel control technologies are key aeropropulsion technology elements where significantR&D remains unsatisfied. Numerous controls and materials research topics require further investment as well, although less uncertainty remains in these areas due to advances made through the shuttle Programmes.
- *Advanced Rotorcraft*: Future rotorcraft will demonstrate increased cruise speeds of 200 kts or greater with tiltrotor speeds approaching 450 kts. These

cruise speeds will be possible at significantly reduced vibration levels and with greatly increased range/fuel economy. Many of the design concepts for attaining these performance improvements are already in development, however much work remains undone.

- *Advanced Rotorcraft Flight Mechanics*: For both conventional helicopter and tiltrotor blades, the wings and propulsion system operate in a very complex aeromechanical environment. Aerodynamics, structures, vibration and acoustics parameters are inseparable and typically drive the design of the entire air vehicle. In trimmed forward flight the advancing blade tip will be moving at near sonic velocities whilst the retreating blade is often in near stall conditions.

Advanced Design and Development

General aviation aircraft pose specific design challenges in all aspects of their design and fabrication. Increasing availability of low cost and high performance avionics, advanced composite designs and powerplant integration all offer opportunities for general aviation aircraft designers and builders.

Many of the technologies being furthered for use in military unmanned aerial vehicles will be of pertinence to general aviation aircraft.

Low cost gas turbine technologies and composite structures development and certification issues will likely be the technologies of greatest interest.

The development of technologies for military purposes will underwrite some of the costs of introduction of those design concepts into general aviation use.

Experimental Assessment and Performance

Analytical design and analysis techniques are a prerequisite to reductions in design cycle time, design and production costs, and improved safety and environmental impact. The development of these analytical or numerical design techniques will remain heavily dependent on experimental validation of design codes and performance targets for another 10-15 years. Whereas in the past, experimental resources such as wind tunnels were used primarily for design development and refinement, in the future they may increasingly be used for the validation of computational design tools. Notwithstanding the foregoing, there will continue to be a requirement for national facilities including wind tunnels, engine test facilities, flight test resources, and specialized resources including icing tunnels and rig test facilities for some time to come.

Experimental design and performance validation technology investment will be required in the following areas to support the aerospace industry in Canada:

- *Data Capture and Analysis Automation*: Automated methods for intelligent data capture and analysis will be required to reduce large facility run times and meet the challenges of design tool validation. This will require investment both in sensors and in computational tools;
- *Experimental Code Development*: Increased data capture rates and fidelity will be required and will necessitate the development of specific codes for experimental design and performance validation. Facilities and infrastructure will have to be maintained or enhanced to achieve these goals; and
- *Infrastructure Support*: The maintenance of critical national facilities will have to be supported in concert with other government departments and industry. The objective will not necessarily be to create new facilities but rather to improve the functionality of existing resources to meet the needs of new technology developments.

Aeropropulsion Performance Assessment

Test cells utilized for Canadian aero-engine Programmes, and also those developed for sale, have typically been sea-level static facilities offering little or no altitude, forward flight velocity or temperature pressure simulation. Some limited flying test bed capability exists in Canada for the testing of engines.

That being said, the National Research Council has participated in numerous international projects in the process ensuring that a world leading test cell capability exists both for engine qualification testing, performance testing and for the development of performance assessment techniques.

Engine test cells take a number of forms. Sea level test facilities are used for Engine Qualification Testing that involves the monitoring of a relatively small number of parameters over long periods where in-service usage is evaluated in a time compressed manner. Qualification testing also involves the ingestion of ice or water to ensure that unacceptable engine degradation does not occur in those instances. The NRC Institute for Aerospace Research has developed world recognized icing testing competencies and icing test facilities that are used by Canadian and off-shore engine manufacturers for qualification testing.

Altitude test cells are used to qualify engines over a full flight envelope as opposed to the endurance type testing previously described.

The National Research Council in colLabouration with Pratt and Whitney Canada have developed and operated one small altitude test cell at NRC for some time. An initiative that began in 2000 will see the development and commissioning of a somewhat larger and more capable altitude facility, again as a colLabourative effort between NRC and P&WC.

Test cells can also be used for the analysis of problems or validation of problem resolution. In these cases the test cells often require enhanced instrumentation suites and a much more careful design to ensure that performance parameters are correctly measured.

World interest in advanced test cell technologies has been directed at those required to support hypersonic vehicles for military uses or for space launch vehicles.

This type of test cell is very resource intensive and highly specialized and will likely be of little interest or utility to any but a limited number of Canadian firms. The Short Take Off and Vertical Landing (STOVL) version of the F35 Joint Strike Fighter has recently posed new challenges in the world of aeropropulsion testing. For this testing, in-flow preparation, exhaust treatment, fan drive systems, and 6 axis thrust measurement in the vertical axis will all pose significant new challenges to the performance assessment community.

Advanced Design Concepts

Analysis and Design Integration

Advanced aerodynamics profile development in Canada will be primarily directed at wing design for subsonic aircraft carrying less than 120 passengers. The objective of work done on advanced aerodynamic profiles will be to increase efficiency and cruise speeds through reduced drag while improving structural and control characteristics. Wing profile, control surface effectiveness, airframe and engine interface effects with the wing and wing tip designs are areas of research and development interest. Also, developments improving wing-flap high lift performance are important areas for minimizing wing size required and hence costs.

Laminar flow control is a term that deserves discussion. Airflow over wings begins as a laminar or ordered flowfield and will transition to a higher drag producing turbulent flow based on flow characteristics such as speed and wing influences including wing shape, surface roughness. It has been estimated that if laminar flow could be maintained on the wings of a large aircraft, fuel savings of up to 25% could be achieved. Wing and flight characteristics of small aircraft are such that laminar flow can be relatively easily maintained over much of the flight envelope. A variety of methods can be used to increase laminar flow regions on aircraft of larger size and having higher Reynolds numbers and sweep angles.

Computational fluid dynamics will be the most important technology relevant to the development of advanced aerodynamic profiles. A number of areas require R&D activity and support for aircraft design particular to Canadian aerospace interests. Large-scaleCFD code refinement and validation is one area requiring work to improve accuracy and reduce computational times for MDO by more rapid design convergence. These CFD codes will also require validation in Labouratories and in wind tunnels.

All-Electric Aircraft Concept Development

The all-electric aircraft will utilize electronic actuators to replace equivalent hydraulic system components. The intent is to save weight and increase reliability. For example, electrical generators would provide power to electric actuators for flight control surface movement rather than equivalent hydraulic powered components.

Electric power cables are lighter and less prone to damage or service induced degradation such as fitting vibration that results in leakage in hydraulic systems. Alternate power supply redundancy is an additional advantage of this concept.

Challenges associated with this type of technology insertion would be related to electromagnetic interference (EMI), and rapid load fluctuations imposed on the power generation engines.

Fly-by-Light Concept Development

Fly-by-Light (FBL) technology involves the replacement of electronic data transmission, mechanical control linkages, and electronic sensors with optical components and subsystems. Benefits include lower initial acquisition and life cycle costs, reduced weight, and increased aircraft performance and reliability.

Fibre-optic cables are essentially immune to electromagnetic interference and therefore not affected by fields generated by other lines or electrical devices in close proximity, nor are they affected by lightning strikes. For flight controls, hydraulic or electric actuators are still employed but receive their command inputs via fibre-optic cables.

Weight reductions are significant as the fibre-optic cables need only be protected from physical damage, whereas electric cables must be insulated and shielded increasing weight cables must be insulated and shielded increasing weight significantly. Also with a FBL connection multiple routes can be readily provided that are well separated to provide control redundancy.

There are a number of enabling technologies that must be developed in order to enable photonics technology insertion. Fibre-optic connectors for in-line and end connections must be developed that are durable and insensitive to in-service maintenance activities. Fibre-optic sensors development will also be necessary to allow the achievement of the full range of benefits that can be obtained in fly-by-light aircraft.

This technology is usually associated with smart structures concepts such as smart skins where fibre-optic cabling can be readily embedded in a composite lay-up to achieve dispersed damage, stress, temperature or vibration sensing capability.

Detection Management and Control Systems

Regional airliners and helicopters operating in lower level airspace are increasingly exposed to hazardous icing conditions. This has increased the need for technologies for proactive and reactive ice detection and protection. Reactive technologies are those related to the detection of runback icing and attempt to monitor real-time or infer likely aerodynamic performance degradation.

Proactive systems forecast the potential for icing conditions and provide on-board avoidance advisory information. Reactive systems provide reasonable protection of the aircraft within the regulated flight envelope but are essentially go/no-go decision aids. Aircraft on Search and Rescue Missions and most civil transport aircraft often do not have the option of avoiding hazardous icing conditions and should have pro-active pilot advisors and ice removal systems.

Reactive ice detection devices include: embedded sensors that are mounted on the wing surface in a critical location and monitor ice build-up; and aerodynamic performance sensors that typically monitor pressure within the boundary layer of the wing to determine lift performance degradation. Proactive systems require the remote measurement of Liquid Water Content (LWC), Outside Air Temperature (OAT) and Mean Volume Diameter (MVD) of the liquid water. Knowledge of these three parameters is required to predict hazardous icing conditions. Additional R&D work on MVD measurement is required.

Ice control and removal systems may use heated air from the engines or electrical heat elements to remove ice from airfoil surfaces. Coatings that are termed"iceophobic" may also be applied to minimize ice build-up. CFD tools are needed to Analyse ice-buildup characteristics, assess aerodynamic degradation, and improve ice removal air supply performance.

This technology area is of particular interest because of the types of aircraft produced in Canada and because of climatic conditions.

Design Techniques

Two issues predominate in the environmental design factors technology category for aeropropulsion systems — external noise and exhaust emissions.

A previously stated objective for noise reduction is in the order of 6 EPNdB (Effective Perceived Noise in dB). This objective can be achieved through the utilization of larger by-pass ratio fans, innovative design concepts for turbo fans and sound conscious designs in the combustor and exhaust nozzles/liners. Generally speaking, noise improvements and fuel efficiency must be improved to meet future regulatory requirements without sacrifice of overall engine efficiency. Of special interest will be advanced ducted propulsors (ADF) that offer both noise attenuation and increased efficiency potential. This technology area will be heavily dependent on computational design techniques and multidisciplinary design optimization.

The reduction in aircraft emissions is also a regulated requirement. While small aircraft engines contribute an insignificant amount of pollution they are still the targets of increased environmental scrutiny. Regulatory requirements are targeted at Nitrous Oxides (NOx), Carbon Monoxide (CO) and visible particulate emissions. CFD analysis techniques specific to combustion processes will be the major tool used to lower aeropropulsion emissions.

DYNAMIC PROGRAMMEMING

INTRODUCTION

Dynamic Programmeming is a method for efficiently solving a broad range of search and optimization problems which exhibit the characteristics of overlappling subproblems and optimal substructure. I'll try to illustrate these characteristics through some simple examples and end with an exercise. Happy coding!

OVERLAPPING SUBPROBLEMS

A problem is said to have overlapping subproblems if it can be broken down into subproblems which are reused multiple times. This is closely related to recursion. To see the difference consider the factorial function, defined as follows (in Python):

```
def factorial(n):
    if n == 0: return 1
    return n*factorial(n-1)
```

Thus the problem of calculating factorial(n) depends on calculating the subproblem factorial(n-1). This problem does not exhibit *overlapping*subproblems since factorial is called exactly once for each positive integer less than n.

Fibonacci Numbers

The problem of calculating the nth Fibonacci number does, however, exhibit overlapping subproblems. The naïve recursive implementation would be

```
def fib(n):
        if n == 0: return 0
        if n == 1: return 1
        return fib(n-1) + fib(n-2)
```

The problem of calculating fib(n) thus depends on both

fib(n–1) and fib(n–2). To see how these subproblems overlap look at how many times fib is called and with what arguments when we try to calculate fib(5):

```
fib(5)
fib(4)  + fib(3)
fib(3)  + fib(2)  + fib(2)  + fib(1)
fib(2)  + fib(1)  + fib(1)  + fib(0)  + fib(1)  +
fib(0)  + fib(1)
fib(1)  + fib(0)  + fib(1)  + fib(1)  + fib(0)  +
fib(1)  + fib(0)  + fib(1)
```

At the kth stage we only need to know the values of fib(k–1) and fib(k–2), but we wind up calling each multiple times. Starting from the bottom and going up we can calculate the numbers we need for the next step, removing the massive redundancy.

```
def fib2(n):
        n2, n1 = 0, 1
        for i in range(n-2):
              n2, n1 = n1, n1 + n2
        return n2+n1
```

In Big-O notation the fib function takes $O(c^n)$ time, i.e., exponential in n, while thefib2 function takes O(n) time. If this is all too abstract take a look at this graph comparing the runtime (in microseconds) of fib and fib2 versus the input parameter.

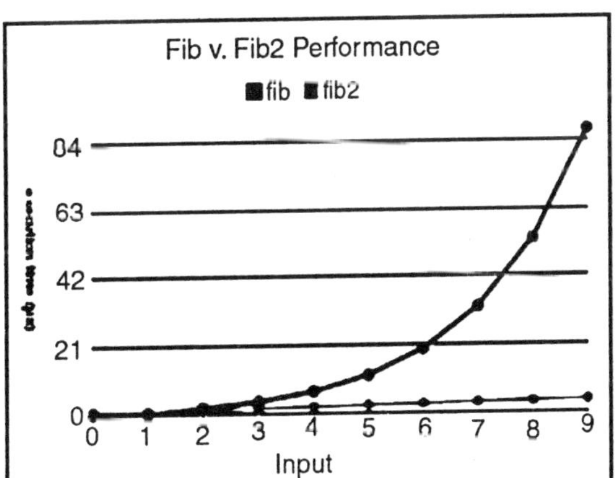

The above problem is pretty easy and for most Programmemers is one of the first examples of the performance issues surrounding recursion versus iteration. In fact, I've seen many instances where the Fibonacci example leads people to believe that recursion is inherently slow. This is not true, but in cases where we can define a problem with overlapping subproblems recursively using the above technique will always reduce the execution time.

Now, for the second characteristic of dynamic Programmeming: optimal substructure.

OPTIMAL SUBSTRUCTURE

A problem is said to have optimal substructure if the globally optimal solution can be constructed from locally optimal solutions to subproblems. The general form of problems in which optimal substructure plays a roll goes something like this. Let's say we have a collection of objects called A. For each object o in A we have a "cost," c(o). Now find the subset of A with the maximum (or minimum) cost, perhaps subject to certain constraints.

The brute-force method would be to generate every subset of A, calculate the cost, and then find the maximum (or minimum) among those values. But if A has n elements in it we are looking at a search space of size 2^n if there are no constraints on A. Oftentimes n is huge making a brute-force method computationally infeasible. Let's take a look at an example.

Maximum Subarry Sum

Let's say we're given an array of integers. What (contiguous) subarray has the largest sum? For example, if our array is [1,2,–5,4,7,–2] then the subarray with the largest sum is [4,7] with a sum of 11. One might think at first that this problem reduces to finding the subarray with all positive entries, if one exists, that maximizes the sum. But consider the array [1,5,–3,4,–2,1]. The subarray with the largest sum is [1, 5, –3, 4] with a sum of 7.

First, the brute-force solution. Because of the constraints

on the problem, namely that the subsets under consideration are contiguous, we only have to check O(n^2) subarrays (why?). Here it is, in Python:

```
def msum(a):
   return max([(sum(a[j:i]), (j,i)) for i in
range(1,len(a)+1) for j inrange(i)])
```

This returns both the sum and the offsets of the subarray. Let's see if we can't find an optimal substructure to exploit.

We are given an input array a. I'm going to use Python notation so that a[0:k] is the subarray starting at 0 and including every element up to and including k-1. Let's say we know the subarray of a[0:i] with the largest sum (and that sum). Using just this information can we find the subarray of a[0:i+1] with the largest sum?

Let a[j:k+1] be the optimal subarray, t the sum of a[j:i], and s the optimal sum. If t+a[i] is greater than s then set a[j:i+1] as the optimal array and set s = t. If t + a[i] is negative, however, the contiguity constraint means that we cannot include a[j:i+1] in our subarray since any such subarray will have a smaller sum than a subarray without it. So, if t+a[i] is negative set t = 0 and set the left-hand bound of the optimal subarray to i+1.

To visualize consider the array [1,2,–5,4,7,-2].

```
Set s = -infinity, t = 0, j = 0, bounds =
(0,0)
(1 2 -5 4 7 -2
(1)| 2 -5 4 7 -2 (set t=1. Since t > s, set
s=1 and bounds = (0,1))
(1 2)|-5 4 7 -2 (set t=3. Since t > s, set
s=3, and bounds = (0,2))
1 2 -5(| 4 7 -2 (set t=-2. Since t < 0, set
t=0 and j = 3)
1 2 -5 (4)| 7 -2 (set t=4. Since t > s, set
s=4 and bounds = (3,4))
1 2 -5 (4 7)|-2 (set t=11. Since t > s, set
s=11 and bounds = (3,5))
1 2 -5 (4 7) -2| (set t=9. Nothing happens
since t < s)
```

This requires only one pass through the array and at each

step we're only keeping track of three variables: the current sum from the left-hand edge of the bounds to the current point (t), the maximal sum (s), and the bounds of the current optimal subarray (bounds). In Python:

```
def msum2(a):
    bounds, s, t, j = (0,0), -
      float('infinity'), 0
    for i in range(len(a)):
        t = t + a[i]
        if t > s: bounds, s = (j, i+1), t
        if t < 0: t, j = 0, i+1
  return (s, bounds)
```

In this problem the "globally optimal" solution corresponds to a subarray with a globally maximal sum, but at each each step we only make a decision relative to what we have already seen.

That is, at each step we know the best solution *thus far*, but might change our decision later based on our previous information and the current information. This is the sense in the problem has optimal substructure. Because we can make decisions locally we only need to traverse the list once, reducing the run-time of the solution to O(n) from O(n^2). Again, a graph:

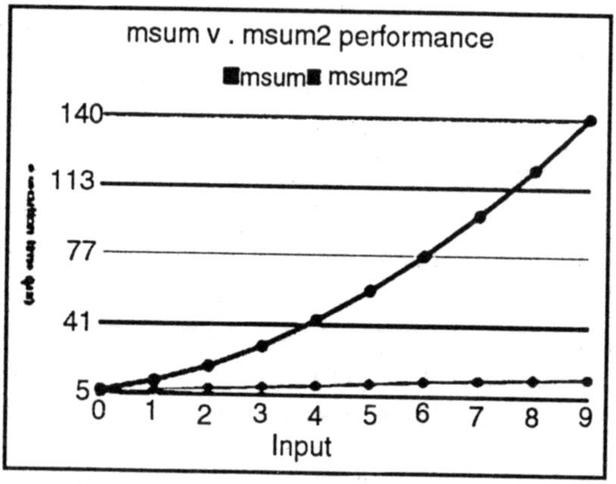

NAPSACK PROBLEM

Let's apply what we're learned so far to a slightly more

interesting problem. You are an art thief who has found a way to break into the impressionist wing at the Art Institute of Chicago. Obviously you can't take everything. In particular, you're constrained to take only what your knapsack can hold — let's say it can only hold W pounds. You also know the market value for each painting. Given that you can only carry W pounds what paintings should you steal in order to maximize your profit?

First let's see how this problem exhibits both overlapping subproblems and optimal substructure. Say there are n paintings with weights $w_1 \dots, w_n$ and market values $v_1 \dots, v_n$. Define A(i,j) as the maximum value that can be attained from considering only the first i items weighting at most j pounds as follows.

Obviously A(0,j) = 0 and A(i,0) = 0 for any i d" n and j d" W. If $w_i > j$ then A(i,j) = A(i-1, j) since we cannot include the ith item. If, however, w_i d" j then A(i,j) then we have a choice: include the ith item or not. If we do not include it then the value will be A(i-1, j). If we do include it, however, the value will be $v_i + A(i-1, j - w_i)$. Which choice should we make? Well, whichever is larger, i.e., the maximum of the two.

Expressed formally we have the following recursive definition,

$$A(i,j) = \begin{cases} 0 & \text{if } i = 0 \text{ or } j = 0 \\ A(i-1,j) & \text{if} w_i > j \\ \max\{A(i-1,j), u_i + A(i-1, j-w_i)\} & \text{if } w_i \le j \end{cases}$$

This problem exhibits both overlapping subproblems and optimal substructure and is therefore a good candidate for dynamic Programmeming. The subproblems overlap because at any stage (i,j) we might need to calculate A(k,l) for several k < i and l < j. We have optimal substructure since at any point we only need information about the choices we have already made.

The recursive solution is not hard to write:

```
def A(w, v, i,j):
```

```
if i == 0 or j == 0: return 0
if w[i-1] > j: return A(w, v, i-1, j)
if w[i-1] ⇐ j: return max(A(w,v, i-1, j),
 v[i-1] + A(w,v, i-1, j - w[i-1]))
```

Remember we need to calculate A(n,W). To do so we're going to need to create an n-by-W table whose entry at (i,j) contains the value of A(i,j). The first time we calculate the value of A(i,j) we store it in the table at the appropriate location. This technique is called memoization and is one way to exploit overlapping subproblems. There's also a Ruby module called memoize which does it for Ruby.

To exploit the optimal substructure we iterate over all i ⇐ n and j ⇐ W, at each step applying the recursion formula to generate the A(i,j) entry by using the memoized table rather than calling A() again. This gives an algorithm which takes O(nW) time using O(nW) space and our desired result is stored in the A(n,W) entry in the table.

The following is an example of global sequence alignment using Needleman/Wunsch techniques. For this example, the two sequences to be globally aligned are

G A A T T C A G T T A (sequence #1)

G G A T C G A (sequence #2)

So M = 11 and N = 7 (the length of sequence #1 and sequence #2, respectively)

A simple scoring scheme is assumed where

- $S_{i,j}$ = 1 if the residue at position i of sequence #1 is the same as the residue at position j of sequence #2 (match score); otherwise
- $S_{i,j}$ = 0 (mismatch score)
- w = 0 (gap penalty)

STEPS IN DYNAMIC PROGRAMMING

- Initialization
- Matrix fill (scoring)
- Traceback (alignment)

Initialization Step

The first step in the global alignment dynamic

Programmeming approach is to create a matrix with M + 1 columns and N + 1 rows where M and N correspond to the size of the sequences to be aligned.

Since this example assumes there is no gap opening or gap extension penalty, the first row and first column of the matrix can be initially filled with 0.

		G	A	A	T	T	C	A	G	T	T	A
	0	0	0	0	0	0	0	0	0	0	0	0
G	0											
G	0											
A	0											
T	0											
C	0											
G	0											
A	0											

Matrix Fill Step

One possible (inefficient) solution of the matrix fill step finds the maximum global alignment score by starting in the upper left hand corner in the matrix and finding the maximal score $M_{i,j}$ for each position in the matrix. In order to find $M_{i,j}$ for any i,j it is minimal to know the score for the matrix positions to the left, above and diagonal to i, j. In terms of matrix positions, it is necessary to know $M_{i-1,j}$, $M_{i,j-1}$ and $M_{i-1,\, j-1}$.

For each position, $M_{i,j}$ is defined to be the maximum score at position i,j; i.e.

$$M_{i,j} = \text{MAXIMUM}[$$
$$M_{i-1,\, j-1} + S_{i,j} \text{ (match/mismatch in the diagonal)},$$
$$M_{i,j-1} + w \text{ (gap in sequence \#1)},$$
$$M_{i-1,j} + w \text{ (gap in sequence \#2)}]$$

Note that in the example, $M_{i-1,j-1}$ will be red, $M_{i,j-1}$ will be green and $M_{i-1,j}$ will be blue.

Using this information, the score at position 1,1 in the matrix can be calculated. Since the first residue in both sequences is a G, $S_{1,1} = 1$, and by the assumptions stated at the beginning, w = 0. Thus, $M_{1,1}$ = MAX[$M_{0,0}$ + 1, $M_{1,0}$ + 0, $M_{0,1}$ + 0] = MAX [1, 0, 0] = 1.

A value of 1 is then placed in position 1,1 of the scoring matrix.

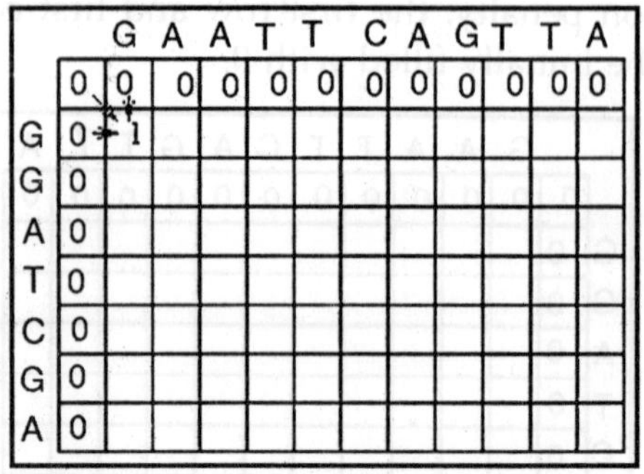

Since the gap penalty (w) is 0, the rest of row 1 and column 1 can be filled in with the value 1. Take the example of row 1. At column 2, the value is the max of 0 (for a mismatch), 0 (for a vertical gap) or 1 (horizontal gap).

The rest of row 1 can be filled out similarly until we get to column 8. At this point, there is a G in both sequences (light blue).

Thus, the value for the cell at row 1 column 8 is the maximum of 1 (for a match), 0 (for a vertical gap) or 1 (horizontal gap). The value will again be 1. The rest of row 1 and column 1 can be filled with 1 using the above reasoning.

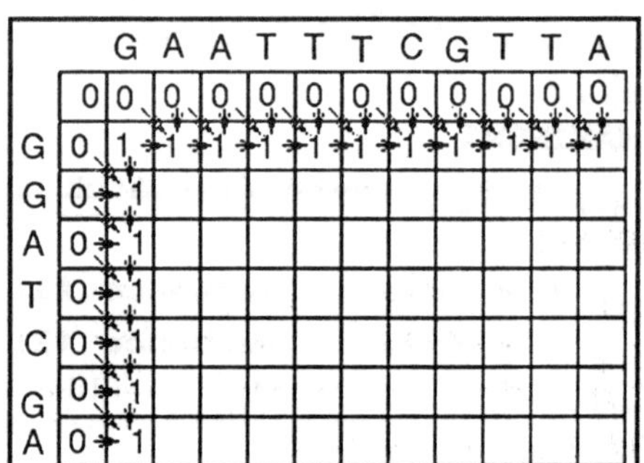

Now let's look at column 2. The location at row 2 will be assigned the value of the maximum of 1(mismatch),

1(horizontal gap) or 1 (vertical gap). So its value is 1. At the position column 2 row 3, there is an A in both sequences. Thus, its value will be the maximum of 2(match), 1 (horizontal gap), 1 (vertical gap) so its value is 2.

Moving along to position colum 2 row 4, its value will be the maximum of 1 (mismatch), 1 (horizontal gap), 2 (vertical gap) so its value is 2.

Note that for all of the remaining positions except the last one in column 2, the choices for the value will be the exact same as in row 4 since there are no matches.

The final row will contain the value 2 since it is the maximum of 2 (match), 1 (horizontal gap) and 2(vertical gap).

		G	A	A	T	T	C	A	G	T	T	A
	0	0	0	0	0	0	0	0	0	0	0	0
G	0	1	1	1	1	1	1	1	1	1	1	1
G	0	1	1									
A	0	1	2									
T	0	1	2									
C	0	1	2									
G	0	1	2									
A	0	1	2									

Using the same techniques as described for column 2, we can fill in column 3.

		G	A	A	T	T	C	A	G	T	T	A
	0	0	0	0	0	0	0	0	0	0	0	0
G	0	1	1	1	1	1	1	1	1	1	1	1
G	0	1	1	1								
A	0	1	2	2								
T	0	1	2	2								
C	0	1	2	2								
G	0	1	2	2								
A	0	1	2	3								

After filling in all of the values the score matrix is as follows:

		G	A	A	T	T	C	A	G	T	T	A
	0	0	0	0	0	0	0	0	0	0	0	0
G	0	1	1	1	1	1	1	1	1	1	1	1
G	0	1	1	1	1	1	1	1	2	2	2	2
A	0	1	2	2	2	2	2	2	2	2	2	3
T	0	1	2	2	3	3	3	3	3	3	3	3
C	0	1	2	2	3	3	3	4	4	4	4	4
G	0	1	2	2	3	3	3	4	4	5	5	5
A	0	1	2	3	3	3	3	4	5	5	5	6

Traceback Step

After the matrix fill step, the maximum alignment score for the two test sequences is 6. The traceback step determines the actual alignment(s) that result in the maximum score. Note that with a simple scoring algorithm such as one that is used here, there are likely to be multiple maximal alignments.

The traceback step begins in the M,J position in the matrix, i.e. the position that leads to the maximal score. In this case, there is a 6 in that location. Traceback takes the current cell and looks to the Neighbour cells that could be direct predacessors. This means it looks to the Neighbour to the left (gap in sequence #2), the diagonal Neighbour (match/ mismatch), and the Neighbour above it (gap in sequence #1). The algorithm for traceback chooses as the next cell in the sequence one of the possible predacessors. In this case, the Neighbours are marked in red. They are all also equal to 5.

		G	A	A	T	T	C	A	G	T	T	A
	0	0	0	0	0	0	0	0	0	0	0	0
G	0	1	1	1	1	1	1	1	1	1	1	1
G	0	1	1	1	1	1	1	1	2	2	2	2
A	0	1	1	2	2	2	2	2	2	2	2	3
T	0	1	2	2	3	3	3	3	3	3	3	3
C	0	1	2	2	3	3	4	4	4	4	4	4
G	0	1	2	2	3	3	4	4	5	5	5	5
A	0	1	2	3	3	3	4	5	5	5	5	6

Since the current cell has a value of 6 and the scores are 1 for a match and 0 for anything else, the only possible predacessor is the diagonal match/mismatch Neighbour. If more than one possible predacessor exists, any can be chosen.

This gives us a current alignment of,

```
(Seq #1)     A
             |
(Seq #2)     A
```

So now we look at the current cell and determine which cell is its direct predacessor. In this case, it is the cell with the red 5.

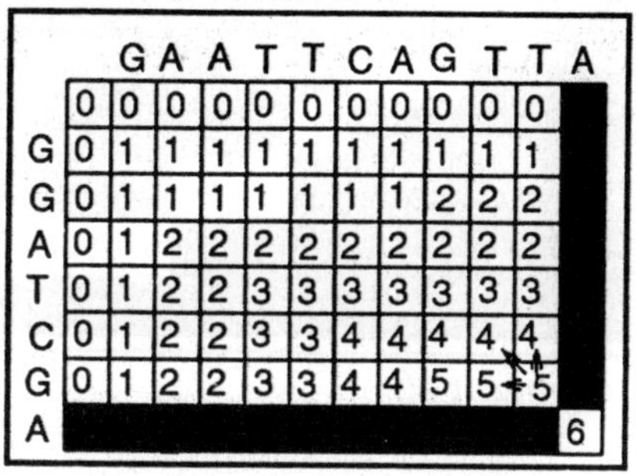

The alignment as described in the above step adds a gap to sequence #2, so the current alignment is

```
(Seq #1)    T A
              |
(Seq #2)    _ A
```

Once again, the direct predacessor produces a gap in sequence #2.

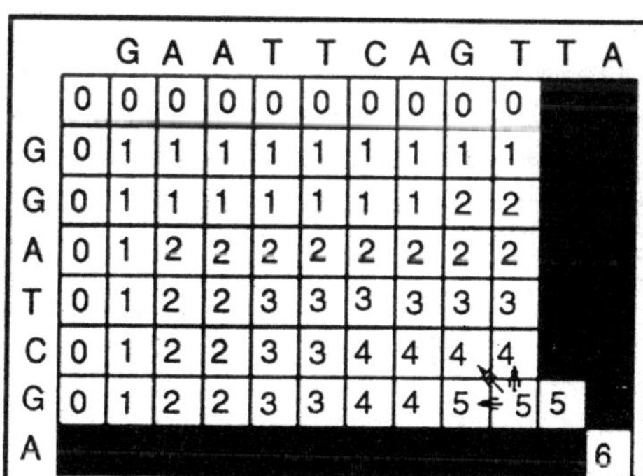

After this step, the current alignment is,

```
(Seq #1)       T T A
                   |
                 _ _ A
```

Continuing on with the traceback step, we eventually get to a position in column 0 row 0 which tells us that traceback is completed. One possible maximum alignment is:

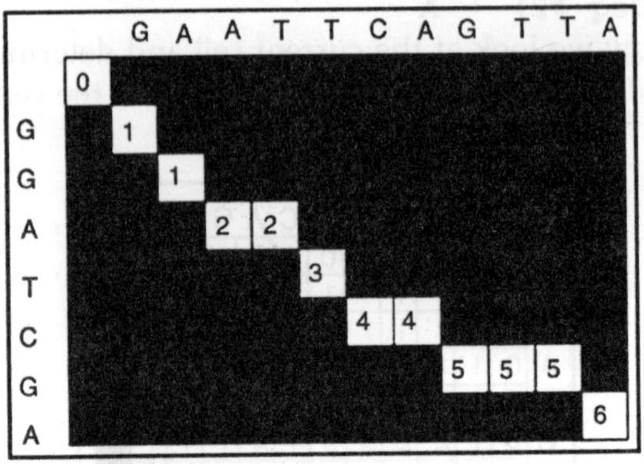

Giving an alignment of:

```
G   A A   T T   C A G T T A
|       |     | |   |            |
G   G A  _  T   C _ G _ _  A
```

FIRST EXAMPLE

Let's begin with a simple capital budgeting problem. A corporation has $5 million to allocate to its three plants for possible expansion. Each plant has submitted a number of proposals on how it intends to spend the money. Each proposal gives the cost of the expansion (c) and the total revenue expected (r). The following table gives the proposals generated:

Table. Investment Possibilities

Proposal	Plant 1.		Plant2.		Plant3	
	c_1	r_1	c_2	r_2	c_3	r_3
1	0	0	0	0	0	0
2	1	5	2	8	1	4
3	2	6	3	9	—	—
4	—	—	4	12	—	—

Each plant will only be permitted to enact one of its proposals. The goal is to maximize the firm's revenues resulting from the allocation of the $5 million. We will assume that any of the $5 million we don't spend is lost (you can work out how a more reasonable assumption will change the problem as an exercise).

A straightforward way to solve this is to try all possibilities and choose the best. In this case, there are only $3 \times 4 \times 2 = 24$ ways of allocating the money. Many of these are infeasible (for instance, proposals 3, 4, and 1 for the three plants costs $6 million). Other proposals are feasible, but very poor (like proposals 1, 1, and 2, which is feasible but returns only $4 million).

Here are some disadvantages of total enumeration:

- For larger problems the enumeration of all possible solutions may not be computationally feasible.
- Infeasible combinations cannot be detected *a priori*, leading to inefficiency.
- Information about previously investigated combinations is not used to eliminate inferior, or infeasible, combinations.

Note also that this problem cannot be formulated as a linear Programme, for the revenues returned are not linear functions.

One method of calculating the solution is as follows:

Let's break the problem into three *stages*: each stage represents the money allocated to a single plant. So stage 1 represents the money allocated to plant 1, stage 2 the money to plant 2, and stage 3 the money to plant 3. We will artificially place an ordering on the stages, saying that we will first allocate to plant 1, then plant 2, then plant 3.

Each stage is divided into *states*. A state encompasses the information required to go from one stage to the next. In this case the states for stages 1, 2, and 3 are

- *{0,1,2,3,4,5}*: The amount of money spent on plant 1, represented as x_1,
- *{0,1,2,3,4,5}*: The amount of money spent on plants 1 and 2 (x_2), and

- *{5}*: The amount of money spent on plants 1, 2, and 3 (x_3).

Unlike linear Programmeming, the x_i do not represent decision variables: they are simply representations of a generic state in the stage.

Associated with each state is a revenue: Note that to make a decision at stage 3, it is only necessary to know how much was spent on plants 1 and 2, not how it was spent. Also notice that we will want x_3 to be 5. Let's try to figure out the revenues associated with each state. The only easy possibility is in stage 1, the states x_1. Table gives the revenue associated with x_1.

Table. Stage 1 Computations.

If the available Capital x_1 is	Then the Optimal Porosal is Proposal is for	And the Revenue Stage1 is
0	1	0
1	2	5
2	3	6
3	3	6
4	3	6
5	3	6

We are now ready to tackle the computations for stage 2. In this case, we want to find the best solution for both plants 1 and 2. If we want to calculate the best revenue for a given x_2, we simply go through all the plant 2 proposals, allocate the given amount of funds to plant 2, and use the above table to see how plant 1 will spend the remainder.

For instance, suppose we want to determine the best allocation for state $x_2 = 4$.

In stage 2 we can do one of the following proposals:

- Proposal 1 gives revenue of 0, leaves 4 for stage 1, which returns 6. Total: 6.
- Proposal 2 gives revenue of 8, leaves 2 for stage 1, which returns 6. Total: 14.
- Proposal 3 gives revenue of 9, leaves 1 for stage 1, which returns 5. Total: 14.
- Proposal 4 gives revenue of 12, leaves 0 for stage 1, which returns 0. Total: 12.

The best thing to do with four units is proposal 1 for plant 2 and proposal 2 for plant 1, returning 14, or proposal 2 for plant 2 and proposal 1 for plant 1, also returning 14. In either case, the revenue for being in state $x_2 = 4$ is 14. The rest of table 3 can be filled out similarly.

Table. Stage 2 Computations.

If the available Capital x_1 is	Then the Optimal Porosal is	And the Revenue for Stage 1 is
0	1	0
1	1	5
2	2	8
3	2	13
4	2 or 3	14
5	4	17

We can now go on to stage 3. The only value we are interested in is $x_3 = 5$. Once again, we go through all the proposals for this stage, determine the amount of money remaining and use Table to decide the value for the previous stages.

So here we can do the following at plant 3:

- Proposal 1 gives revenue 0, leaves 5. Previous stages give 17. Total: 17.
- Proposal 2 gives revenue 4, leaves 4. Previous stages give 14. Total: 18.

Therefore, the optimal solution is to implement proposal 2 at plant 3, proposal 2 or 3 at plant 2, and proposal 3 or 2 (respectively) at plant 1. This gives a revenue of 18.

If you study this procedure, you will find that the calculations are done *recursively*. Stage 2 calculations are based on stage 1, stage 3 only on stage 2. Indeed, given you are at a state, all future decisions are made independent of how you got to the state. This is the *principle of optimality* and all of dynamic Programmeming rests on this assumption.

We can sum up these calculations in the following formulas:

Denote by $r(k_j)$ the revenue for proposal k_j at stage *j*, and by $t_j(x_j)$ the corresponding cost. Let x_j be the revenue of state x_j in stage *j*. Then we have the following calculations

$$f_1(x_1) = \max_{k_1 x(k_1) \le x_1} \{r(k_1)\}$$

and

$$f_j(x_j) = \max_{k_j x(k_j) \le x_j} \{r(k_{j-1}) + f_{j-1}(x_j - c(k_j))\} \text{ for } j = 2, 3.$$

All we were doing with the above calculations was determining these functions.

The computations were carried out in a forward procedure. It was also possible to calculate things from the "last" stage back to the first stage.

We could define,

- y_1 = amount allocated to stages 1, 2, and 3,
- y_2 = amount allocated to stages 2 and 3, and
- y_3 = amount allocated to stage 3.

This defines a *backward recursion*. Graphically, this is illustrated in Figure 1.

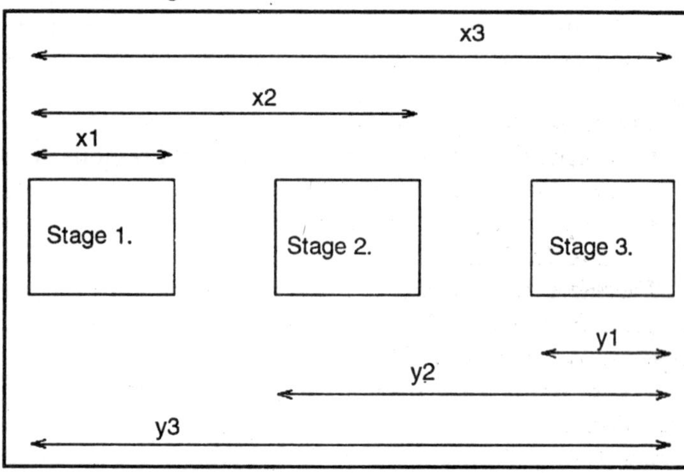

Fig. Forward vs. Backward Recursion

Corresponding formulas are:

- Let $f_3(y_3)$ be the optimal revenue for stage 3, given y_3,
- $f_2(y_2)$be the optimal revenue for stages 2 and 3, given y_3, and

- $f_1(y_1)$ be the optimal revenue for stages 1, 2, and 3, given y_1.

The recursion formulas are:

$$f_3(y_3) = \max_{k_3 : c(k_s) \leq ys} \{r(k_3)\}$$

and

$$f_j(y_j) = \max_{kj : c(k_j) \leq y_j} \{r(k_3) + f_{j+1}(y_j - c(k_j))\}$$

If you carry out the calculations, you will come up with the same answer. Therefore, in the future, I will be presenting only the backward recursion, except in cases where I wish to contrast the two recursions.

SECOND EXAMPLE

Dynámic Programmeming may look somewhat familiar. Both our shortest path algorithm and our method for CPM project scheduling have a lot in common with it. Let's look at a particular type of shortest path problem. Suppose we wish to get from A to J in the road network of Figure 2.

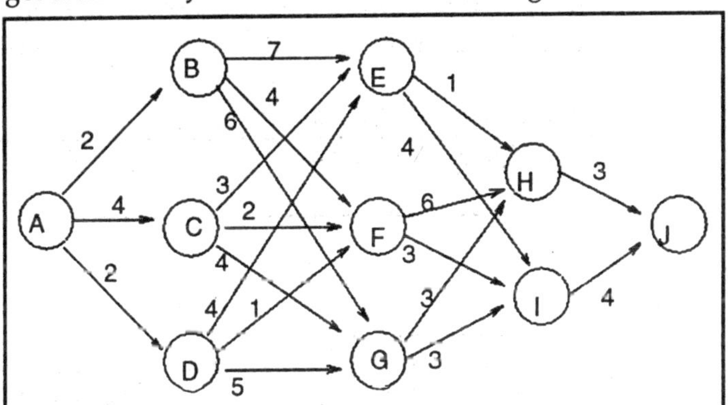

Fig. Road Network

The numbers on the arcs represent distances. Due to the special structure of this problem, we can break it up into stages. Stage 1 contains node A, stage 2 contains nodes B, C, and D, stage 3 contains node E, F, and G, stage 4 contains H and I, and stage 5 contains J.

The states in each stage correspond just to the node names. So stage 3 contains states E, F, and G. If we let *S* denote a node in stage *j* and let $f_j(S)$ be the shortest distance from node *S* to the destination *J*, we can write

$$f_j(S) = \max_{\text{nodes } z \text{ in stage } j+1} \{C_{SZ} + f_{j+1}(Z)\}$$

where c_{SZ} denotes the length of arc *SZ*. This gives the recursion needed to solve this problem. We begin by setting $f_5(J) = 0$.

Here are the rest of the calculations:

Stage 4.

During stage 4, there are no real decisions to make: you simply go to your destination *J*. So you get:

- $f_4(H) = 3$ by going to J,
- $f_4(I) = 4$ by going to J.

Stage 3.

Here there are more choices. Here's how to calculate $f_3(F)$. From F you can either go to H or I. The immediate cost of going to H is 6. The following cost is $f_4(H) = 3$. The total is 9. The immediate cost of going to I is 3.

The following cost is $f_4(I) = 4$ for a total of 7. Therefore, if you are ever at F, the best thing to do is to go to I. The total cost is 7, so $f_3(F) = 7$.

The next table gives all the calculations:

S_3	$CS_3 Z_3 + f_4(Z_3)$		$F_3(S_3)$	Decision Go to
	H	I		
E	4	8	4	H
F	9	7	7	I
G	6	7	6	H

You now continue working back through the stages one by one, each time completely computing a stage before continuing to the preceding one.

The results are:

Stage 1.

S_1	$CS_1Z_1 + f_2(Z_1)$			f_2S_1	Decision go to
	B	C	D		
A	13	11	11	11	Cor D

Stage 2.

S_2	$CS_2Z_2 + f_3(S_2)$			$f_2(S_2)$	Decision Go to
	E	F	G		
B	11	11	12	11	E or F
C	7	9	10	7	E
D	8	8	11	8	E or F

COMMON CHARACTERISTICS

There are a number of characteristics that are common to these two problems and to all dynamic Programmeming problems.

These are:

- The problem can be divided into *stages* with a *decision* required at each stage.
  In the capital budgeting problem the stages were the allocations to a single plant. The decision was how much to spend. In the shortest path problem, they were defined by the structure of the graph. The decision was were to go next.
- Each stage has a number of *states* associated with it.
  The states for the capital budgeting problem corresponded to the amount spent at that point in time. The states for the shortest path problem was the node reached.
- The decision at one stage transforms one state into a state in the next stage.
  The decision of how much to spend gave a total amount spent for the next stage. The decision of where to go next defined where you arrived in the next stage.
- Given the current state, the optimal decision for each of the remaining states does not depend on the previous states or decisions.
  In the budgeting problem, it is not necessary to know how the money was spent in previous stages, only how much was spent. In the path problem, it was not necessary to know how you got to a node, only that you did.

- There exists a recursive relationship that identifies the optimal decision for stage *j*, given that stage *j*+1 has already been solved.
- The final stage must be solvable by itself.

  The last two properties are tied up in the recursive relationships given above.

The big skill in dynamic Programmeming, and the art involved, is to take a problem and determine stages and states so that all of the above hold. If you can, then the recursive relationship makes finding the values relatively easy. Because of the difficulty in identifying stages and states, we will do a fair number of examples.

KNAPSACK PROBLEM

The knapsack problem is a particular type of integer Programme with just one constraint. Each item that can go into the knapsack has a size and a benefit. The knapsack has a certain capacity. What should go into the knapsack so as to maximize the total benefit? As an example, suppose we have three items as shown in Table , and suppose the capacity of the knapsack is 5.

Table. Knapsack Items

Item (j)	Weight (w_j)	Benfit (b_j)
1	2	65
2	3	80
3	1	30

The stages represent the items: we have three stages *j*=1,2,3. The state y_j at stage *j* represents the total weight of items *j* and all following items in the knapsack. The decision at stage *j* is how many items *j* to place in the knapsack.

Call this value k_j. This leads to the following recursive formulas: Let $f_j(y_j)$ be the value of using units of capacity for items *j* and following.

Let y_j represent the largest integer less than or equal to *a*.

- $f_3(y_j) = 30y_j$
- $f_j(y_j) = \max k_j \leq \lfloor y_j / w_j \rfloor \{b_j k_j + f_{j+1}(y_j - w_j k_j)\}$

ALTERNATIVE FORMULATION

There is another formulation for the knapsack problem. This illustrates how arbitrary our definitions of stages, states, and decisions are. It also points out that there is some flexibility on the rules for dynamic Programmeming. Our definitions required a decision at a stage to take us to the next stage (which we would already have calculated through backwards recursion). In fact, it could take us to any stage we have already calculated. This gives us a bit more flexibility in our calculations. The recursion I am about to present is a forward recursion. For a knapsack problem, let the stages be indexed by *w*, the weight filled. The decision is to determine the last item added to bring the weight to *w*. There is just one state per stage. Let *g*(*w*) be the maximum benefit that can be gained from a *w* pound knapsack. Continuing to use b_j and w_j as the weight and benefit, respectively, for item *j*, the following relates *g*(*w*) to previously calculated *g* values:

$$g(w) = \max_{j} \left\{ b_j + g\left(w - w_j\right) \right\}$$

Intuitively, to fill a *w* pound knapsack, we must end off by adding some item. If we add item *j*, we end up with a knapsack of size $w - w_j$ to fill.

To illustrate on the above example:

- $g(0) = 0$
- $g(1) = 30$ add item 3.
- $g(2) = \max\{65 + g(0) = 65, 30 + g(1) = 60\} = 65$ add item

$g(3) = \max\{65 + g(1) = 95, 80 + g(0) = 80, 30 + g(2) = 95\} = 95$ add item 1 or 3.

- $g(4) = \max\left\{\begin{matrix} 65 + g(2) = 130, 80 + g(1) = \\ 110, 30 + g(3) = 125 \end{matrix}\right\} = 130$ add item 1.
- $g(5) = \max\left\{\begin{matrix} 65 + g(3) = 160, 80 + g(2) = \\ 145, 30 + g(4) = 160 \end{matrix}\right\} = 160$ add item 1 or 3.

This gives a maximum of 160, which is gained by adding 2 of item 1 and 1 of item 3.

EQUIPMENT REPLACEMENT

In the network homework, you already saw how to formulate and solve an equipment replacement problem using a shortest path algorithm. Let's look at an alternative dynamic Programmeming formulation.

Suppose a shop needs to have a certain machine over the next five year period. Each new machine costs \$1000. The cost of maintaining the machine during its *i*th year of operation is as follows:

$$m_1 = \$60,\ m_2\ \$80,\ \text{and}\ m_3 = \$120.$$

A machine may be kept up to three years before being traded in. The trade in value after *i* years is $s_1 = \$800$, $s_2 = \$600$, and $s_3 = \$500$. How can the shop minimize costs over the five year period?

Let the stages correspond to each year. The state is the age of the machine for that year. The decisions are whether to keep the machine or trade it in for a new one. Let $f_t(x)$ be the minimum cost incurred from time *t* to time 5, given the machine is *x* years old in time *t*.

Since we have to trade in at time 5,

$$f_5(x) = -s_x.$$

Now consider other time periods. If you have a three year old machine in time *t*, you must trade in, so

$$f_t(3) = -500 + 1000 + 60 + f_{t+1}(1)\ \text{(Trade)}.$$

If you have a two year old machine, you can either trade or keep.

- Trade costs you $-600 + 1000 + 60\ f_{t+1}(1)$.
- Keep costs you $120 + f_{t+1}(3)$.

So the best thing to do with a two year old machine is the minimum of the two.

Similarly,

$$f_t(1) = \min\{-800 + 1000 + 60 + f_{t+1}(1), 80 + f_{t+1}(2)\}.$$

Finally, at time zero, we have to buy, so

$$f_o(0) = 1000 + 60\ f_1(1)$$

This is solved with backwards recursion as follows:

Stage 0.

Age x	Trade	Keep	$f_1(x)$	Decision
0		1280	1280	Keep

Stage 1.

Age x	Trade	Keep	$f_1(x)$	Decision
1	220	220	220	Trade or Keep

Stage 2.

Age x	Trade	Keep	$f_2(x)$	Decision
1	–40	–40	–40	Trade or Keep
2	160	140	140	Keep

Stage 3.

Age x	Trade	Keep	$f_3(x)$	Decision
1	–280	–300	–300	Keep
2	–80	–120	–120	Keep
3	20		20	Trade

Stage 4.

Age x	Trade	Keep	$f_4(x)$	Decision
1	–540	–520	–540	Trade
2	–340	–380	–380	Keep
3	–240		–240	Trade

Stage 5.

Age x	$f_5(x)$
1	–800
2	–600
3	–500

So the cost is 1280, and one solution is to trade in years 1 and 2. There are other optimal solutions.

TRAVELING SALESPERSON PROBLEM

We have seen that we can solve one type of integer Programmeming (the knapsack problem) with dynamic Programmeming.

The traveling salesperson problem is to visit a number of cities in the minimum distance. For instance, a politician begins in New York and has to visit Miami, Dallas, and Chicago before returning to New York. How can she minimize the distance traveled? The distances are as in Table.

Table. TSP Example Problem.

	New York	Miami	Dallas	Chicago
1. New York	—	1334	1559	809
2. Miami	1334	—	1343	1397
3. Dallas	1559	1343	—	921
4. Chicago	809	1397	921	—

The real problem in solving this is to define the stages, states, and decisions. One natural choice is to let stage t represent visiting t cities, and let the decision be where to go next. That leaves us with states. Imagine we chose the city we are in to be the state. We could not make the decision where to go next, for we do not know where we have gone before. Instead, the state has to include information about all the cities visited, plus the city we ended up in. So a state is represented by a pair (i,S) where S is the set of t cities already visited and i is the last city visited (so i must be in S). This turns out to be enough to get a recursion.

The stage 3 calculations are,

- $f_3(2,\{2, 3, 4\}) = 1334$
- $f_3(3,\{2, 3, 4\}) = 1559$
- $f_3(4, \{2, 3, 4\}) = 809$

For other stages, the recursion is,

$$f_t(i,S) = \min_{j \neq 1 \text{ and } j \notin S} \left\{C_{ij} + f_{t+1}(j, S \cup j)\right\}.$$

You can continue with these calculations. One important aspect of this problem is the so called *curse of dimensionality*. The state space here is so large that it becomes impossible to solve even moderate size problems.

For instance, suppose there are 20 cities. The number of states in the 10th stage is more than a million. For 30 cities, the number of states in the 15th stage is more than a billion. And for 100 cities, the number of states at the 50th stage is more than 5,000,000,000,000,000,000,000,000,000,000. This is not the sort of problem that will go away as computers get better.

NONADDITIVE RECURSIONS

Not every recursion must be additive. Here is one example where we multiply to get the recursion.

A student is currently taking three courses. It is important that he not fail all of them. If the probability of failing French is P_1, the probability of failing English is P_3, and the probability of failing Statistics is P_2, then the probability of failing all of them is $P_1P_2P_3$. He has left himself with four hours to study. How should he minimize his probability of failing all his courses? The following gives the probability of failing each course given he studies for a certain number of hours on that subject, as shown in Table.

Table. Student Failure Probabilities.

Hours	French	English	Statistatics
0	.8	.75	.9
1	.7	.7	.7
2	.65	.67	.6
3	.62	.65	.55
4	.6	.62	.5

What kind of student is this? We let stage 1 correspond to studying French, stage 2 for English, and stage 3 for Statistics. The state will correspond to the number of hours studying for that stage and all following stages. Let $f_t(x)$ be the probability of failing *t* and all following courses, assuming *x* hours are available. Denote the entries in the above table as $P_t(k)$, the probability of failing course *t* given *k* hours are spent on it.

The final stage is easy:

$$f_3(x) = p_3(x)$$

The recursion is as follows:

$$f_t(x) = \min_{k : k \leq x} \{p_t(k) f_{t+1}(x-k)\}.$$

We can now solve this recursion:

Stage 1.

X	k=0	k=1	k=2	k=3	k=4	$f_1(x)$
4	.8(.37)=.30	.7(.41)=.287	.65(.45)=.293	62.(.52)=.32	.6(.68)=.41	.287

Stage 2.

x	k=0	k=1	k=2	k=3	k=4	f_2 (x)
0	–75(.9) =.68					

Stage 3.

x	$f_3(x)$
0	.9
1	.7
2	.6
3	.55
4	.5

So, the optimum way of dividing time between studying English and Statistics is to spend it all on Statistics.

The overall optimal strategy is to spend one hour on French, and three on Statistics. The probability of failing all three courses is about 29%.

STOCHASTIC DYNAMIC PROGRAMMEMING

In deterministic dynamic Programmeming, given a state and a decision, both the immediate payoff and next state are known.

If we know either of these only as a probability function, then we have a stochastic dynamic Programme. The basic ideas of determining stages, states, decisions, and recursive formulae still hold: they simply take on a slightly different form.

Uncertain Payoffs

Consider a supermarket chain that has purchased 6 gallons of milk from a local dairy. The chain must allocate the 6 gallons to its three stores.

If a store sells a gallon of milk, then the chain receives revenue of $2. Any unsold milk is worth just $.50. Unfortunately, the demand for milk is uncertain, and is given in the following table:

Store	Demand	Probability
1	1	.60
	2	.00
	3	.40
2	1	.5
	2	.1
	3	.4
3	1	.4
	2	.3
	3	.3

The goal of the chain is to maximize the expected revenue from these 6 gallons. (This is not the only possible objective, but a reasonable one.)

Note that this is quite similar to some of our previous resource allocation problems: the only difference is that the revenue is not known for certain. We can, however, determine an expected revenue for each allocation of milk to a store. For instance, the value of allocating 2 gallons to store 1 is:

$$f_3(x) = r_3(x)$$

$$f_i(x) = \max_{k \le x}\{r_i(k) + f_{i+1}(x-k)$$

We can do this for all allocations to get the following values:

Store	Allocation	Value
1	1	2
	2	3.1
	3	4.2
2	1	2
	2	3.25
	3	4.35
3	1	2
	2	.3.4
	3	4.35

We have changed what looked to be a stochastic problem into a deterministic one! We simply use the above expected values. The resulting problem is identical to our previous resource allocation problems. We have a stage for each store. The states for stage 3 are the number of gallons given to store

3 (0, 1, 2, 3); the states for stage 2 are the number of gallons given to stores 2 and 3 (0, 1, 2, 3, 4, 5, 6) and the state for stage 1 is the number of gallons given to stores 1, 2, and 3 (6). The decision at stage *i* is how many gallons to give to store *i*. If we let the above table be represented by $r_i(k)$ (the value of giving *k* gallons to store *i*, then the recursive formulae are

$$f_3(x) = r_3(x)$$

$$f_i(x) = \max_{k \le x} \{r_i(k) + f_{i+1}(x-k)$$

If you would like to work out the values, you should get a valuation of \$9.75, with one solution assigning 1 gallon to store 1, 3 gallons to store 2 and 2 gallons to store 3.

Uncertain States

A more interesting use of uncertainty occurs when the state that results from a decision is uncertain. For example, consider the following coin tossing game: a coin will be tossed 4 times. Before each toss, you can wager \$0, \$1, or \$2 (provided you have sufficient funds). You begin with \$1, and your objective is to maximize the probability you have \$5 at the end. of the coin tosses.

We can formulate this as a dynamic Programme as follows: create a stage for the decision point before each flip of the coin, and a "final" stage, representing the result of the final coin flip. There is a state in each stage for each possible amount you can have. For stage 1, the only state is "1", for each of the others, you can set it to "0,1,2,3,4,5" (of course, some of these states are not possible, but there is no sense in worrying too much about that). Now, if we are in stage *i* and bet *k* and we have *x* dollars, then with probability.5, we will have *x–k* dollars, and with probability.5 we will have *x+k* dollars next period. Let $f_i(x)$ be the probability of ending up with at least \$5 given we have \$*x* before the *i*th coin flip.

This gives us the following recursion:

$$f_i(x) = \max_{k \le x_j k \le 2} 0.5 f_{i+1}(x+k) + 0.5 f_{i+1}(x-k)$$

$$f_5(5) = 1; f_5(x) = 0 \text{ for } \le 4$$

Note that the next state is not known for certain, but is a

probabilistic mixing of states. We can still easily determine f_4 from f_5, and f_3 from f_4 and so on back to $f_1(1)$.

Another example comes from the pricing of stock options. Suppose we have the option to buy Netscape stock at \$150. We can exercise this option anytime in the next 10 days (american option, rather than a european option that could only be exercised 10 days from now). The current price of Netscape is \$140. We have a model of Netscape stock movement that predicts the following: on each day, the stock will go up by \$2 with probability.4, stay the same with probability.1 and go down by \$2 with probability.4. Note that the overall trend is downward (probably conterfactual, of course). The value of the option if we exercise it at price *x* is *x*-150 (we will only exercise at prices above 150).

We can formulate this as a stochastic dynamic Programme as follows: we will have stage *i* for each day *i*, just before the exercise or keep decision.

The state for each stage will be the stock price of Netscape on that day. Let $f_i(x)$ be the expected value of the option on day *i* given that the stock price is *x*.

Then, the optimal decision is given by:

$$f_i(x) = \max\{x - 150, 0.4f_{i+1}(x+2) + 0.1f_{i+1}f(x) + 0.5f_{i+1}(x-2)\}$$

and

$$f_{10}(x) = \max\{0, x - 150\}$$

Given the size of this problem, it is clear that we should use a spreadsheet to do the calculations.

There is one major difference between stochastic dynamic Programmes and deterministic dynamic Programmes: in the latter, the complete decision path is known. In a stochastic dynamic Programme, the actual decision path will depend on the way the random aspects play out. Because of this, "solving" a stochastic dynamic Programme involves giving a decision rule for every possible state, not just along an optimal path.

Linear Decision Making

Many decision problems (and some of the most frustrating ones), involve choosing one out of a number of choices where future choices are uncertain. For example, when getting (or not getting!) a series of job offers, you may have to make a decision on a job before knowing if another job is going to be offered to you. Here is a simplification of these types of problems:

Suppose we are trying to find a parking space near a restaurant. This restaurant is on a long stretch of road, and our goal is to park as close to the restaurant as possible. There are *T* spaces leading up to the restaurant, one spot right in front of the restaurant, and *T* after the restaurant as follows:

–T	–(T–1)	...	–1	0	1	...	T–1	T

Each spot can either be full (with probability, say.9) or empty (.1). As we pass a spot, we need to make a decision to take the spot or try for another (hopefully better) spot. The value for parking in spot *t* is $|t|$. If we do not get a spot, then we slink away in embarrasment at large cost *M*. What is our optimal decision rule?

We can have a stage for each spot *t*. The states in each stage are either *e* (for empty) or *o* (for occupied). The decision is whether to park in the spot or not (cannot if state is *o*). If we let $f_t(e)$ and $f_t(o)$ be the values for each state, then we have:

$$f_T(e) = T$$
$$f_T(o) = M$$
$$f_t(e) = \max\{|t|, .9f_{t+1}(o) + .1f_{t+1}(e)\}$$
$$f_t(o) = .9f_{t+1}(o) + .1f_{t+1}(e)$$

In general, the optimal rule will look something like, take the first empty spot on or after spot *t* (where *t* will be negative).

GREEDY ALGORITHM

INTRODUCTION

Greedy algorithms are simple and straightforward. They are shortsighted in their approach in the sense that they take decisions on the basis of information at hand without worrying about the effect these decisions may have in the future. They are easy to invent, easy to implement and most of the time quite efficient. Many problems cannot be solved correctly by greedy approach. Greedy algorithms are used to solve optimization problems

GREEDY APPROACH

Greedy Algorithm works by making the decision that seems most promising at any moment; it never reconsiders this decision, whatever situation may arise later.

As an example consider the problem of "Making Change".

Coins available are:

- Dollars (100 cents)
- Quarters (25 cents)
- Dimes (10 cents)
- Nickels (5 cents)
- Pennies (1 cent)

Problem Make a change of a given amount using the smallest possible number of coins.

Informal Algorithm

- Start with nothing.
- At every stage without passing the given amount.
  - Add the largest to the coins already chosen.

Formal Algorithm

Make change for n units using the least possible number of coins.

```
MAKE-CHANGE                                  (n)
C ¬ {100, 25, 10, 5, 1}// constant.
Sol ¬ {};// set that will hold the solution
 set.
Sum ¬ 0 sum of item in solution set
WHILE sum not = n
x = largest item in set C such that sum + x £
 n
IF no such item THEN
 RETURN "No Solution"
S ¬ S {value of x}
sum ¬ sum + x
RETURN S
```

Example Make a change for 2.89 (289 cents) here n = 2.89 and the solution contains 2 dollars, 3 quarters, 1 dime and 4 pennies. The algorithm is greedy because at every stage it chooses the largest coin without worrying about the consequences. Moreover, it never changes its mind in the sense that once a coin has been included in the solution set, it remains there.

CHARACTERISTICS AND FEATURES

To construct the solution in an optimal way. Algorithm maintains two sets. One contains chosen items and the other contains rejected items.

The greedy algorithm consists of four (4) function:

- A function that checks whether chosen set of items provide a solution.
- A function that checks the feasibility of a set.
- The selection function tells which of the candidates is the most promising.
- An objective function, which does not appear explicitly, gives the value of a solution.

STRUCTURE GREEDY ALGORITHM

- Initially the set of chosen items is empty i.e., solution set.
- At each step
  - item will be added in a solution set by using selection function.
  - IF the set would no longer be feasible
    a) Reject items under consideration (and is never consider again).
  - ELSE IF set is still feasible THEN
    a) Add the current item.

DEFINITIONS OF FEASIBILITY

A feasible set (of candidates) is promising if it can be extended to produce not merely a solution, but an optimal solution to the problem. In particular, the empty set is always promising why? (because an optimal solution always exists)

Unlike Dynamic Programmeming, which solves the subproblems bottom-up, a greedy strategy usually progresses in a top-down fashion, making one greedy choice after another, reducing each problem to a smaller one.

Greedy-Choice Property

The "greedy-choice property" and "optimal substructure" are two ingredients in the problem that lend to a greedy strategy.

Greedy-Choice Property

It says that a globally optimal solution can be arrived at by making a locally optimal choice.

SAMPLE PROBLEM

There is a long list of stalls, some of which need to be covered with boards. You can use up to N (1 ⇐ N ⇐ 50) boards, each of which may cover any number of consecutive stalls. Cover all the necessary stalls, while covering as few total stalls as possible.

THE IDEA

The basic idea behind greedy algorithms is to build large solutions up from smaller ones. Unlike other approaches, however, greedy algorithms keep only the best solution they find as they go along.

Thus, for the sample problem, to build the answer for N = 5, they find the best solution for N = 4, and then alter it to get a solution for N = 5. No other solution for N = 4 is ever considered.

Greedy algorithms are fast, generally linear to quadratic and require little extra memory. Unfortunately, they usually aren't correct. But when they do work, they are often easy to implement and fast enough to execute.

PROBLEMS

There are two basic problems to greedy algorithms.

How to Build

How does one create larger solutions from smaller ones? In general, this is a function of the problem. For the sample problem, the most obvious way to go from four boards to five boards is to pick a board and remove a section, thus creating two boards from one. You should choose to remove the largest section from any board which covers only stalls which don't need covering (so as to minimize the total number of stalls covered).

To remove a section of covered stalls, take the board which spans those stalls, and make into two boards: one of which covers the stalls before the section, one of which covers the stalls after the second.

WORK

The real challenge for the Programmemer lies in the fact that greedy solutions don't always work. Even if they seem to work for the sample input, random input, and all the cases you can think of, if there's a case where it won't work, at least one (if not more!) of the judges' test cases will be of that form.

For the sample problem, to see that the greedy algorithm described above works, consider the following:

Assume that the answer doesn't contain the large gap which the algorithm removed, but does contain a gap which is smaller. By combining the two boards at the end of the smaller gap and splitting the board across the larger gap, an answer is obtained which uses as many boards as the original solution but which covers fewer stalls. This new answer is better, so therefore the assumption is wrong and we should always choose to remove the largest gap.

If the answer doesn't contain this particular gap but does contain another gap which is just as large, doing the same transformation yields an answer which uses as many boards and covers as many stalls as the other answer. This new answer is just as good as the original solution but no better, so we may choose either.

Thus, there exists an optimal answer which contains the large gap, so at each step, there is always an optimal answer which is a superset of the current state. Thus, the final answer is optimal.

CONCLUSIONS

If a greedy solution exists, use it. They are easy to code, easy to debug, run quickly, and use little memory, basically defining a good algorithm in contest terms. The only missing element from that list is correctness. If the greedy algorithm finds the correct answer, go for it, but don't get suckered into thinking the greedy solution will work for all problems.

Algorithm

The sequence has three parts: the part which will be 1 when in sorted order, 2 when in sorted order, and 3 when in sorted order. The greedy algorithm swaps as many as possible of the 1's in the 2 part with 2's in the 1 part, as many as possible 1's in the 3 part with 3's in the 1 part, and 2's in the 3 part with 3's in the 2 part.

Once none of these types remains, the remaining elements out of place need to be rotated one way or the other in sets of 3. You can optimally sort these by swapping all the 1's into place and then all the 2's into place.

Analysis: Obviously, a swap can put at most two elements in place, so all the swaps of the first type are optimal. Also, it is clear that they use different types of elements, so there is no "interference" between those types. This means the order does not matter. Once those swaps have been performed, the best you can do is two swaps for every three elements not in the correct location, which is what the second part will achieve (for example, all the 1's are put in place but no others; then all that remains are 2's in the 3's place and vice-versa, and which can be swapped).

Friendly Coins - A Counterexample [Abridged]

Given the denominations of coins for a newly founded country, the Dairy Republic, and some monetary amount, find the smallest set of coins that sums to that amount. The Dairy Republic is guaranteed to have a 1 cent coin.

Algorithm: Take the largest coin value that isn't more than the goal and iterate on the total minus this value.

(Faulty) Analysis: Obviously, you'd never want to take a smaller coin value, as that would mean you'd have to take more coins to make up the difference, so this algorithm works.

Maybe not: Okay, the algorithm usually works. In fact, for the U.S. coin system {1, 5, 10, 25}, it always yields the optimal set. However, for other sets, like {1, 5, 8, 10} and a goal of 13, this greedy algorithm would take one 10, and then three 1's, for a total of four coins, when the two coin solution {5, 8} also exists.

Topological Sort

Given a collection of objects, along with some ordering constraints, such as "A must be before B," find an order of the objects such that all the ordering constraints hold.

Algorithm: Create a directed graph over the objects, where there is an arc from A to B if "A must be before B." Make a pass through the objects in arbitrary order. Each time you find an object with in-degree of 0, greedily place it on the end of the current ordering, delete all of its out-arcs, and recurse on its (former) children, performing the same check. If this algorithm gets through all the objects without putting every object in the ordering, there is no ordering which satisfies the constraints.

AMORTIZED ANALYSIS

DEFINITION

Amortized analysis means analyzing time-averaged cost for a sequence of operations. Motivation is that traditional worst-case-per-operation analysis can give overly pessimistic bound if the only way of having an expensive operation is to have a lot of cheap ones before it.

Note: this is DIFFERENT from our usual notion of "average case analysis" — we're not making any assumptions about inputs being chosen at random — we're just averaging over time.

The approach is going to be to somehow assign an artificial cost to each operation in the sequence. This artificial cost is called the _amortized cost_ of an operation. The key property required of amortized cost is that the total real cost of the sequence should be bounded by the total of the amortized costs of all the operations. Then, for purposes of analyzing an algorithm that, say, accesses a data structure, it is okay to just use the amortized cost instead of the actual cost of the operation. This will give you correct results.

Note: There is sometimes flexibility in the assignment of amortized costs.

There are going to be three approaches that we call:

The aggregate method The banker's method (tokens in the data structure) The physicist's method (potential functions) (The physicist's method is just a slightly more formal version of the banker's method, as we'll see.).

We'll illustrate these methods through some examples.

*Example*1: a binary counter. Say we want to store a big binary counter in an array A: Start all entries at 0. The operation we are going to implement and Analyse is that of counting.

The algorithm we'll use for incrementing this counter is the usual one. We toggle bit A[0]. If it changed from 0 to 1, then we toggle bit A[1], etc. We stop when a bit changes from 0 to 1. The cost of an increment is the number of bits that change.

A[m]	A[m-1]......	A[3]	A[2]	A[1]	A[0]	cost
0	0	0	0	0	0	1
0	0	0	0	0	1	2
0	0	0	0	1	0	1
0	0	0	0	1	1	3
0	0	0	1	0	0	1
0	0	0	1	0	1	2
0	0	0	1		1	0

The number of bits that change when the increment produces a number n is at most 1+floor(lg n). (That's just the number of bits in the binary representation of n.) Thus, in a sequence of n increments, worst-case cost per increment is bounded by n(1+floor(lg n)) = O(n log n).

But, what is our *amortized* cost per increment?

Answer: 2.

Proof 1 (aggregate method): how often do we flip A[0]?

Answer: every time. how often do we flip A[1]?

Answer: every other time. How often do we flip A[2]?

Answer: every 4th time. Etc. So, total cost spent on flipping A[0] is n, total cost of A[1] is floor(n/2), total cost on A[2] is floor(n/4), etc. So, the total cost is: total cost = n + floor(n/2) + floor(n/4) +... total cost ⇐ n + n/2 + n/4 + n/8 +... ⇐ 2n

So the total cost is 2n, which means the amortized cost of an increment is 2.

Proof 2 (banker's method): Let's us a kind of accounting trick. On every bit that is a 1, let's keep a dollar on that bit. So for example, if the current count is 6, we'd have:

```
                             $   $
array: 0....    0     1      1   0
```

We'll use the convention that whenever we toggle a bit, we must pay a dollar to do that.

Let's say we allocate $2 to do an increment. Let's see how much it costs to do the increment. In general, a bunch of low order bits change from 1 to 0, and then one bit changes from a 0 to a 1, and the process terminates. For each of the bits that changes from 1 to 0, we have a dollar sitting on the bit to pay for toggling that bit. For the bit that changes from a 0 to a 1, we have to pay a dollar to toggle the bit, then put a dollar on that bit (for future use).

Thus, having allocated $2 for the increment always guarantees that we will have enough money to pay for the work, no matter how costly the increment actually is. This completes proof 2 that the amortized cost of the increment is 2.

Example 2: Implementing a FIFO queue with two stacks Say you have a stack data type, and you need to implement a FIFO queue. The stack has the usual POP and PUSH operations, and the cost of each operation is 1.

We can implement a FIFO queue using two stacks as follows. The FIFO has two operations: ENQUEUE and DEQUEUE: *ENQUEUE(x)*: Push x onto stack1.

DEQUEUE(): If stack2 is empty, then we POP the entire

contents of stack1 and PUSH it into stack2. Now simply POP from stack2 and return the result.

It's easy to see that this algorithm is correct. Here we'll just worry about the running time. (I'm going to ignore the cost of checking of stack2 is empty, and only measure the cost in terms of the number of PUSHs and POPs that are done.)

Claim: the amortized cost of ENQUEUE is 3 and DEQUEUE is 1.

Proof 1 (aggregate method): As an element flows through the two-stack data structure, it's PUSHed at most twice and POPPed at most twice. This shows that we can assign an amortized cost of 4 to ENQUEUE and 0 to DEQUEUE.

To get the desired result, note that if an element is not DEQUEUED it's only PUSHED twice and POPPED once. So the cost of 3 is paid for by the cost of 3 per ENQUEUE. The last POP is paid for by the DEQUEUE (if it happens).

Proof 2 (banker's method): Maintain a collection of tokens on stack1. In fact, keep 2 tokens for each thing in the stack.

When we ENQUEUE, we have three tokens to work with. We use one to push the element onto stack1, and the other two are put on the element for future use. When we have to move stack1 into stack2, we have enough tokens in the stack to pay for the move (one POP and one PUSH for each element).

Finally, the last pop done by the DEQUEUE is paid for by the 1 we allocated for it. QED.

Example 3: doubling array

We'll use an array to implement a stack that allows push and pop operations. We represent the stack as an array, A[] and an integer variable top that points to the top of the stack.

Here is a naive implementation of push and pop:

push(x): top++; A[top] = x;

pop; top—; return A[top+1]

These operations are both constant time (cost=1). The problem is, what happens when the array gets full? To deal with this, we keep another variable L, storing the size of the array, and a variable k keeping count of the number of elements of the array that are in use. When we are about to overflow the available space (k=L), we allocate an array twice as large, move the data over to the new array, free the old array, and double L. This operation is called "doubling". It will be convenient to Analyse it as thought it was a separate operation on the data strucure, that occurs only when k=L.

If the stack is full, and has size L, and we apply the doubling operation, the cost of the operation is L, because we have to move L items into the new array. (The cost of allocating and freeing the arrays is O(L).)

Starting from an empty stack, doing any sequence n pushes and pops, how much does this cost?

First analysis: Total cost for pushes and pops is n.

Total cost for doubling is at worst 1 + 2 + 4 +... n/2 + n < 2n So, the total cost is 3n. Therefore we can say that the amortized cost of an operation is 3. *Second analysis*: Again, we use the financial approach. We'll keep money lying around the data structure in the following way.

```
                    $ $ $ $
                    $ $ $ $
             +-----------------+
|x|x|x|x|x|x|x|x|x|x|x|x|  |  |  |  |
               +-----------------+
                        ^
                        |
                    midpoint
```

We'll keep $2 on each element stored in the stack that is Beyond The Midpoint of the current array. In the normal case when we do a push (the array is not full), we need $1 to do the work, and then at most $2 to put onto the the new item we just pushed. Thus the cost is $3. (pop is even cheaper.) Now what happens if we have to do a doubling operation?

Before doubling:

```
                    $ $ $ $ $ $ $ $
                    $ $ $ $ $ $ $ $
                  +-------------------+
|x|x|x|x|x|x|x|x|x|x|x|x|x|x|x|x|
                   -------------------+
                          ^
                          !
```

```
                    midpoint
              <---------L--------->
 After doubling:
          +-------------------+-------------------+
|x|x|x|x|x|x|x|x|x|x|x|x|x|x|x|x|  |  |  |  |  |  |
|  |  |  |  |  |  |  |  |  |  |
          +-------------------+-------------------+
                                 ^
                                 |
                             midpoint
```

You can see that the money that we had on the items (L) was sufficient to pay for all the work of doubling the array (L). We conclude that if we allocate $3 for each operation, we'll never run out of money. Thus the amortized cost of an operation is 3.

In these examples, the financial model was not really necessary to get the desired results. However, later we'll see examples where this approach is necessary.

THE PHYSICIST'S METHOD

Let's say that instead of distributing our money all over the data structure (as we did above), we keep it all in a piggy bank. What's really important is how much money is in the piggy bank. We'll call the amount of money in this bank the "potential function" (Phi) for the problem.

So for the two problems above, we used the following two potential functions:

```
Phi(counter) = # of one bits in the counter
Phi(queue) = 2 * the size of stack 1.
[2(k-L/2) if k Þ L/2
Phi(stack) = [
[0 otherwise
```

(Here L is the current array size, and k is the number of elements currently in the stack.) Using this formalism we can define the amortized cost of an operation. Say the system changes from state S to state S′ as a result of doing some operation.

We define the amortized cost of the operation as follows:

```
amortized cost = actual cost + Delta(Phi) =
= actual cost + Phi(S') - Phi(S)
```

This is simply the amount of additional money that we need to maintain our piggy bank and to pay for the work.

For the counter, with the potential function given above: amortized cost of increment ⇐ 2

For the stack, with the potential function given above: amortized cost of pop ⇐ 3

How is this amortized cost related to actual cost? Let's sum the above definition of amortized cost over all the operations:

Sigma(amortized cost) = Sigma(actual cost) + Phi(final) - Phi(initial) or Sigma(actual cost) = Sigma(amortized cost) + Phi(initial) - Phi(final) If the potential is always non-negative, and starts at zero (as it is in our examples), then Sigma(actual cost) ⇐ Sigma(amortized cost) In this more general framework, the potential can be negative, and may not start at 0. So in general we have to worry about the initial and final potentials.

Summary of using potential functions to do amortized analysis:

- Pick a potential function that's going to work (this is art)
- Using your potential function, bound the amortized cost of the operations you're interested in.
- Bound Phi(initial) - Phi(final) In terms of (1), one obvious point is that if the actual cost of an operation is HIGH, and you want the amortized cost to be LOW, then in this case the potential must DECREASE by a lot to pay for it. This is illustrated in both of the examples in this lecture.

We'll see in the next lecture just how essential this formalism is for analyzing splay trees.

DYNAMIC ARRAY

When an array becomes full, just copy the array elements to a larger array

Array→ pointer to an array

Number → number of items in the array

Size → size of the array

```
AddToTable(x)
   if Number == Size then
      allocate NewArray with size 2*Size
      insert all items from Table to NewArray
      free Array
      Array= NewArray
     Size = 2 * Size
  end if
  insert x into Array
  Number = Number + 1
  end insert
```

In a sequence of operations on a data structure often the worst case can not occur in each operation.

The worst case cost of inserting an element in a dynamic array is N + 1.

N = size of the array before the insertion

But you can't get two worst cases in a row!

Amortized Analysis gives the average performance of each operation in the worst case

Three methods used in amortized analysis:

- Aggregate Method
- Accounting Method
- Potential Method

Example: Incrementing a k-bit binary counter

Let A[0..k-1] be an array of bits representing a number X

A[0] - low order bit, so

$$X = \sum_{J=0}^{K-1} A[J]2^J$$

length[A] = k

Start with X = 0

```
Increment (A)
   J = 0
   while J < length[A] and A[J] == 1 do
        A[J] = 0
        J = J + 1
```

```
end while
if J < length[A] then
    A[J] = 1
  end if
end Increment
```

Count bits flipped.
Worst Case.
Increment flips k bits in worst case.
Sequence of n Increment operations takes O(nk).

AGGREGATE METHOD

T(n) = all work done in worst case in sequence of n operations Amortized cost per operation is T(n)/n

X	A[4]	A[3]	A[2]	A[1]	A[0]	Total Cost
0	0	0	0	0	*0*	0
1	0	0	0	*0*	1	1
2	0	0	0	1	*0*	3
3	0	0	*0*	1	1	4
4	0	0	1	0	*0*	7
5	0	0	1	*0*	1	8
6	0	0	1	1	*0*	10
7	0	*0*	1	1	1	11
8	0	1	0	0	*0*	15
9	0	1	0	*0*	1	16

A[0] flips each time Increment is called n

A[1] flips every other time:

$$\left\lfloor \frac{n}{2} \right\rfloor$$

A[1] flips every fourth time:

$$\left\lfloor \frac{n}{2^2} \right\rfloor$$

A[J] flips every 2^J time:

$$\left\lfloor \frac{n}{2^J} \right\rfloor$$

Total number of flips is:

$$\sum_{J=0}^{\lfloor \lg n \rfloor} \left\lfloor \frac{n}{2^J} \right\rfloor < n\sum_{J=0}^{\infty} \frac{1}{2^J} = 2n$$

So amortized cost of each operation is 2 = O(1)

ACCOUNTING METHOD

Assign an amortized cost to each operation Amortized cost may be more or less than the actual cost. If amortized cost is more than the actual cost of the operation assign the difference to part of the data structure as a credit, No negative credit allowed. Total amortized cost is ⇒ total worst case cost.

Example - binary Counter

Amortized cost of setting bit to 1 2 units
1 unit to pay for setting bit to 1
1 unit stored with bit
Amortized cost of setting bit to 0 0 units
Only a 1-bit is set to 0,
All 1-bits have credit of one unit
This pays for setting bit to 0

Example Continued

```
Increment (A)
 J = 0
 while J < length[A] and A[J] == 1 do
     A[J] = 0
  Cost 0
     J = J + 1
     end while
     if J < length[A] then
       A[J] = 1
   Cost 2
     end if
 end Increment
```

X	A[4]	A[3]	A[2]	A[1]	A[0]	Amortized cost
0	0	0	0	0	0	0
1	0	0	0	0	1 (1)	2
2	0	0	0	1 (1)	0	4

3	0	0	0	1 (1)	1 (1)	6
4	0	0	1 (1)	0	0	8
5	0	0	1 (1)	0	1 (1)	10
6	0	0	1 (1)	1 (1)	0	12
7	0	0	1 (1)	1 (1)	1 (1)	14
8	0	1 (1)	0	0	0	16
9	0	1 (1)	0	0	1 (1)	18

POTENTIAL METHOD

Assign an amortized cost to each operation: If amortized cost is more than the actual cost of the operation assign the difference the entire data structure as potential energy ck= actual cost of operation k

$\hat{c}_k$ = amortized cost of operation k

Dk = the state of the data structure after applying k'th operation to Dk,

Φ (D_k) = potential associated with Dk

$$\hat{c}_k + \Phi(D_k) - \Phi(D_{k-1})$$

$$\sum_{k=1}^{n} \hat{C}_k = \sum_{k=1}^{n} (c_k + \Phi(D_k) - \Phi(D_{k-1}))$$

$$= \sum_{k=1}^{n} c_k + \Phi(Dn) - \Phi(D_0)$$

So if $\Phi(D_n) \Rightarrow 0$ then $\Phi(D_0) \Rightarrow 0$ is an upper bound on total cost of the algorithm

Example - binary counter

Potential = number of 1's in the counter

if the k'th operation sets t_k bits to 0 the actual cost is t_k+1

$$\Phi(D_k) - \Phi(D_{k-1}) = 1 - t_k$$

so,

$$\hat{c}_k = c_k + \Phi(D_k) - \Phi(D_{k-1}) = 2$$

How to find $\Phi(D_k)$?

DYNAMIC TABLES

Table $\rightarrow$ pointer to a table

```
Number → number of items in the table
Size → size of the table
AddToTable(x)
if Number == Size then
allocate NewTable with size 2*Size
insert all items from Table to newTable
free Table
Table = NewTable
Size = 2 * Size
end if
insert x into Table
Number = Number + 1
end insert
```

INSERTS DONE BY N ADDTOTABLE

Amortized Cost per AddToTable 3 inserts Table after moving from size 4 to size 8 Perform 4 AddToTable operations

X	X	X	X				
X	X	X	X	Y(2)			
X	X	X	X	Y(2)	Y(2)		
X	X	X	X	Y(2)	Y(2)	Y(2)	
X	X	X	X	Y(2)	Y(2)	Y(2)	Y(2)

1/2 the table has 2 credits One credit per item to pay for the move to next size table

X	X	X	X	Y	Y	Y	Y

TABLE EXPANSION AND CONTRACTION

Policy

When table becomes full move to table twice the size When table contracts to 1/4 full, move to table 1/2 size Let load = (Size of table)/ (number of items in the table) Amortized Cost:

Inserting when load ⇒ 1/2

3 units

Inserting when load < 1/2

0 units

Deleting when load > 1/2

0 units
Deleting when load ⇐ 1/2
2 units

X	X	X	X	
X	X	X	X	Y(2)
X	X	X	X	
X	X	X	(1)	
X	X	(1)	(1)	
X	X			

LINKED LIST VS. DYNAMIC ARRAY LIST

Table. Amortized Costs Per Operation over n Operations

	linked List	**Dynamic Array]**
Insertion	1 call to new	lg(n)/n call to new
set two links	3 data moves	
Deletion	two links	3 data moves
after find		
	1 delete	lg(n)/n call to delete

BACKTRACKING

SOLUTION SPACES

Backtracking is a refinement of the brute force approach, which systematically searches for a solution to a problem among all available options. It does so by assuming that the solutions are represented by vectors ($v_1 \ldots, v_m$) of values and by traversing, in a depth first manner, the domains of the vectors until the solutions are found.

When invoked, the algorithm starts with an empty vector. At each stage it extends the partial vector with a new value. Upon reaching a partial vector ($v_1 \ldots, v_i$) which can't represent a partial solution, the algorithm backtracks by removing the trailing value from the vector, and then proceeds by trying to extend the vector with alternative values.

```
ALGORITHM try(v1...,vi)
   IF (v1...,vi) is a solution THEN RETURN
   (v1...,vi)
```

```
  FOR each v DO
     IF (v1...,vi,v) is acceptable vector THEN
        sol = try(v1...,vi,v)
        IF sol != () THEN RETURN sol
     END
END
RETURN ()
```

If S_i is the domain of v_i, then $S_1 \times ... \times S_m$ is the solution space of the problem. The validity criteria used in checking for acceptable vectors determines what portion of that space needs to be searched, and so it also determines the resources required by the algorithm.

The traversal of the solution space can be represented by a depth-first traversal of a tree. The tree itself is rarely entirely stored by the algorithm in discourse; instead just a path toward a root is stored, to enable the backtracking.

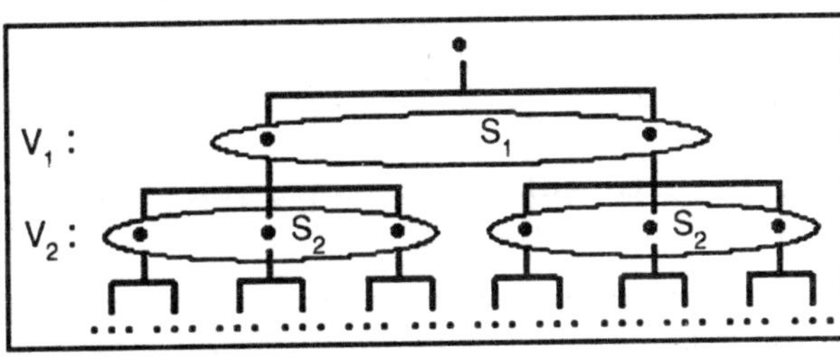

TRAVELING SALESPERSON

The problem assumes a set of *n* cities, and a salesperson which needs to visit each city exactly once and return to the base city at the end. The solution should provide a route of minimal length. The route (a, b, d, c) is the shortest one for the following one, and its length is 51.

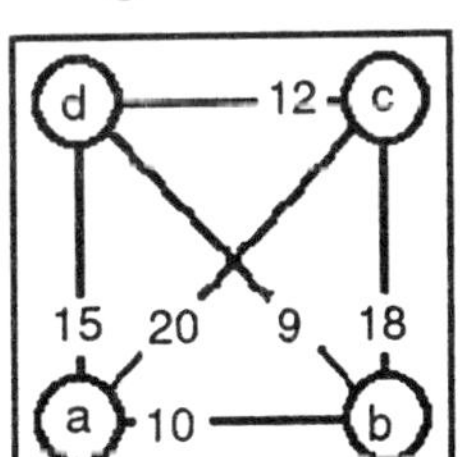

The traveling salesperson problem is an NP-hard problem, and so no polynomial time algorithm is available for it. Given an instance G = (V, E) the backtracking algorithm may search for a vector of cities $(v_1 ..., v_{|V|})$ which represents the best route.

The validity criteria may just check for number of cities in of the routes, pruning out routes longer than $|V|$. In such a case, the algorithm needs to investigate $|V|^{|V|}$ vectors from the solution space.

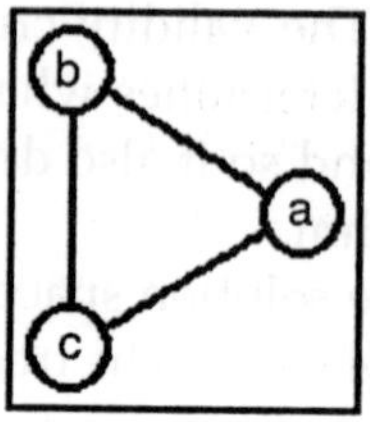

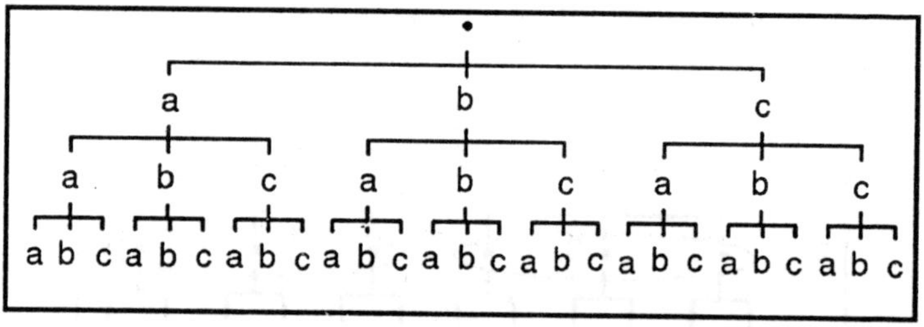

On the other hand, the validity criteria may check for repetition of cities, in which case the number of vectors reduces to $|V|!$.

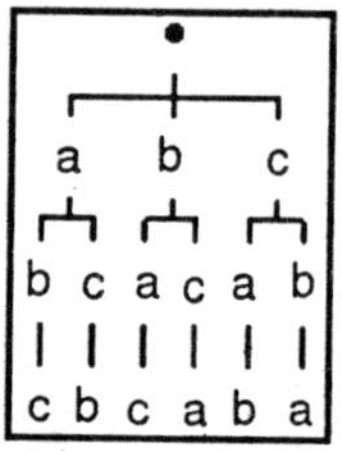

THE QUEENS PROBLEM

Consider a n by n chess board, and the problem of placing n queens on the board without the queens threatening one another.

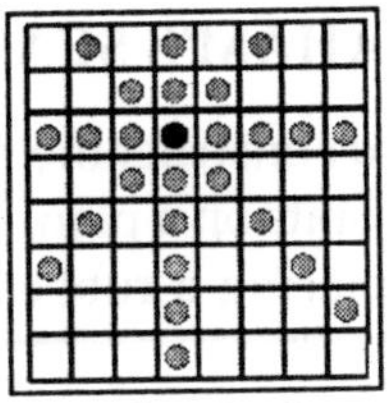

The solution space is $\{1, 2, 3..., n\}^n$. The backtracking algorithm may record the columns where the different queens are positioned. Trying all vectors $(p_1..., p_n)$ implies n^n cases. Noticing that all the queens must reside in different columns reduces the number of cases to $n!$.

For the latter case, the root of the traversal tree has degree n, the children have degree n - 1, the grand children degree n - 2, and so forth.

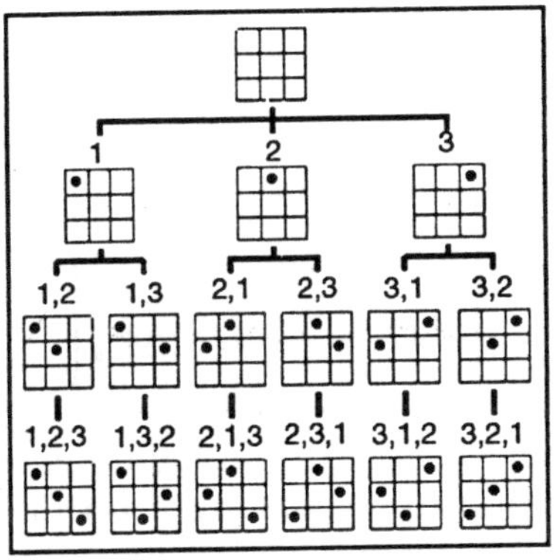

Checking for threatening positions along the way my further reduce the number of visited configurations.

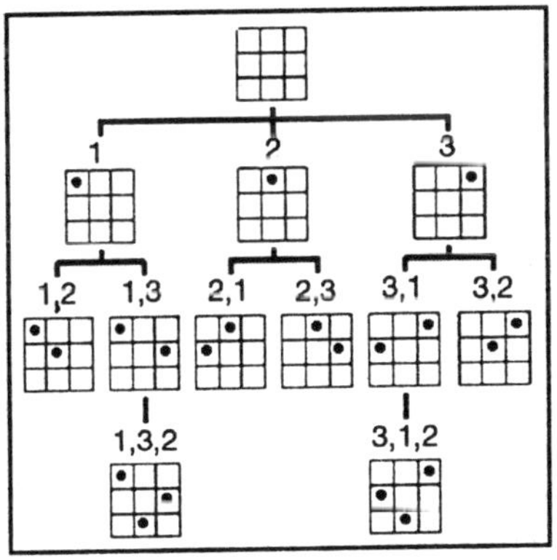

CONVEX HULL (GRAHAM'S SCAN)

The problem asks to construct the shortest polygon which encloses a given set of points on a plan. Intuitively, the polygon can be determined by placing a rubber around the set.

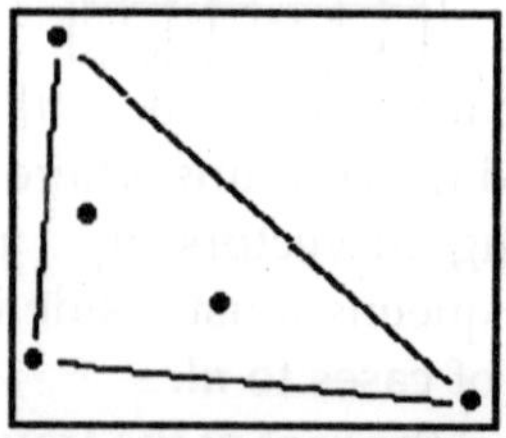

Determine an extreme point with the largest x coordinate. Sort the points in order of increasing angles, relatively to the extreme point.

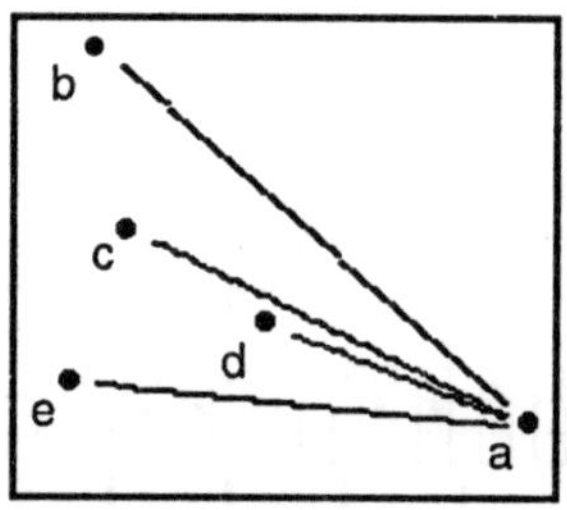

Traverse the points in the sorted order, adding them to the partial solution upon making a turn of less than 180 degrees, and backtracking when making a larger turn.

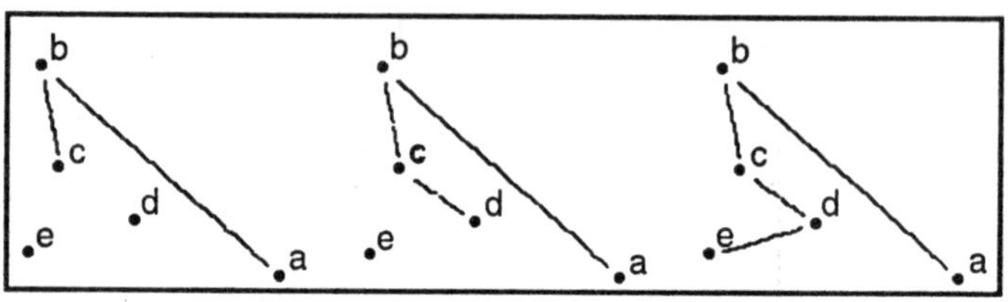

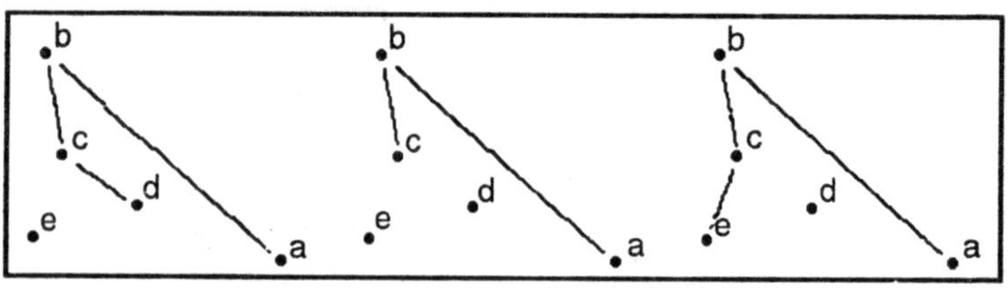

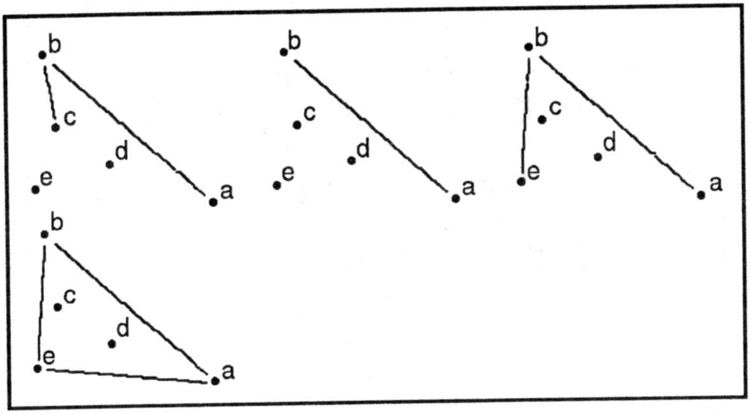

The algorithm requires $O(n \log n)$ time for sorting the points, and $O(n)$ time to select an appropriate subset.

GENERATING PERMUTATIONS

A permutation can be obtained by selecting an element in the given set and recursively permuting the remaining elements.

$$P(\alpha_1,\ldots,\alpha_N)=\begin{cases}\alpha_i,(\alpha_1,\ldots,\alpha_{i-1},\alpha_{i+1},\ldots,a_N) & \text{if } N>1\\ a_N & \text{if } N=1\end{cases}$$

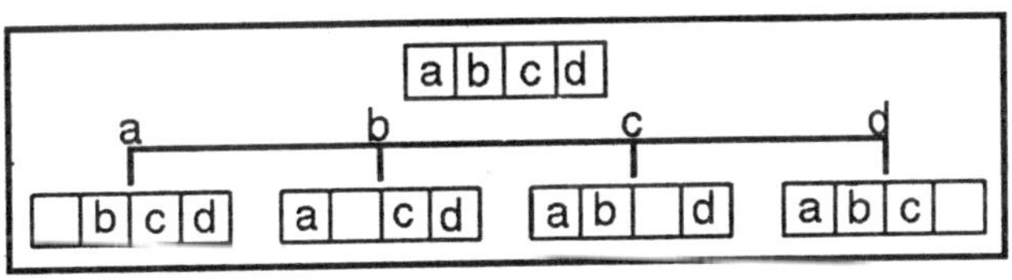

At each stage of the permutation process, the given set of elements consists of two parts: a subset of values that already have been processed, and a subset that still needs to be processed.

This logical seperation can be physically Realised by exchanging, in the i'th step, the i'th value with the value being chosen at that stage.

That approaches leaves the first subset in the first i locations of the outcome.

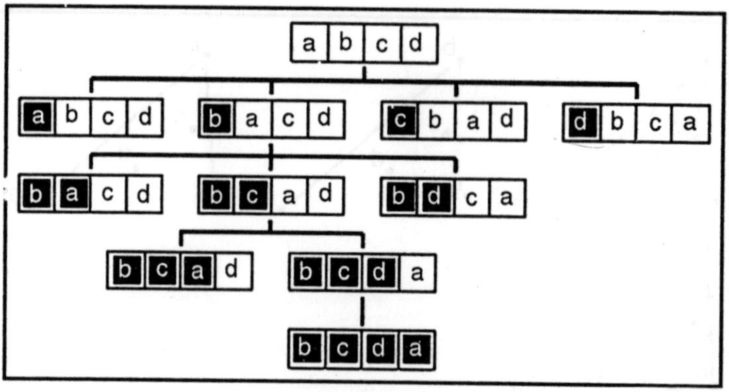


```
permute(i)
   if i == N output A[N]
   else
      for j = i to N do
           swap(A[i], A[j])
           permute(i+1)
           swap(A[i], A[j])
```

Chapter 4

Graph Algorithms

ALGORITHM

Te graph algorithms contained in LEDA, basic graph algorithms for reachability problems, shortest path algorithms, matching algorithms, flow algorithms....

All graph algorithms are generic, i.e., they accept instances of any user defined parameterized graph type *GRAPH< vtype, etype>* as arguments.

All graph algorithms are available by including the header file <LEDA/graph/graph_alg.h>. Alternatively, one may include a more specific header file.

An important subclass of graph algorithms are network algorithms. The input to most network algorithms is a graph whose edges or nodes are labeled with numbers, e.g., shortest path algorithms get edge costs, network flow algorithms get edge capacities, and min cost flow algorithms get edge capacities and edge costs. We use*NT* to denote the number type used for the edge and node labels.

Most network algorithms come in three kinds: A templated version in which *NT* is a template parameter, and reinstantiated and precompiled versions for the number types *int* (always) and *double* (except for a small number of functions). The function name of the templated version ends in _T. Thus MAX_FLOW_T is the name of the templated version of the max flow algorithm and MAX_FLOW is the name of the instantiated version.

In order to use the templated version a file <LEDA/graph/templates/XXX.h> must be included, e.g., in order to use the templated version of the maxflow algorithm, one must include <LEDA/graph/templates/max_flow.h>

Special care should be taken when using network algorithms with a number type *NT* that can incur rounding error, e.g., the type *double*. The functions perform correctly if the arithmetic is exact. This is the case if all numerical values in the input are integers (albeit stored as a number of type *NT*), if none of the intermediate results exceeds the maximal integer representable by the number type (2^{52} in the case of *doubles*), and if no round-off errors occur during the computation. We give more specific information on the arithmetic demand for each function below. If the arithmetic incurs rounding error, the computation may fail in two ways: give a wrong answer or run forever.

GRAPH SEARCHS

Breadth First Search

Search a graph (directed or not) in breadth first; this is done by using a queue where the vertices found are stored.

Here is a brief description of the BFS algorithm:

```
bfs (Graph G)
{
   all vertices of G are first painted white
   the graph root is painted gray and put in
   a queue
   while the queue is not empty
    {
       a vertex u is removed from the queue
         for all white successors v of u
          {
             v is painted gray
             v is added to the queue
          }
          u is painted black
       }
 }
```

And now watch it run — click the applet to start/stop the

search. You may want to have a look at the corresponding Java code.

Depth First Search

The general idea is the same, but we now use a stack instead of a queue. With recursion of course, so the stack management is all done by Java.

Here is a brief description of the DFS algorithm:

```
dfs-visit (Graph G, Vertex u)
{
    the vertex u is painted gray
    for all white successors v of u
   {
      dfs-visit(G, v)
   }
   u is painted black
}
 dfs (Graph G)
 {
    all vertices of G are first painted white
    dfs-visit(G, root of G)
}
```

Watch it run with this applet: You may want to have a look at the corresponding Java code.

COMMENTS

DFS seems cleaner than BFS: recursive, it doesn't make use of an external data structure (a queue), and is shorter too. But it is important to Realise these two algorithms address very different needs. An example of BFS usage, instead of DFS, is to implement a Web robot; a Depth First Search performed on the World Wide Web (a neat graph, isn't it?) would quickly overload any given web server with an ever growing number of requests. Therefore a Breadth First Search is preferred, since it dispatches requests to many servers at a time.

ELEMENTARY GRAPH

Presents methods for representing a graph and for

searching a graph. Searching a graph means systematically following the edges of the graph so as to visit the vertices of the graph. A graph-searching algorithm can discover much about the structure of a graph. Many algorithms begin by searching their input graph to obtain this structural information.

Other graph algorithms are organized as simple eLabourations of basic graph-searching algorithms. Techniques for searching a graph are at the heart of the field of graph algorithms.

Discusses the two most common computational representations of graphs: as adjacency lists and as adjacency matrices. Section 23.2 presents a simple graph-searching algorithm called breadth-first search and shows how to create a breadth-first tree. Section presents depth-first search and proves some standard results about the order in which depth-first search visits vertices. Section provides our first real application of depth-first search: topologically sorting a directed acyclic graph.

REPRESENTATIONS OF GRAPHS

There are two standard ways to represent a graph G = (V, E): as a collection of adjacency lists or as an adjacency matrix. The adjacency-list representation is usually preferred, because it provides a compact way to represent sparse graphs--those for which |E| is much less than |V|2. Most of the graph algorithms presented in this book assume that an input graph is represented in adjacency-list form.

An adjacency-matrix representation may be preferred, however, when the graph isdense--|E| is close to |V|2 -- or when we need to be able to tell quickly if there is an edge connecting two given vertices. For example, two of the all-pairs shortest-paths algorithms presented in Chapter 26 assume that their input graphs are represented by adjacency matrices.

The adjacency-list representation of a graph G = (V, E) consists of an array Adj of |V| lists, one for each vertex in V. For each u V, the adjacency list Adj[u] contains (pointers to) all the vertices v such that there is an edge (u,v) E. That is,

Adj[u] consists of all the vertices adjacent to u in G. The vertices in each adjacency list are typically stored in an arbitrary order

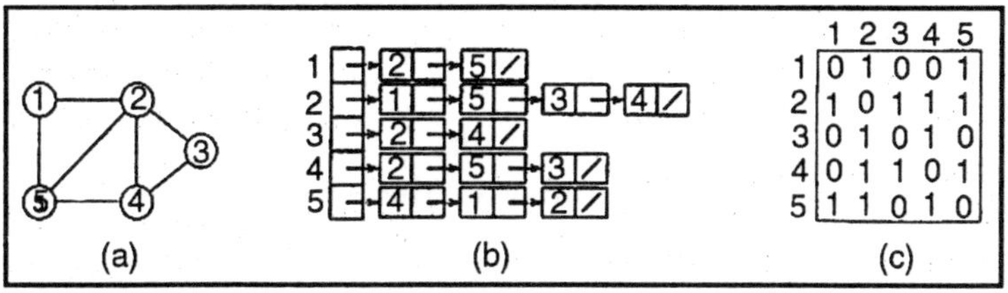

Fig. Two Representations of an Undirected Graph.

(a) An Undirected Graph G Having Five Vertices and Seven Edges.
(b) An Adjacency-list Representation of G.
(c) The Adjacency-matrix Representation of G.

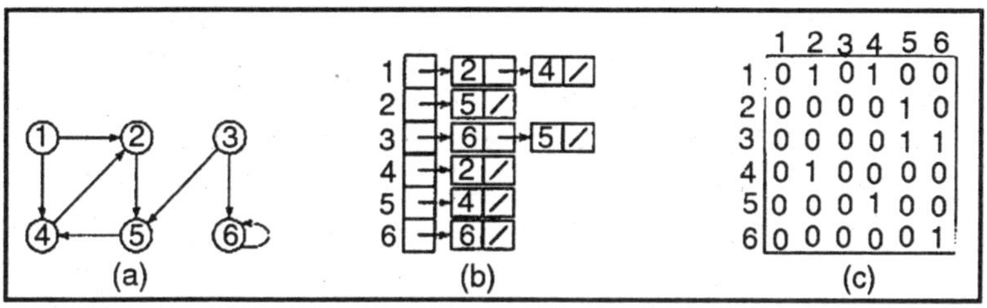

Fig. Two Representations of a Directed Graph.

(a) A Directed Graph G Having six Vertices and Eight Edges.
(b) An Adjacency-list Representation of G.
(c) The Adjacency-matrix Representation of G.

If G is a directed graph, the sum of the lengths of all the adjacency lists is |E|, since an edge of the form (u,v) is represented by having v appear in Adj[u]. If G is an undirected graph, the sum of the lengths of all the adjacency lists is 2|E|, since if (u,v) is an undirected edge, then u appears in v's adjacency list and vice versa. Whether a graph is directed or not, the adjacency-list representation has the desirable property that the amount of memory it requires is O(max(V, E)) = O(V + E).

Adjacency lists can readily be adapted to represent weighted graphs, that is, graphs for which each edge has an associated weight, typically given by a weight function w: E R. For example, let G = (V, E) be a weighted graph with weight function w. The weight w(u,v) of the edge (u,v) E is simply stored with vertex v in u's adjacency list. The adjacency-list representation is quite robust in that it can be modified to support many other graph variants.

A potential disadvantage of the adjacency-list representation is that there is no quicker way to determine if a given edge (u,v) is present in the graph than to search for v in the adjacency list Adj[u]. This disadvantage can be remedied by an adjacency-matrix re presentation of the graph, at the cost of using asymptotically more memory.

For the adjacency-matrix representation of a graph G = (V, E), we assume that the vertices are numbered 1, 2..., |V| in some arbitrary manner. The adjacency-matrix representation of a graph G then consists of a |V| |V| matrix A = (aij) such that,

$$a_{ij} = \begin{cases} 1 \text{ if } (i,j) \in E, \\ 0 \text{ other wise.} \end{cases}$$

Figures are the adjacency matrices of the undirected and directed graphs in Figures 23.1(a) and 23.2(a), respectively. The adjacency matrix of a graph requires (V^2) memory, independent of the number of edges in the graph.

Observe the symmetry along the main diagonal of the adjacency matrix in Figure. We define the the *transpose* of a matrix $A = (a_{ij})$ to be the matrix,

$$A^{\tau} = \left(a_{ij}^{\tau}\right)$$

given by $a_{ij}^{\tau} = a_{ij}$. Since in an undirected graph, (u,v) and (v,u) represent the same edge, the adjacency matrix A of an undirected graph is its own transpose: $A = A^T$. In some applications, it pays to store only the entries on and above the diagonal of the adjacency matrix, thereby cutting the memory needed to store the graph almost in half.

Like the adjacency-list representation of a graph, the adjacency-matrix representation can be used for weighted graphs. For example, if $G = (V, E)$ is a weighted graph with edge-weight function w, the weight $w(u, v)$ of the edge (u,v) E is simply stored as the entry in row u and column v of the adjacency matrix. If an edge does not exist, a NIL value can be stored as its corresponding matrix entry, though for many problems it is convenient to use a value such as 0 or.

Although the adjacency-list representation is asymptotically at least as efficient as the adjacency-matrix representation, the simplicity of an adjacency matrix may make it preferable when graphs are reasonably small. Moreover, if the graph is unweighted, there is an additional advantage in storage for the adjacency-matrix representation. Rather than using one word of computer memory for each matrix entry, the adjacency matrix uses only one bit per entry.

MINIMUM SPANNING TREE

SPANNING TREES

A *spanning tree* of a graph is just a subgraph that contains all the vertices and is a tree. A graph may have many spanning trees; for instance the complete graph on four vertices

```
o---o
|\ /|
| X |
|/ \|
o---o
```

has sixteen spanning trees:

```
o---o   o---o   o   o   o---o
|   |   |       |   |       |
|   |   |       |   |       |
|   |   |       |   |       |
o   o   o---o   o---o   o---o

o---o   o   o   o   o   o   o
 \ /    |\ /     \ /     \ /|
  X     | X       X       X |
 / \    |/ \     / \     / \|
o   o   o   o   o---o   o   o
```

MINIMUM SPANNING TREES

Now suppose the edges of the graph have weights or

lengths. The weight of a tree is just the sum of weights of its edges. Obviously, different trees have different lengths. The problem: how to find the minimum length spanning tree?

MINIMUM SPANNING TREES

The standard application is to a problem like phone network design. You have a business with several offices; you want to lease phone lines to connect them up with each other; and the phone company charges different amounts of money to connect different pairs of cities.

You want a set of lines that connects all your offices with a minimum total cost. It should be a spanning tree, since if a network isn't a tree you can always remove some edges and save money.

A less obvious application is that the minimum spanning tree can be used to approximately solve the traveling salesman problem. A convenient formal way of defining this problem is to find the shortest path that visits each point at least once.

Note that if you have a path visiting all points exactly once, it's a special kind of tree. For instance in the example above, twelve of sixteen spanning trees are actually paths. If you have a path visiting some vertices more than once, you can always drop some edges to get a tree. So in general the MST weight is less than the TSP weight, because it's a minimization over a strictly larger set.

On the other hand, if you draw a path tracing around the minimum spanning tree, you trace each edge twice and visit all points, so the TSP weight is less than twice the MST weight. Therefore this tour is within a factor of two of optimal. There is a more complicated way (*Christofides' heuristic*) of using minimum spanning trees to find a tour within a factor of 1.5 of optimal; I won't describe this here but it might be covered in ICS 163 (graph algorithms) next year.

FIND MINIMUM SPANNING TREE

The stupid method is to list all spanning trees, and find minimum of list. We already know how to find minima... But there are far too many trees for this to be efficient. It's also not really an algorithm, because you'd still need to know how to list all the trees.

A better idea is to find some key property of the MST that lets us be sure that some edge is part of it, and use this property to build up the MST one edge at a time.

For simplicity, we assume that there is a unique minimum spanning tree. (Problem 4.3 of Baase is related to this assumption). You can get ideas like this to work without this assumption but it becomes harder to state your theorems or write your algorithms precisely.

Lemma: Let X be any subset of the vertices of G, and let edge e be the smallest edge connecting X to G-X. Then e is part of the minimum spanning tree.

Proof: Suppose you have a tree T not containing e; then I want to show that T is not the MST. Let e=(u,v), with u in X and v not in X. Then because T is a spanning tree it contains a unique path from u to v, which together with e forms a cycle in G. This path has to include another edge f connecting X to G-X. T+e-f is another spanning tree (it has the same number of edges, and remains connected since you can replace any path containing f by one going the other way around the cycle). It has smaller weight than t since e has smaller weight than f. So T was not minimum, which is what we wanted to prove.

KRUSKAL'S ALGORITHM

We'll start with Kruskal's algorithm, which is easiest to understand and probably the best one for solving problems by hand.

```
Kruskal's algorithm:
sort the edges of G in increasing order by
length
keep a subgraph S of G, initially empty
for each edge e in sorted order
   if the endpoints of e are disconnected in S
   add e to S
return S
```

Note that, whenever you add an edge (u,v), it's always the smallest connecting the part of S reachable from u with the rest of G, so by the lemma it must be part of the MST. This algorithm is known as a *greedy algorithm*, because it chooses at each step the cheapest edge to add to S. You should be very careful when trying to use greedy algorithms to solve other problems, since it usually doesn't work. E.g. if you want to find a shortest path from a to b, it might be a bad idea to keep taking the shortest edges. The greedy idea only works in Kruskal's algorithm because of the key property we proved.

Analysis: The line testing whether two endpoints are disconnected looks like it should be slow (linear time per iteration, or O(mn) total). But actually there are some complicated data structures that let us perform each test in close to constant time; this is known as the *union-find* problem and is discussed in Baase section 8.5 (I won't get to it in this class, though). The slowest part turns out to be the sorting step, which takes O(m log n) time.

PRIM'S ALGORITHM

Rather than build a subgraph one edge at a time, Prim's algorithm builds a tree one vertex at a time.

```
  Prim's algorithm:
  let T be a single vertex x
 while (T has fewer than n vertices)
 {
 find the smallest edge connecting T to
       G-T
         add it to T
 }
```

Since each edge added is the smallest connecting T to G-T, the lemma we proved shows that we only add edges that should be part of the MST.

Again, it looks like the loop has a slow step in it. But again, some data structures can be used to speed this up. The idea is to use a heap to remember, for each vertex, the smallest edge connecting T with that vertex.

```
Prim with heaps:
make a heap of values (vertex,edge,weight(edge))
     initially (v,-,infinity) for each vertex
```

```
    let tree T be empty
while (T has fewer than n vertices)
 {
    let (v,e,weight(e)) have the smallest weight
    in the heap
    remove (v,e,weight(e)) from the heap
    add v and e to T
    for each edge f=(u,v)
    if u is not already in T
        find value (u,g,weight(g)) in heap
        if weight(f) < weight(g)
        replace (u,g,weight(g)) with
        (u,f,weight(f))
  }
```

Analysis: We perform n steps in which we remove the smallest element in the heap, and at most 2m steps in which we examine an edge f=(u,v).

For each of those steps, we might replace a value on the heap, reducing it's weight. (You also have to find the right value on the heap, but that can be done easily enough by keeping a pointer from the vertices to the corresponding values.) I haven't described how to reduce the weight of an element of a binary heap, but it's easy to do in O(log n) time. Alternately by using a more complicated data structure known as a Fibonacci heap, you can reduce the weight of an element in constant time. The result is a total time bound of O(m + n log n).

- *Step* 0: Pick any vertex as a starting vertex. (Call it S). Mark it with any given colour, say red.
- *Step* 1 Find the nearest neighbour of S (call it P_1). Mark both P_1 and the edge SP_1 red. cheapest unmarked (uncoloured) edge in the graph that doesn't close a coloured circuit. Mark this edge with same colour of Step 1.
- *Step* 2 Find the nearest uncoloured neighbour to the red subgraph (i.e., the closest vertex to any red vertex). Mark it and the edge connecting the vertex to the redsubgraph in red.

- *Step* 3: Repeat Step 2 until all vertices are marked red. The red subgraph is a minimum spanning tree.
- Interactive Prim's Algorithm

Given the graph G below:

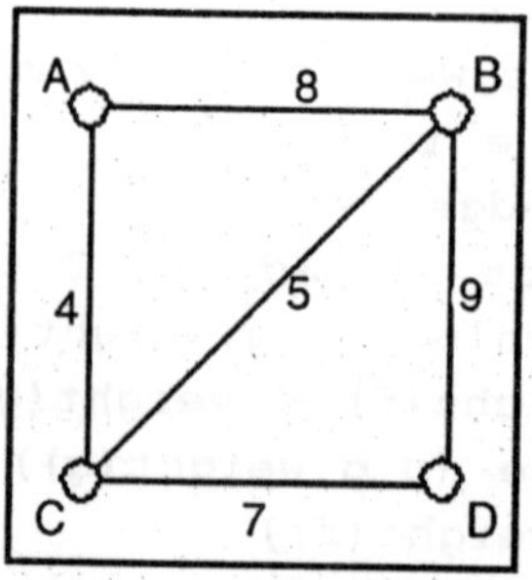

- Find a spanning subgraph of G and draw it below.
- Draw all the different spanning trees of G
- Of those you had in # 2, which one(s) is (are) minimum spanning trees. (i.e., those that have a minimum sum of their weighted edges.)

Given the weighted graph below:

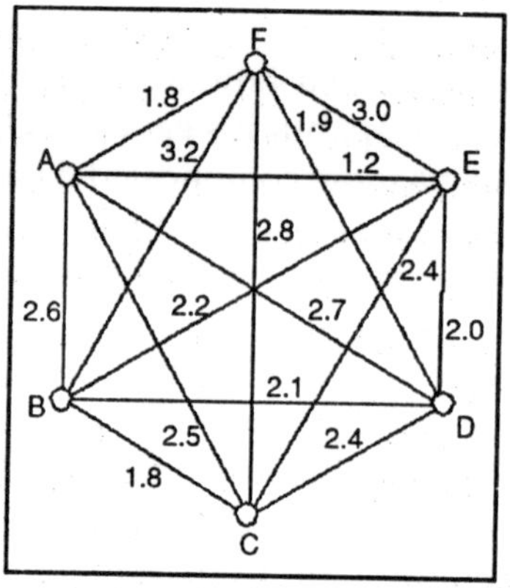

- Use Kruskal's algorithm to find a minimum spanning tree and indicate the edges in the graph shown below: Indicate on the edges that are selected the order of their selection.
- Use Prim's algorithm to find the minimum spanning tree and indicate the edges in the graph shown below.

Indicate on the edges that are selected the order of their selection.

BORUVKA'S ALGORITHM

(Actually Boruvka should be spelled with a small raised circle accent over the "u".) Although this seems a little complicated to explain, it's probably the easiest one for computer implementation since it doesn't require any complicated data structures. The idea is to do steps like Prim's algorithm, in parallel all over the graph at the same time.

```
Boruvka's algorithm:
make a list L of n trees, each a single
vertex
while (L has more than one tree)
  for each T in L, find the smallest edge
  connecting T to G-T
  add all those edges to the MST
  (causing pairs of trees in L to merge)
```

As we saw in Prim's algorithm, each edge you add must be part of the MST, so it must be ok to add them all at once.

Analysis: This is similar to merge sort. Each pass reduces the number of trees by a factor of two, so there are O(log n) passes. Each pass takes time O(m) (first figure out which tree each vertex is in, then for each edge test whether it connects two trees and is better than the ones seen before for the trees on either endpoint) so the total is O(m log n).

A HYBRID ALGORITHM

This isn't really a separate algorithm, but you can combine two of the classical algorithms and do better than either one alone. The idea is to do O(log log n) passes of Boruvka's algorithm, then switch to Prim's algorithm. Prim's algorithm then builds one large tree by connecting it with the small trees in the list L built by Boruvka's algorithm, keeping a heap which stores, for each tree in L, the best edge that can be used to connect it to the large tree. Alternately, you can think of collapsing the trees found by Boruvka's algorithm into "supervertices" and running Prim's algorithm on the resulting smaller graph. The point is that this reduces the number of remove min operations in the heap used by Prim's algorithm, to equal the number of trees left in L after Boruvka's algorithm, which is O(n/ log n).

Analysis: O(m log log n) for the first part, O(m + (n/log n) log n) = O(m + n) for the second, so O(m log log n) total.

SINGLE SOURCE

CONDITION

- The induction hypothesis is that both (a) and (b) hold just before we add a new vertex v to S.
- For every node already in S before adding v, nothing changes, so condition (a) is still true.
- We have to only show (a) for v which is just added to S.

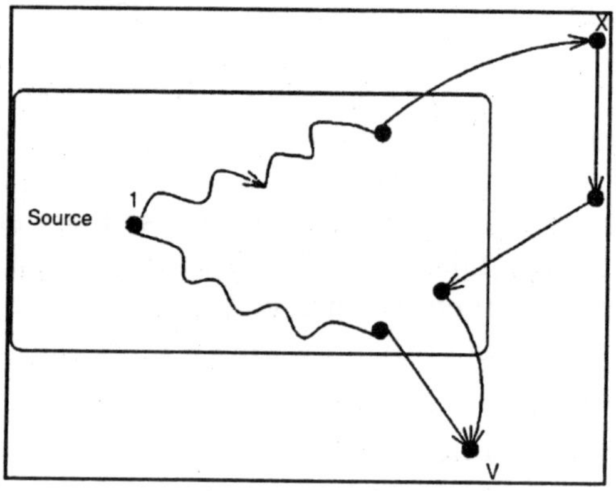

Fig. The Shortest Path to v Cannot Visit x

- Before adding it to S, we must check that D[v] gives the length of the shortest path from source to v. By the induction hypothesis, D[v] certainly gives the length of the shortest special path. We therefore have to verify that the shortest path from the source to v does not pass through any nodes that do not belong to S.
- Suppose to the contrary. That is, suppose that when we follow the shortest path from source to v, we

encounter nodes not belonging to S. Let x be the first such node encountered. The initial segment of the path from source to x is a special path and by part (b) of the induction hypothesis, the length of this path is D[x]. Since edge weights are no-negative, the total distance to v via x is greater than or equal to D[x]. However since the algorithm has chosen v ahead of x, D[x] ≥D[v]. Thus the path via x cannot be shorter than the shortest special path leading to v.

Induction step for condition (b): Let ω≠ v and ω∈ S.

When v is added to S, these are two possibilities for the shortest special path from source to w:

- It remains as before
- It now passes through v (and possibly other nodes in S)

In the first case, there is nothing to prove. In the second case, let y be the last node of S visited before arriving at w. The length of such a path is D[y] + C[y,w].

- At first glance, to compute the new value of d[w], it looks as if we should compare the old value of D[w] with D[y] + C[y,w] for every *y* ∈ *S* (including v)
- This comparison was however made for all *y* ∈ *S* except v, when y was added to S in the algorithm. Thus the new value of D[w] can be computed simply by comparing the old value with D[v] + C[v,w]. This the algorithm does.

When the algorithm stops, all the nodes but one are in S and it is clear that the vector D[1], D[2]..., D[n]) contains the lengths of the shortest paths from source to respective vertices.

Example: Consider the digraph in Figure 7.5.

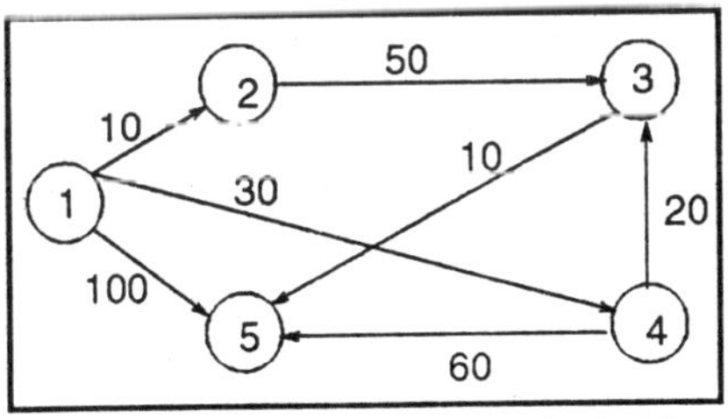

Fig. A Digraph Example for Dijkstra's Algorithm

Initially:

$S = \{1\}$ $D[2] = 10$ $D[3] = \infty$ $D[4] = 30$ $D[5] = 100$

Iteration 1

Select w = 2, so that S = {1, 2}

$D[3] = \min(\infty, D[2] + C[2, 3]) = 60$

$D[4] = \min(30, D[2] + C[2, 4]) = 30$

$D[5] = \min(100, D[2] + C[2, 5]) = 100$

Iteration 2

Select w = 4, so that S = {1, 2, 4}

$D[3] = \min(60, D[4] + C[4, 3]) = 50$

$D[5] = \min(100, D[4] + C[4, 5]) = 90$

Iteration 3

Select w = 3, so that S = {1, 2, 4, 3}

$D[5] = \min(90, D[3] + C[3, 5]) = 60$

Iteration 4

Select w = 5, so that S = {1, 2, 4, 3, 5}

$D[2] = 10$

$D[3] = 50$

$D[4] = 30$

$D[5] = 60$

COMPLEXITY OF DIJKSTRA'S ALGORITHM

With adjacency matrix representation, the running time is O(n2) By using an adjacency list representation and a partially ordered tree data structure for organizing the set V - S, the complexity can be shown to be O(elog n) where e is the number of edges and n is the number of vertices in the digraph.

SHORTEST PATHS

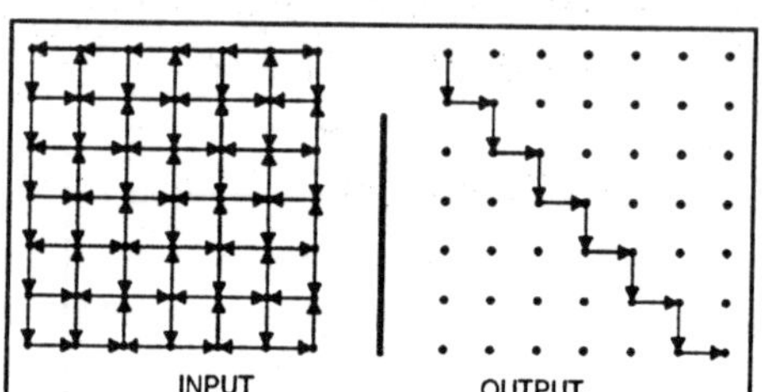

Input Description: An edge-weighted graph *G*, with start vertex *s* and end vertex *t*.

Problem: Find the shortest path from *s* to *t* in *G*.

Excerpt from The Algorithm Design Manual.

The problem of finding shortest paths in a graph has a surprising variety of applications:

- The most obvious applications arise in transportation or communications, such as finding the best route to drive between Chicago and Phoenix or figuring how to direct packets to a destination across a network.
- Consider the problem of image segmentation, that is, separating two characters in a scanned, bit-mapped image of printed text. We need to find the separating line between two points that cuts through the fewest number of black pixels. This grid of pixels can be modeled as a graph, with any edge across a black pixel given a high cost. The shortest path from top to bottom defines the best separation between left and right.
- A major problem in speech recognition is distinguishing between words that sound alike (homophones), such as *to, two,* and *too.* We can construct a graph whose vertices correspond to possible words, with an edge between possible Neighbouring words. If the weight of each edge measures the likelihood of transition, the shortest path across the graph defines the best interpretation of a sentence.
- Suppose we want to draw an informative picture of a graph. The Centre of the page should cooorespond to the "Centre" of the graph, whatever that means. A good definition of the Centre is the vertex that minimizes the maximum distance to any other vertex in the graph. Finding this Centre point requires knowing the distance (i.e. shortest path) between all pairs of vertices.

ALL PAIRS SHORTEST PATHS

ALL PAIRS SHORTEST PATHS PROBLEM

Given A Digraph G = (V, E) in which each are v → w has a Nonnegative cost C[v, w]

To find For each Ordereed Pair of Vertices (v, w), the Smallest Length of any Path from v to w

FLOYD'S ALGORITHM

- This is an $O(n^3)$ algorithm, where n is the number of vertices in the digraph.
- Uses the principle of Dynamic Programmeming.
- Let $V = \{1, 2..., n\}$. The algorithm uses a matrix $A[1..n][1..n]$ to compute the lengths of the shortest paths.
- Initially,

$A[i, j] = C[i, j]$ if $i \neq j$

$= 0$ if $i = j$

Note that $C[i, j]$ is taken as ∞ if there is no directed arc from i to j.

- The algorithm makes n passes over A. Let $A_0, A_1..., A_n$ be the values of A on the n passes, with A_0 being the initial value. Just after the k-1th iteration,

$A_{k-1}[i, j]$ = Smallest Length of any Path from vertex i to vertex j that Does not pass through the vertices k, k + 1...,n (i.e. that only passes through possibly 1, 2...k–1)

The kth pass explores whether the vertex k lies on an optimal path from i to j, $\forall\ i, j$

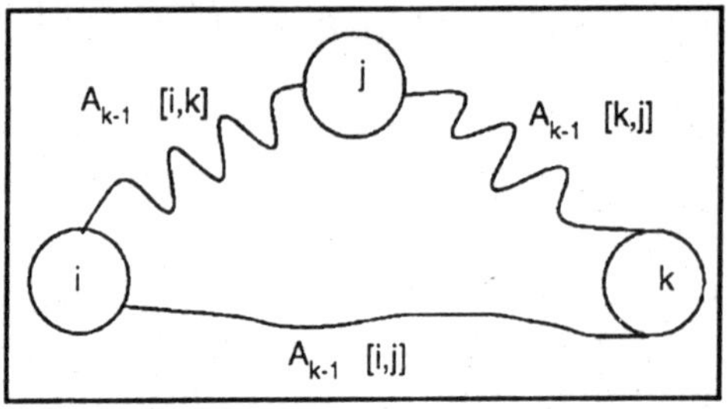

Fig. Principle of Floyd's Algorithm

- We use

$$A_k[i, j] = \min \begin{cases} A_{k-1}[i, j] \\ A_{k-1}[i, k] + A_{k-1}[k, j] \end{cases}$$

- The algorithm:

```
void Floyd (floatC[n - 1][n - 1], A[n - 1][n -
```

```
 1])
{int i, j, k;
{for(i = 0, i £ n - 1;i + +)
for(j = 0;j £ n - 1, j + +)
A[i, j] = C[i, j];
for(i = 0;i £ n - 1;i + +)
A[i, i] = 0;
for(k = 0;k £ n - 1;k + +);
{
for(i = 0;i £ n - 1;i + +)
{
for(j = 0;j £ n - 1, j + +)
if(A[i, k] + A[k, j] < A[i, j])
A[i, j] = A[i, k] + A[k, j]
}
}
}
}
```

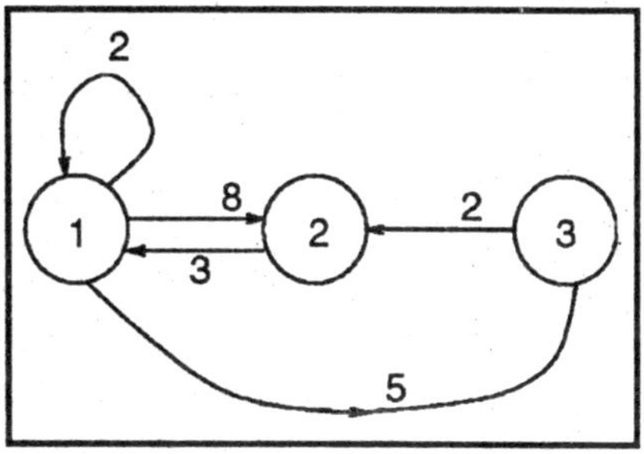

Fig. A Digraph Example for Floyd's Algorithm

Example

$$C = \begin{bmatrix} 2 & 8 & 5 \\ 3 & \infty & \infty \\ \infty & 2 & \infty \end{bmatrix}$$

$$A_0 = \begin{bmatrix} 0 & 8 & 5 \\ 3 & 0 & \infty \\ \infty & 2 & 0 \end{bmatrix}$$

$$A_1 = \begin{bmatrix} 0 & 8 & 5 \\ 3 & 0 & 8 \\ \infty & 2 & 0 \end{bmatrix}$$

$$A_2 = \begin{bmatrix} 0 & 8 & 5 \\ 3 & 0 & 8 \\ 5 & 2 & 0 \end{bmatrix}$$

$$A_3 = \begin{bmatrix} 0 & 8 & 5 \\ 3 & 0 & 8 \\ 5 & 2 & 0 \end{bmatrix}$$

- With adjacency matrix representation, Floyd's algorithm has a worst case complexity of $O(n^3)$ where n is the number of vertices
- If Dijkstra's algorithm is used for the same purpose, then with an adjacency list representation, the worst case complexity will be $O(ne\log n)$. Thus if e is $O(n^2)$, then the complexity will be $O(n^3\log n)$ while if e is $O(n)$, then the complexity is $O(n^2\log n)$.

MAXIMUM FLOW

This article covers a problem that often arises in real life situations and, as expected, in Programmeming contests, with Top Coder being no exception.

It is addressed mostly to coders who are not familiar with the subject, but it may prove useful to the more experienced as well.

Lots of papers have been written, and there are many algorithms known to solve this problem.

While they are not the fastest, the algorithms presented here have the advantage of being simple and efficient, and because of this they are usually preferred during a contest setup. The reader is advised to read the article on graph theory first, as the concepts presented there are needed to understand those presented here.

STANDARD MAXIMUM FLOW PROBLEM

So, what are we being asked for in a max-flow problem? The simplest form that the statement could take would be something along the lines of: "A list of pipes is given, with different flow-capacities.

These pipes are connected at their endpoints. What is the maximum amount of water that you can route from a given starting point to a given ending point?" or equivalently "A company owns a factory located in city X where products are manufactured that need to be transported to the distribution Centre in city Y.

You are given the one-way roads that connect pairs of cities in the country, and the maximum number of trucks that can drive along each road.

What is the maximum number of trucks that the company can send to the distribution Centre?"

A first observation is that it makes no sense to send a truck to any other city than Y, so every truck that enters a city other than Y must also leave it.

A second thing to notice is that, because of this, the number of trucks leaving X is equal to the number of trucks arriving in Y.

Rephrasing the statement in terms of graph theory, we are given a network - a directed graph, in which every edge has a certain capacity *c* associated with it, a starting vertex (the source, X in the example above), and an ending vertex (the sink).

We are asked to associate another value *f* satisfying *f d" c* for each edge such that for every vertex other than the source and the sink, the sum of the values associated to the edges that enter it must equal the sum of the values associated to the edges that leave it.

We will call *f* the flow along that edge. Furthermore, we are asked to maximize the sum of the values associated to the arcs leaving the source, which is the total flow in the network.

The image below shows the optimal solution to an instance of this problem, each edge being labeled with the values f/c associated to it.

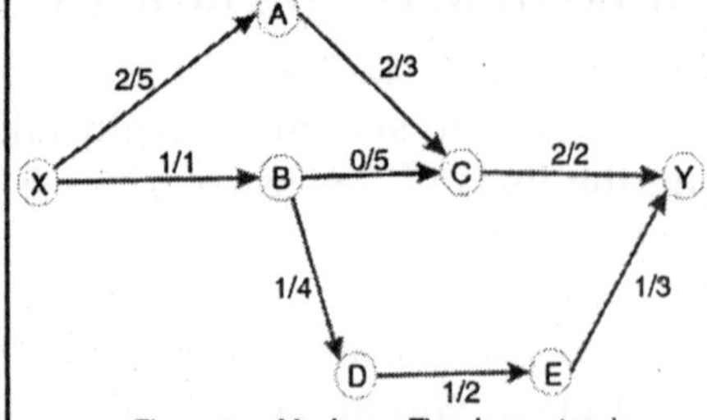

Figure 1a - Maximum Flow in a network

Fig. Maximum Flow in a Network

SOLVE

Now how do we actually solve the problem? First, let us define two basic concepts for understanding flow networks: residual networks and augmenting paths. Consider an arbitrary flow in a network. The residual network has the same vertices as the original network, and one or two edges for each edge in the original. More specifically, if the flow along the edge x-y is less than the capacity there is a forward edge x-y with a capacity equal to the difference between the capacity and the flow (this is called the residual capacity), and if the flow is positive there is a backward edge y-x with a capacity equal to the flow on x-y. An augmenting path is simply a path from the source to the sink in the residual network, whose purpose is to increase the flow in the original one.

It is important to understand that the edges in this path can point the "wrong way" according to the original network. The path capacity of a path is the minimum capacity of an edge along that path. Let's take the following example:

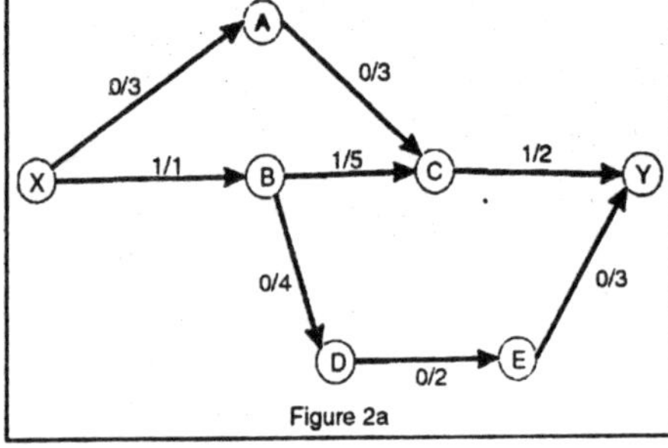

Figure 2a

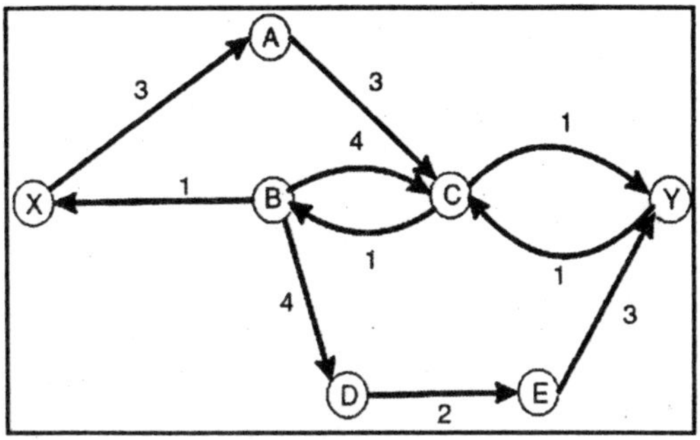

Fig. The Residual Network of the Network in 2a

By considering the path X_A_C_Y, we can increase the flow by 1 - the edges X_A and A_C have capacity of 3, as in the original network, but the edge C_Y has capacity 1, and we take the minimum of these values to get the path capacity. Increasing the flow along this path with 1 yields the flow below:

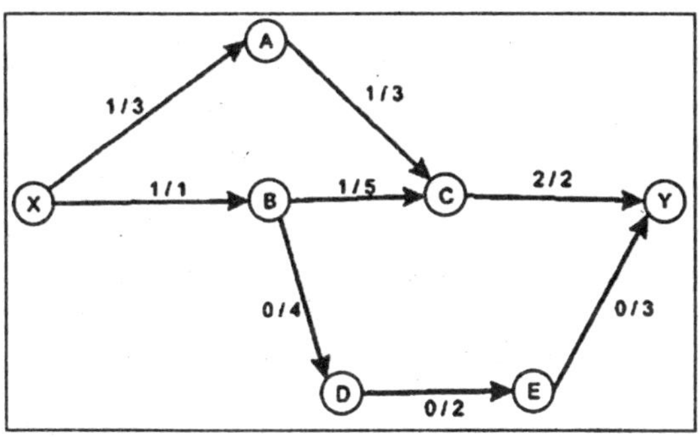

The value of the current flow is now 2, and as shown in Figure, we could do better. So, let's try to increase the flow. Clearly, there is no point in considering the directed paths X_A_C Y or X_B_D_E_Y as the edges C_Y and X_B, respectively, are filled to capacity.

As a matter of fact, there is no directed path in the network shown above, due to the edges mentioned above being filled to capacity.

At this point, the question that naturally comes to mind is: is it possible to increase the flow in this case? And the answer is yes, it is. Let's take a look at the residual network:

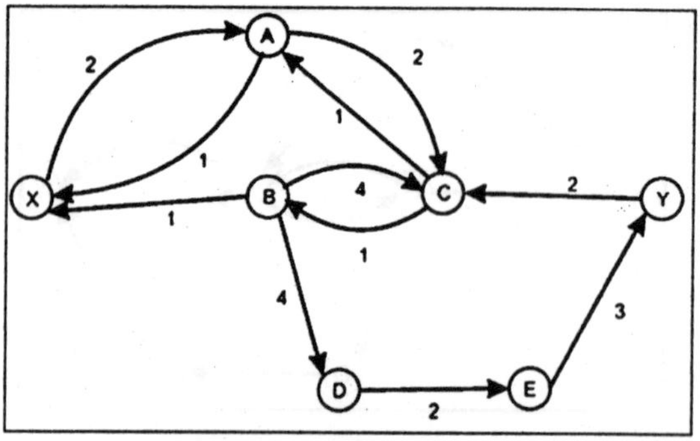

Fig. The residual Network of the Network in 3a

Let's consider the only path from X to Y here: X_A_C_B_D_E_Y. Note that this is not a path in the directed graph, because C_B is walked in the opposite way. We'll use this path in order to increase the total flow in the original network. We'll "push" flow on each of the edges, except for C_B which we will use in order to "cancel" flow on B_C. The amount by which this operation can be performed is limited by the capacities of all edges along the path (as shown in Figure 3b). Once again we take the minimum, to conclude that this path also has capacity 1. Updating the path in the way described here yields the flow shown in Figure. We are left with the following residual network where a path between the source and the sink doesn't exist:

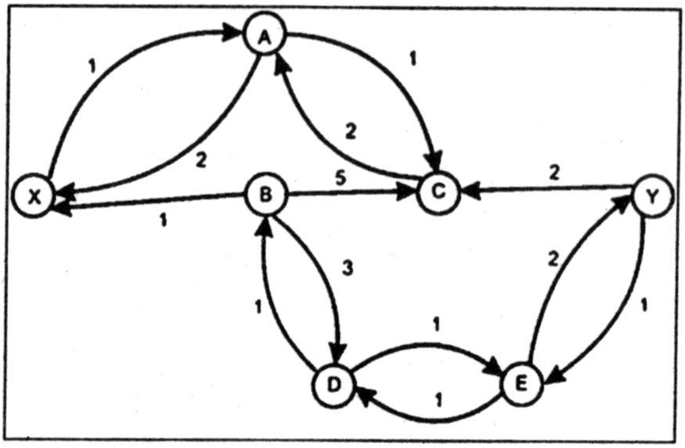

Fig. The Residual Network **of the** Network in 1a

This example suggests the following algorithm: start with no flow everywhere and increase **the total** flow in the network while there is an augmenting path from the source to the sink with no full forward edges or empty backward edges - a path in the residual network.

The algorithm (known as the Ford-Fulkerson method) is guaranteed to terminate: due to the capacities and flows of the edges being integers and the path-capacity being positive, at each step we get a new flow that is closer to the maximum. As a side note, the algorithm isn't guaranteed to even terminate if the capacities are irrationals.

What about the correctness of this algorithm? It is obvious that in a network in which a maximum flow has been found there is no augmenting path, otherwise we would be able to increase the maximum value of the flow, contradicting our initial assumption. If the converse of this affirmation is true, so that when there is no augmenting path, the value of the flow has reached its maximum, we can breathe a sigh of relief, our algo is correct and computes the maximum flow in a network. This is known as the max-flow min-cut theorem and we shall justify its correctness in a few moments.

A cut in a flow network is simply a partition of the vertices in two sets, let's call them A and B, in such a way that the source vertex is in A and the sink is in B. The capacity of a cut is the sum of the capacities of the edges that go from a vertex in A to a vertex in B. The flow of the cut is the difference of the flows that go from A to B (the sum of the flows along the edges that have the starting point in A and the ending point in B), respectively from B to A, which is exactly the value of the flow in the network, due to the entering flow equals leaving flow - property, which is true for every vertex other than the source and the sink.

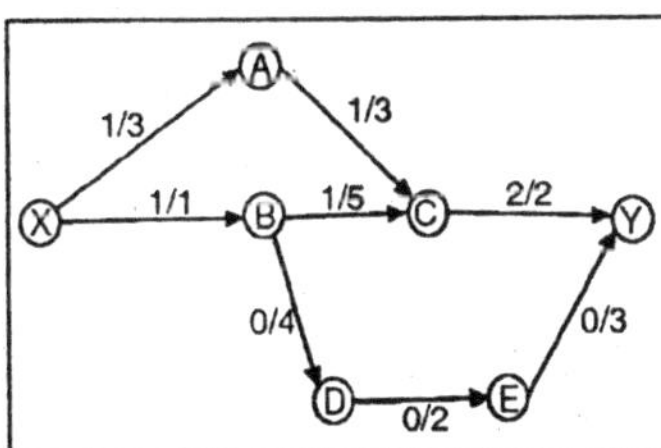

The Yellow vertices are in set A and those in blue are in set B.
The Capacity of the cut is the sum of the capacities of the edges XB and CY: 1+2=3.
The flow of the cut is the sum of the flow along the edges XB and CY minus the flow on BC: 1+2-1=2. and is equal to the value of the flow

Fig. Cut in a Network

Notice that the flow of the cut is less or equal to the capacity of the cut due to the constraint of the flow being less or equal to the capacity of every edge. This implies that the maximum flow is less or equal to every cut of the network. This is where the max-flow min-cut theorem comes in and states that the value of the maximum flow through the network is exactly the value of the minimum cut of the network. Let's give an intuitive argument for this fact. We will assume that we are in the situation in which no augmenting path in the network has been found. Let's Colour in yellow, like in the figure above, every vertex that is reachable by a path that starts from the source and consists of non-full forward edges and of non-empty backward edges.

Clearly the sink will be Coloured in blue, since there is no augmenting path from the source to the sink. Now take every edge that has a yellow starting point and a blue ending point. This edge will have the flow equal to the capacity, otherwise we could have added this edge to the path we had at that point and Colour the ending point in yellow. Note that if we remove these edges there will be no directed path from the source to the sink in the graph. Now consider every edge that has a blue starting point and a yellow ending point. The flow on this edge must be 0 since otherwise we could have added this edge as a backward edge on the current path and Colour the starting point in yellow. Thus, the value of the flow must equal the value of the cut, and since every flow is less or equal to every cut, this must be a maximum flow, and the cut is a minimum cut as well.

In fact, we have solved another problem that at first glance would appear to have nothing to do with maximum flow in a network, ie. given a weighted directed graph, remove a minimum-weighted set of edges in such a way that a given node is unreachable from another given node. The result is, according to the max-flow min-cut theorem, the maximum flow in the graph, with capacities being the weights given. We are also able to find this set of edges in the way described above: we take every edge with the starting point marked as reachable in the last traversal of the graph and with an unmarked ending point. This edge is a member of the minimum cut.

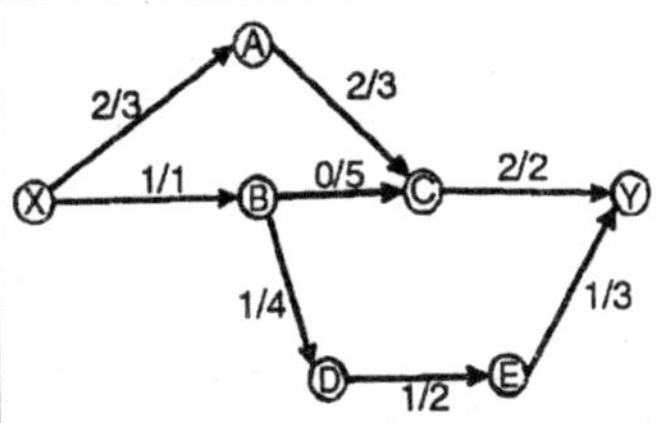

Fig.-AMinimum Out in Network

AUGMENTING-PATH ALGORITHMS

The neat part of the Ford-Fulkerson algorithm described above is that it gets the correct result no matter how we solve (correctly!!) the sub-problem of finding an augmenting path. However, every new path may increase the flow by only 1, hence the number of iterations of the algorithm could be very large if we carelessly choose the augmenting path algorithm to use. The function *max_flow* will look like this, regardless of the actual method we use for finding augmenting paths:

```
int max_flow()
   result = 0
      while (true)
 // the function find_path returns the path
 capacity of the
 augmenting path found
 path_capacity = find_path()
 // no augmenting path found
 if (d = 0) exit while
 else result += path_capacity
end while
return result
```

To keep it simple, we will use a 2-dimensional array for storing the capacities of the residual network that we are left with after each step in the algorithm. Initially the residual network is just the original network. We will not store the flows along the edges explicitly, but it's easy to figure out how to find them upon the termination of the algorithm: for each edge x-y in the original network the flow is given by the capacity of the backward edge y-x in the residual network. Be careful though; if the reversed arc y-x also exists in the original network, this will fail, and it is recommended that the initial capacity of each arc be stored somewhere, and then the flow along the edge is the difference between the initial and the residual capacity.

We now require an implementation for the function *find_path*. The first approach that comes to mind is to use a depth-first search (DFS), as it probably is the easiest to implement. Unfortunately, its performance is very poor on some networks, and normally is less preferred to the ones discussed next.

The next best thing in the matter of simplicity is a breadth-first search (BFS). Recall that this search usually yields the shortest path in an un-weighted graph. Indeed, this also applies here to get the shortest augmenting path from the source to the sink. In the following pseudocode we will basically: find a shortest path from the source to the sink and compute the minimum capacity of an edge (that could be a forward or a backward edge) along the path - the path capacity. Then, for each edge along the path we reduce its capacity and increase the capacity of the reversed edge with the path capacity.

```
int bfs()
   queue Q
    push source to Q
    mark source as visited
    keep an array from with the
    semnification: from[x] is the
    previous vertex visited in the shortest
    path from the source to x;
    initialize from with -1 (or any other
    sentinel value)
     while Q is not empty
        where = pop from Q
     for each vertex next adjacent to where
```

```
        if next is not visited and
        capacity[where][next] > 0
           push next to Q
           mark next as visited
           from[next] = where
           if next = sink
              exit while loop
      end for
  end while
  // we compute the path capacity
  where = sink, path_cap = infinity
  while from[where] > -1
     prev = from[where]// the previous vertex
     path_cap = min(path_cap,
           capacity[prev][where])
     where = prev
   end while
     // we update the residual network; if no
     path is found the while
     loop will not be entered
     where = sink
        while from[where] > -1
          prev = from[where]
          capacity[prev][where] -= path_capacity
             capacity[where][prev] +=
               path_capacity
     where = prev
   end while
   // if no path is found, path_cap is infinity
   if path_cap = infinity
      return 0
   else return path_cap
```

As we can see, this is pretty easy to implement. As for its performance, it is guaranteed that this takes at most $N * M/2$ steps, where N is the number of vertices and M is the number of edges in the network. This number may seem very large, but it is over-estimated for most networks. For example, in the network we considered 3 augmenting paths are needed which is significantly less than the upper bound of 28. Due to the $O(M)$ running time of BFS (implemented with adjacency lists) the worst-case running time of the shortest-augmenting path max-flow algorithm is $O(N * M^2)$, but usually the algorithm performs much better than this.

Next we will consider an approach that uses a priority-first search (PFS), that is very similar to the Dijkstra heap method explained here. In this method the augmenting path with a maximum path capacity is preferred. Intuitively this would lead to a faster algorithm, since at each step we increase the flow with the maximum possible amount. However, things are not always so, and the BFS implementation has better running times on some networks.

We assign as a priority to each vertex the minimum capacity of a path (in the residual network) from the source to that vertex. We process vertices in a greedy manner, as in Dijkstra's algorithm, in decreasing order of priorities. When we get to the sink, we are done, since a path with a maximum capacity is found. We would like to implement this with a data structure that allows us to efficiently find the vertex with the highest priority and increase the priority of a vertex (when a new better path is found) - this suggests the use of a heap which has a space complexity proportional to the number of vertices.

In TopCoder matches we may find it faster and easier to implement this with a priority queue or some other data structure that approximates one, even though the space required might grow to being proportional with the number of edges. This is how the following pseudocode is implemented. We also define a structure node that has the members vertex and prioritywith the above significance. Another field from is needed to store the previous vertex on the path.

```
int pfs()
  priority queue PQ
  push node(source, infinity, -1) to PQ
  keep the array from as in bfs()
  // if no augmenting path is found, path_cap
```

```
    will remain 0
    path_cap = 0
    while PQ is not empty
        node aux = pop from PQ
        where = aux.vertex, cost = aux.priority
        if we already visited where continue
        from[where] = aux.from
        if where = sink
          path_cap = cost
          exit while loop
         mark where as visited
         for each vertex next adjacent to where
            if capacity[where][next] > 0
               new_cost = min(cost,
                 capacity[where][next])
               push node(next, new_cost, where)
to               PQ
        end for
    end while
    // update the residual network
    where = sink
    while from[where] > -1
       prev = from[where]
       capacity[prev][where] -= path_cap
       capacity[where][prev] += path_cap
       where = prev
    end while
       return path_cap
```

The analysis of its performance is pretty complicated, but it may prove worthwhile to remember that with PFS at most $2M1gU$ steps are required, where U is the maximum capacity of an edge in the network.

As with BFS, this number is a lot larger than the actual number of steps for most networks. Combine this with the $O(M$ $1g$ $M)$complexity of the search to get the worst-case running time of this algorithm.

Now that we know what these methods are all about, which of them do we choose when we are confronted with a max-flow problem? The PFS approach seems to have a better worst-case performance, but in practice their performance is pretty much the same. So, the method that one is more familiar with may prove more adequate. Personally, I prefer the shortest-path method, as I find it easier to implement during a contest and less error prone.

MAXIMUM FLOW PROBLEM

The maximum flow problem is again structured on a network; but here the arc capacities, or upper bounds, are the only relevant parameters.

The problem is to find the maximum flow possible from some given source node to a given sink node. A network model is in Fig. All arc costs are zero, but the cost on the arc leaving the sink is set to -1. Since the goal of the optimization is to minimize cost, the maximum flow possible is delivered to the sink node.

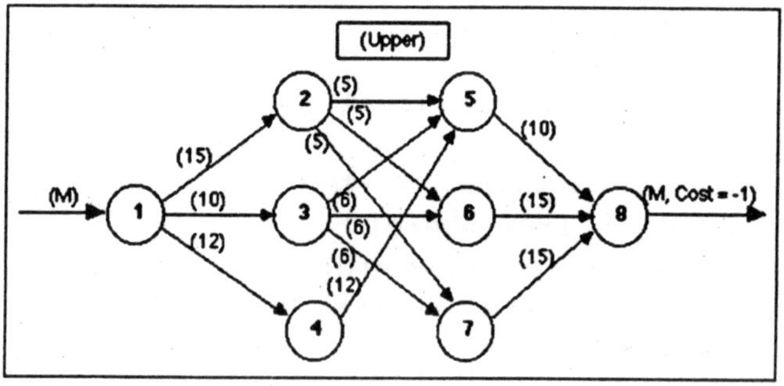

Fig. Network Model for the Maximum Flow Problem.

The solution to the example is in Fig. The maximum flow from node 1 to node 8 is 30 and the flows that yield this flow are shown on the figure. The heavy arcs on the figure are called the minimal cut.

These arcs are the bottlenecks that are restricting the maximum flow. The fact that the sum of the capacities of the arcs on the minimal cut equals the maximum flow is a famous theorem of network theory called the max flow min cut theorem. The arcs on the minimum cut can be identified using sensitivity analysis.

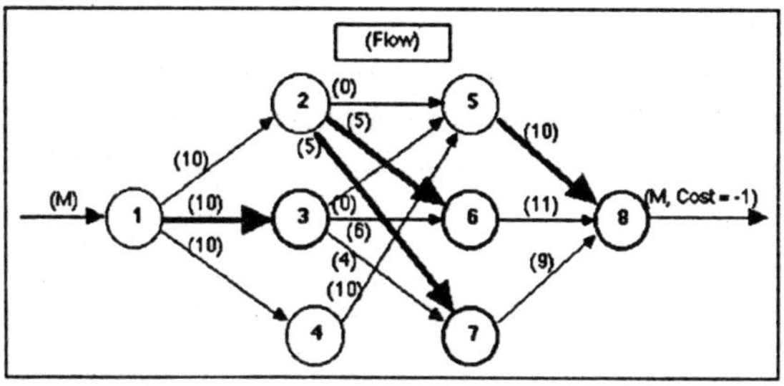

MAX-FLOW/MIN-CUT RELATED PROBLEMS

How to recognize max-flow problems? Often they are hard to detect and usually boil down to maximizing the movement of something from a location to another. We need to look at the constraints when we think we have a working solution based on maximum flow - they should suggest at least an $O(N^3)$ approach. If the number of locations is large, another algorithm (such as dynamic Programmeming or greedy), is more appropriate.

The problem description might suggest multiple sources and/or sinks. For example, in the sample statement in the beginning of this article, the company might own more than one factory and multiple distribution Centres. How can we deal with this? We should try to convert this to a network that has a unique source and sink.

In order to accomplish this we will add two "dummy" vertices to our original network - we will refer to them as super-source and super-sink. In addition to this we will add an edge from the super-source to every ordinary source (a factory). As we don't have restrictions on the number of trucks that each factory can send, we should assign to each edge an infinite capacity.

Note that if we had such restrictions, we should have assigned to each edge a capacity equal to the number of trucks each factory could send. Likewise, we add an edge from every ordinary sink (distribution Centres) to the super-sink with infinite capacity.

A maximum flow in this new-built network is the solution to the problem - the sources now become ordinary vertices, and they are subject to the entering-flow equals leaving-flow property. You may want to keep this in your bag of tricks, as it may prove useful to most problems.

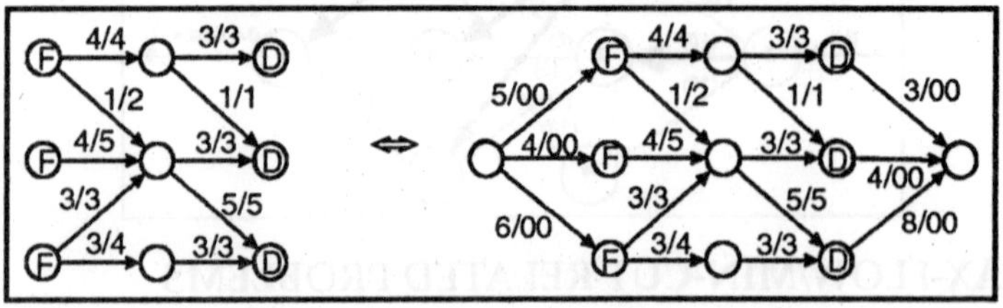

Fig. Reduction of a Multiple-source/ Muitiple-sink Max-flow Proble

What if we are also given the maximum number of trucks that can drive through each of the cities in the country (other than the cities where the factory and the distribution Centre are located)? In other words we have to deal with vertex-capacities too. Intuitively, we should be able to reduce this to maximum-flow, but we must find a way to take the capacities from vertices and put them back on edges, where they belong.

Another nice trick comes into play. We will build a network that has two times more vertices than the initial one. For each vertex we will have two nodes: an in-vertex and an out-vertex, and we will direct each edge x-y from the out-vertex of x to the in-vertex of y.

We can assign them the capacities from the problem statement. Additionally we can add an edge for each vertex from the in to the out-vertex.

The capacity this edge will be assigned is obviously the vertex-capacity. Now we just run max-flow on this network and compute the result.

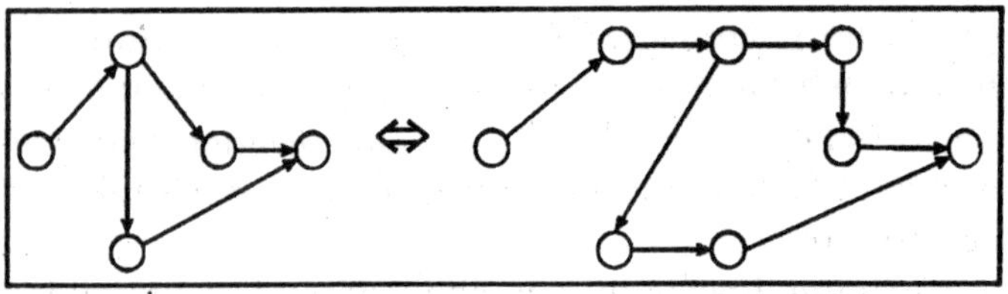

Fig. Eliminating Vertex-Capacities

Maximum flow problems may appear out of nowhere. Let's take this problem for instance:"You are given the in and out degrees of the vertices of a directed graph.

Your task is to find the edges (assuming that no edge can appear more than once)." First, notice that we can perform this simple test at the beginning.

We can compute the number M of edges by summing the out-degrees or the in-degrees of the vertices. If these numbers are not equal, clearly there is no graph that could be built. This doesn't solve our problem, though.

There are some greedy approaches that come to mind, but none of them work.

We will combine the tricks discussed above to give a max-flow algorithm that solves this problem. First, build a network that has 2 (in/out) vertices for each initial vertex. Now draw an edge from every out vertex to every in vertex. Next, add a super-source and draw an edge from it to every out-vertex. Add a super-sink and draw an edge from every in vertex to it. We now need some capacities for this to be a flow network. It should be pretty obvious what the intent with this approach is, so we will assign the following capacities: for each edge drawn from the super-source we assign a capacity equal to the out-degree of the vertex it points to.

As there may be only one arc from a vertex to another, we assign a 1 capacity to each of the edges that go from the outs to the ins.

As you can guess, the capacities of the edges that enter the super-sink will be equal to the in-degrees of the vertices. If the maximum flow in this network equals M - the number of edges, we have a solution, and for each edge between the out and in vertices that has a flow along it (which is maximum 1, as the capacity is 1) we can draw an edge between corresponding vertices in our graph.

Note that both x-y and y-x edges may appear in the solution. This is very similar to the maximum matching in a bipartite graph that we will discuss later. An example is given below where the out-degrees are (2, 1, 1, 1) and the in-degrees (1, 2, 1, 1).

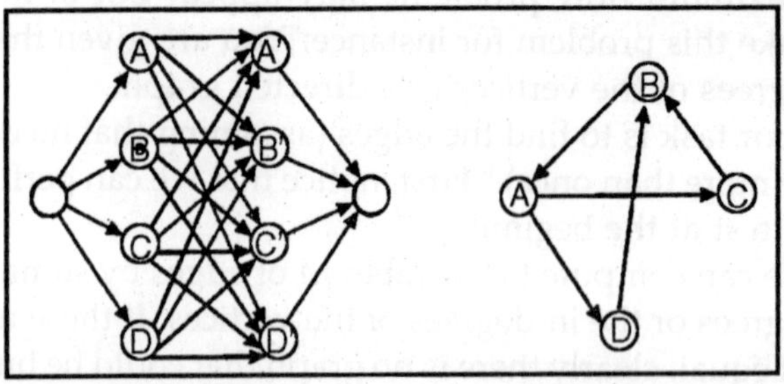

Some other problems may ask to separate two locations minimally. Some of these problems usually can be reduced to minimum-cut in a network. Two examples will be discussed here, but first let's take the standard min-cut problem and make it sound more like a TopCoder problem. We learned earlier how to find the value of the min-cut and how to find an arbitrary min-cut. In addition to this we will now like to have a minimum-cut with the minimum number of edges. An idea would be to try to modify the original network in such a way that the minimum cut here is the minimum cut with the minimum edges in the original one.

Notice what happens if we multiply each edge capacity with a constant T. Clearly, the value of the maximum flow is multiplied by T, thus the value of the minimum cut is T times bigger than the original. A minimum cut in the original network is a minimum cut in the modified one as well. Now suppose we add 1 to the capacity of each edge. Is a minimum cut in the original network a minimum cut in this one? The answer is no, as we can see in Figure shown below, if we take T = 2.

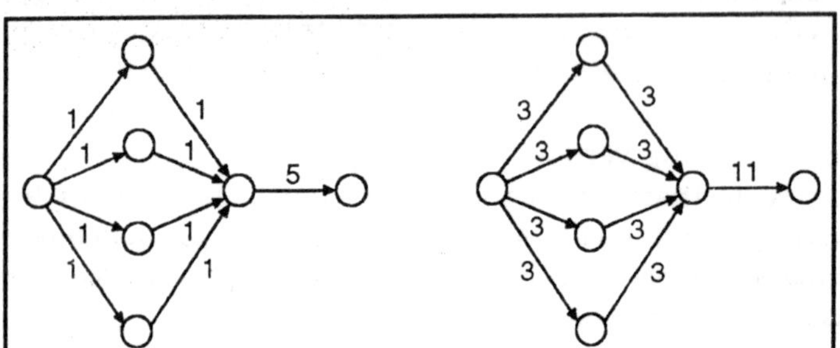

Fig. The Minnimum-cut Before/After

Why did this happen? Take an arbitrary cut. The value of the cut will be T times the original value of the cut, plus the number of edges in it.

Thus, a non-minimum cut in the first place could become minimum if it contains just a few edges. This is because the constant might not have been chosen properly in the beginning, as is the case in the example above. We can fix this by choosing T large enough to neutralize the difference in the number of edges between cuts in the network.

In the above example T = 4 would be enough, but to generalize, we take T = 10, one more than the number of edges in the original network, and one more than the number of edges that could possibly be in a minimum-cut. It is now true that a minimum-cut in the new network is minimum in the original network as well. However the converse is not true, and it is to our advantage. Notice how the difference between minimum cuts is now made by the number of edges in the cut. So we just find the min-cut in this new network to solve the problem correctly.

Let's illustrate some more the min-cut pattern: "An undirected graph is given. What is the minimum number of edges that should be removed in order to disconnect the graph?" In other words the problem asks us to remove some edges in order for two nodes to be separated. This should ring a bell - a minimum cut approach might work. So far we have only seen maximum flow in directed graphs, but now we are facing an undirected one.

This should not be a very big problem though, as we can direct the graph by replacing every (undirected) edge x-y with two arcs: x-y and y-x. In this case the value of the min-cut is the number of edges in it, so we assign a 1 capacity to each of them. We are not asked to separate two given vertices, but rather to disconnect optimally any two vertices, so we must take every pair of vertices and treat them as the source and the sink and keep the best one from these minimum-cuts.

An improvement can be made, however. Take one vertex, let's say vertex numbered 1. Because the graph should be disconnected, there must be another vertex unreachable from it. So it suffices to treat vertex 1 as the source and iterate through every other vertex and treat it as the sink.

What if instead of edges we now have to remove a minimum number of vertices to disconnect the graph? Now we are asked for a different min-cut, composed of vertices. We must somehow convert the vertices to edges though. Recall the problem above where we converted vertex-capacities to edge-capacities. The same trick works here. First "un-direct" the graph as in the previous example.

Next double the number of vertices and deal edges the same way: an edge x-y is directed from the out-x vertex to in-y. Then convert the vertex to an edge by adding a 1-capacity arc from the in-vertex to the out-vertex.

Now for each two vertices we must solve the sub-problem of minimally separating them. So, just like before take each pair of vertices and treat the out-vertex of one of them as the source and the in-vertex of the other one as the sink (this is because the only arc leaving the in-vertex is the one that goes to the out-vertex) and take the lowest value of the maximum flow. This time we can't improve in the quadratic number of steps needed, because the first vertex may be in an optimum solution and by always considering it as the source we lose such a case.

MAXIMUM BIPARTITE MATCHING

This is one of the most important applications of maximum flow, and a lot of problems can be reduced to it. A matching in a graph is a set of edges such that no vertex is touched by more than one edge. Obviously, a matching with a maximum cardinality is a maximum matching. For a general graph, this is a hard problem to deal with.

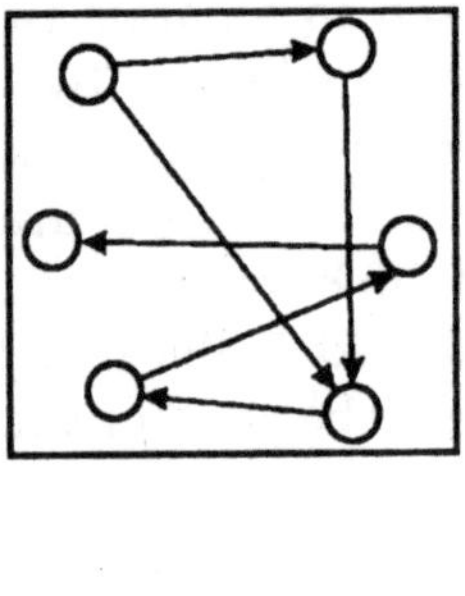

Let's direct our attention towards the case where the graph is bipartite - its vertices can be split into two sets such that there is no edge connecting vertices from the same set. In this case, it may sound like this: "Each of your employees can handle a given set of jobs. Assign a job to as many of them as you can."

A bipartite graph can be built in this case: the first set consists of your employees while the second one contains the jobs to be done. There is an edge from an employee to each of the jobs he could be assigned.

An example is given below:

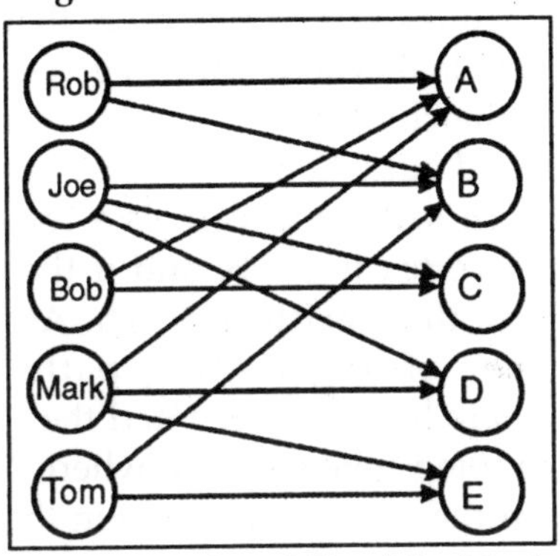

So, Joe can do jobs B, C and D while Mark wouldn't mind being assigned jobs A, D or E. This is a happy case in which each of your employees is assigned a job:

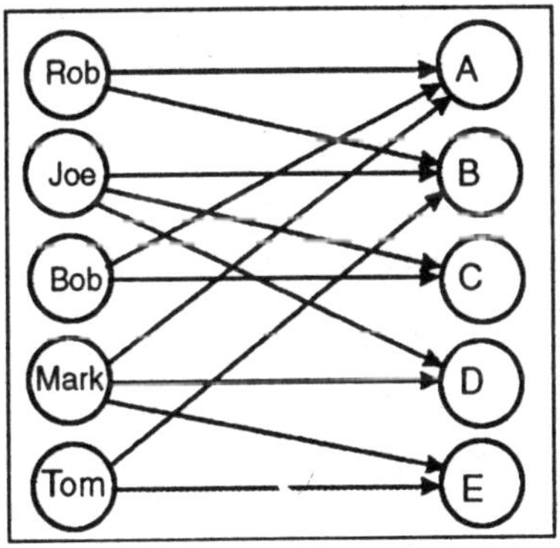

In order to solve the problem we first need to build a flow network. Just as we did in the multiple-source multiple-sink problem we will add two "dummy" vertices: a super-source and a super-sink, and we will draw an edge from the super-source to each of the vertices in set A (employees in the example above) and from each vertex in set B to the super-sink. In the end, each unit of flow will be equivalent to a match between an employee and a job, so each edge will be assigned a capacity of 1.

If we would have assigned a capacity larger than 1 to an edge from the super-source, we could have assigned more than one job to an employee. Likewise, if we would have assigned a capacity larger than 1 to an edge going to the super-sink, we could have assigned the same job to more than one employee. The maximum flow in this network will give us the cardinality of the maximum matching.

It is easy to find out whether a vertex in set B is matched with a vertex x in set A as well. We look at each edge connecting x to a vertex in set B, and if the flow is positive along one of them, there exists a match. As for the running time, the number of augmenting paths is limited by $\min(|A|,|B|)$, where by $|X|$ is denoted the cardinality of set X, making the running time $O(N \cdot M)$, where N is the number of vertices, and M the number of edges in the graph.

An implementation point of view is in place. We could implement the maximum bipartite matching just like in the pseudocode given earlier. Usually though, we might want to consider the particularities of the problem before getting to the implementation part, as they can save time or space. In this case, we could drop the 2-dimensional array that stored the residual network and replace it with two one-dimensional arrays: one of them stores the match in set B (or a sentinel value if it doesn't exist) for each element of set A, while the other is the other way around. Also, notice that each augmenting path has capacity 1, as it contributes with just a unit of flow. Each element of set A can be the first (well, the second, after the super-source) in an augmenting path at most once, so we can just iterate through each of them and try to find a match in set B. If an augmenting path exists, we follow it. This might lead to de-matching other elements along the way, but because we are following an augmenting path, no element will eventually remain unmatched in the process.

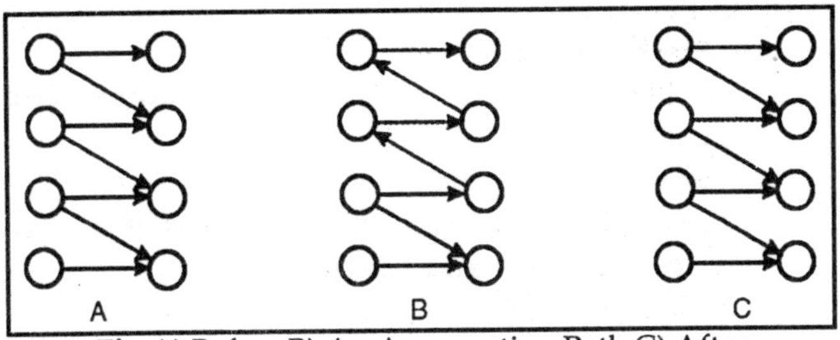

Fig A) Before B) An Augmenting Path C) After

Now let's solve some TopCoder problems!

ROOKATTACK

This problem asks us to place a maximum number of rooks on a *rows x cols* chessboard with some squares cut out. The idea behind this might be a little hard to spot, but once this is done, we get into a standard maximum bipartite-matching problem.

Notice that at most one rook can be placed on each row or column. In other words, each row corresponds at most to one column where a rook can be placed. This suggests a bipartite matching where set A is composed of elements corresponding to every row of the board, while set B consists of the columns.

For each row add edges to every column if the corresponding square is not cut out of the board. Now we can just run maximum bipartite-matching in this network and compute the result. Since there are at most *rows* * *cols* edges, the time complexity of the algorithm is:$O(rows^2 * cols)$

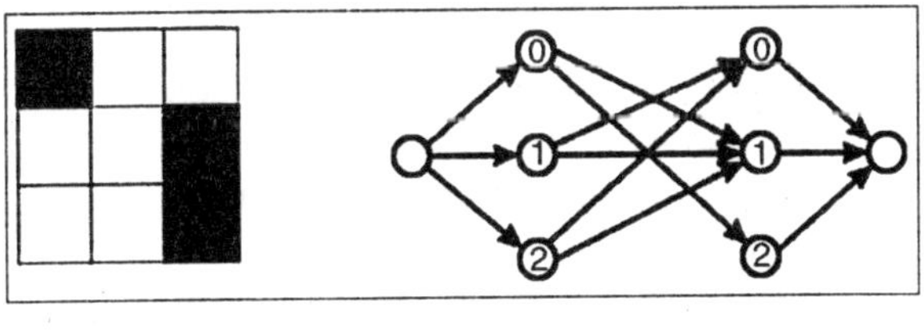

Fig. The Corresponding Network

In the C++ code below BFS is used for finding an augmenting-path:

```
class RookAttack
 {// a list of the non-empty squares for
  each row
     vector lst[300];
   // in this arrays we keep matches found
   to every row and column
  int row_match[300], col_match[300];
   // we search for an augmenting path
  starting with row source
   bool find_match(int source) {
  // from[x] = the row-vertex that precedes
    x in the path
  int from[300], where, match;
  memset(from, -1, sizeof(from));
     from[source] = source;
     deque q;
     q.push_back(source);
     bool found_path = false;
     while (!found_path && !q.empty()) {
       // where = current row-vertex we are
       in
       where = q.front(); q.pop_front();
      // we take every uncut square in the
      current row
      for (int i = 0; i < lst[where].size();
      ++ i) {
       match = lst[where][i];
      // next = the row matched with column
      match
     int next = col_match[match];
     if (where != next) {
       // no row matched with column match
       thus
we found an augmenting path
       if (next == -1) {
          found_path = true;
```

```
              break;
            }
          // a check whether we already visited
 the row-vertex next
          if (from[next] == -1) {
          q.push_back(next);
          from[next] = where;
        }
      }
    }
  }
  if (!found_path)
    return false;
  while (from[where] != where) {
      // we de-match where from its current
        match (aux)
and match it with match
       int aux = row_match[where];
       row_match[where] = match;
       col_match[match] = where;
       where = from[where];
       match = aux;
    }
    // at this point where = source
    row_match[where] = match;
    col_match[match] = where;
    return true;
 }
  public:
  int howMany(int rows, int cols, vector
  cutouts)
  {// build lst from cutouts; column j should
  appear in
 row's i list if square (i, j) is present on
 the board
    int ret = 0;
    memset(row_match, -1, sizeof(row_match));
    memset(col_match, -1, sizeof(col_match));
```

```
    // we try to find a match for each row
    for (int i = 0; i < rows; ++ i)
        ret += find_match(i);
    return ret;
  }
};
```

Let's take a look at the DFS version, too. We can implement the *find_match* function like this: for each non-empty square in the current row try to match the row with its corresponding column and call *find_match* recursively to attempt to find a new match for the current match (if the current match exists - if not, an augmenting path is found) of this column.

If one is found, we can perform the desired match. Note that to make this run in time we must not visit the same column (or row) twice. Notice the C++ code below is extremely short:

```
   bool find_match(int where) {
       // the previous column was not matched
   if (where == -1)
      return true;
  for (int i = 0; i < lst[where].size(); ++
  i) {
  int match = lst[where][i];
  if (visited[match] == false) {
   visited[match] = true;
   if (find_match(col_match[match])) {
      col_match[match] = where;
      return true;
    }
   }
 }
 return false;
}
```

This runs in time because the number of augmenting paths is the same for both versions. The only difference is that BFS finds the shortest augmenting-path while DFS finds a longer one. As implementation speed is an important factor in TopCoder matches, in this case it would be a good deal to use the slower, but easier DFS version. The following version of the problem is left as an exercise for the reader: to try and place as many rooks as possible on the board in such a way that the number of rooks on each row is equal to the number of rooks on each column (it is allowed for two rooks to attack each other).

GRADUATION

In this problem we are given a set of requirements, each stating that a number of classes should be taken from a given set of classes. Each class may be taken once and fulfills a single requirement. Actually, the last condition is what makes the problem harder, and excludes the idea of a greedy algorithm. We are also given a set of classes already taken. If it weren't for this, to ensure the minimality of the return, the size of the returned string would have been (if a solution existed) the sum of the number of classes for each requirement. Now as many classes as possible must be used from this set.

At first glance, this would have been a typical bipartite-matching problem if every requirement had been fulfilled by taking just a single class. Set A would have consisted of the classes available (all characters with ASCII code in the range 33-126, except for the numeric characters '0'-'9'), while the set of requirements would have played the role of set B. This can be taken care of easily. Each requirement will contribute to set B with a number of elements equal to the number of classes that must be taken in order to fulfill it - in other words, split each requirement into several requirements. At this point, a bipartite-matching algorithm can be used, but care should be allotted to the order in which we iterate through the set of classes and match a class with a requirement.

It is important to understand that any order to iterate through set A can be considered when solving the standard bipartite-matching problem. For example, it doesn't matter what element from set A we choose to be the first one to be matched.

Consider the solution found by the algorithm containing this element x from A, matched with an element y from B. Also, we should consider any optimal solution. Clearly, in the optimal, y must be matched with an element z from A, otherwise we can add the pair x-y to the matching, contradicting the fact that the solution is optimal. Then, we can just exchange z with x to come with a solution of the same cardinality, which completes the proof.

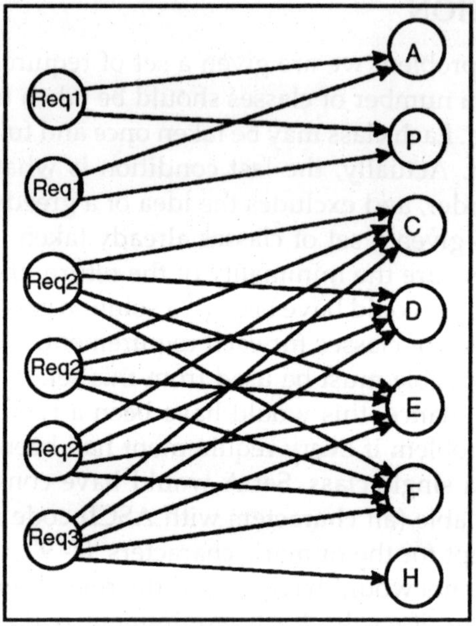

Fig. The Problem Statement

That being said, to gain as much as possible from the classes already taken we first must match each of these with a requirement. If, after completing this step, all requirements are fulfilled, we just need to return the empty string, as there is no need for taking more classes. Now we have to deal with the requirement that the return must be the first in lexicographic order.

It should be obvious now that the other classes must be considered in increasing order. If a match is found for a class, that class is added to the return value. In the end, if not every requirement is fulfilled, we don't have a solution. The implementation is left as an exercise for the reader.

As a final note, it is possible to speed things up a bit. To achieve this, we will drop the idea of splitting each requirement. Instead we will modify the capacities of the edges connecting those with the super-sink. They will now be equal to the number of classes to be taken for each requirement. Then we can just go on with the same approach as above.

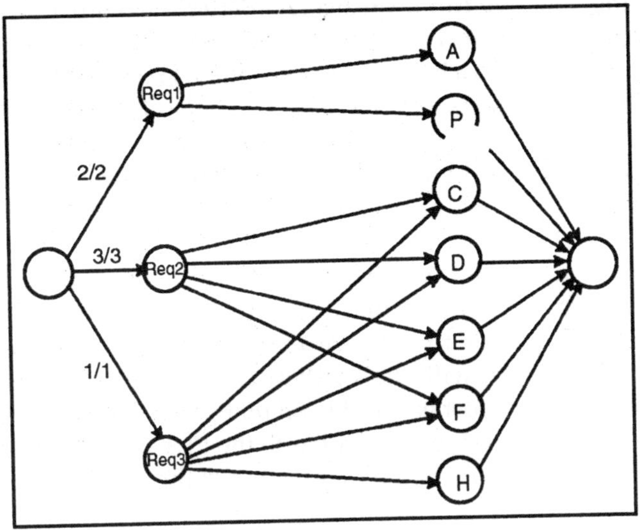

Fig. The Problem Statement

PARKING

In this problem we have to match each of the cars with a parking spot. Additionally the time it takes for all cars to find a parking spot must be minimized. Once again we build a bipartite graph: set A is the set that consists of the cars and set B contains the parking spots. Each edge connecting elements from different sets has as the cost (and not the capacity!) the time required for the car to get to the parking spot. If the spot is unreachable, we can assign it an infinite cost (or remove it). These costs are determined by running breadth-first search.

For solving it, assume that the expected result is less than or equal to a constant D. Then, there exists a matching in which each edge connecting a car and a parking spot has the cost less than or equal to D. Thus, removing edges with cost greater than D will have no effect on the solution. This suggests a binary search on D, removing all edges with cost greater than D, and then performing a maximum bipartite-matching algorithm.

If a matching exists in which every car can drive to a parking spot, we can decrease D otherwise we must increase it. However, there is a faster and more elegant solution using a priority-first search. Instead of keeping D fixed as above, we could try to successively increase D whenever we find that it is too low.

We will start with D = 0. Then we iterate through each of the cars and try to find an augmenting path in which no edge has a cost larger than D.

If none exists, we increase D until one path exists. Obviously, we will increase it with the smallest possible amount. In order to achieve this, we will search for the augmenting path with the smallest cost - the cost of the path is the maximum cost of an edge on that path. This can be done with a priority-first search similar to the PFS augmenting-path algorithm presented in the first section of the article. C++ code follows:

```
struct node {
   int where, cost, from;
   node(int _where, int _cost, int _from):
   where(_where),
cost(_cost), from(_from) {};
};
bool operator < (node a, node b) {
   return a.cost > b.cost;
}
int minTime(vector park)
{
   // build a cost matrix cost[i][j] = cost of
   getting from car i to
parking spot j, by doing a BFS
 // vertices 0, 1..., N - 1 will represent
 the cars, and
```

```
 vertices N, N + 1..., N + M - 1 will
represent
  //the parking spots; N + M will be the
  super-sink
    int D = 0, sink = N + M;
    int car_match[105], park_match[105];
    memset(car_match, -1, sizeof(car_match));
    memset(park_match, -1, sizeof(park_match));
    for (int source = 0; source < N; ++ source)
    {
      bool visited[210];
      memset(visited, false, sizeof(visited));
      int from[210];
      memset(from, -1, sizeof(from));
      priority_queue pq;
      pq.push(node(source, 0, -1));
      while (!pq.empty()) {
         int cst = pq.top().cost, where =
         pq.top().where,
   _from = pq.top().from;
        pq.pop();
        if (visited[where]) continue;
        visited[where] = true;
        from[where] = _from;
        // if where is a car try all M parking
        spots
         if (where < N) {
           for (int i - 0; i < M; ++ i) {
             // if the edge doesn't exist or
             this car
 is already matched with this parking spot
     if (cost[where][i] == infinity ||
car_match[where] == i) continue;
    int ncst = max(cst, cost[where][i]);
  // the i-th parking spot is N + i
  pq.push(node(N + i, ncst, where));
 }
}
```

```
else {
  // if this parking spot is unmatched we
  found
the augmenting path with minimum cost
  if (park_match[where - N] == -1) {
     from[sink] = where;
     // if D needs to be increased, increase
     it
     D = max(D, cst);
     break;
 }
 // otherwise we follow the backward edge
 int next = park_match[where - N];
 int ncst = max(cst, cost[next][where]);
 pq.push(node(next, ncst, where));
 }
}
int where = from[sink];
// if no augmenting path is found we have no
solution
if (where == -1)
  return -1;
// follow the augmenting path
while (from[where] > -1) {
  int prev = from[where];
  // if where is a parking spot the edge
(prev, where)
is a forward edge and the match must be
updated
 if (where ⇒ N) {
    car_match[prev] = where;
    park_match[where - N] = prev;
 }
    where = prev;
 }
}
return D;
}
```

TRAVELING SALESMAN PROBLEM

The travelling salesman problem consists in finding the shortest (or a nearly shortest) path connecting a number of locations (perhaps hundreds), such as cities visited by a travelling salesman on his sales route.

The Traveling Salesman Problem is typical of a large class of "hard" optimization problems that have intrigued mathematicians and computer scientists for years.

Most important, it has applications in science and engineering. For example, in the manufacture of a circuit board, it is important to determine the best order in which a laser will drill thousands of holes. An efficient solution to this problem reduces production costs for the manufacturer.

The impetus behind the SA algorithm is its analogy to the statistical mechanics of annealing solids... When a physical system is at a high temperature, the atoms in the system are in a highly disordered state, and consequently the associated ensemble energy of the system is also high.

Lowering the temperature of the system results in the atoms of the system acquiring a more orderly state, thus reducing the energy of the system.

For example, to grow a crystal, which is highly ordered, the system needs to be heated to a temperature which allows many atomic rearrangements.

Then the system must be carefully cooled, ensuring a thermal equilibrium is reached at each temperature stage, until the system is 'frozen' into a good crystal.

This process of cooling is known as annealing. If the cooling process is performed too quickly, extensive irregularities can be locked into the crystals structure, with the resulting energy level far greater than in a perfect crystal.

The Metropolis algorithm..., developed to simulate the behaviour of atoms in thermal equilibrium at a particular temperature, begins with an initial configuration with energy E_0. Each subsequent iteration involves performing a small random perturbation to the current configuration i (with associated energyE_i), then the energy, E_j, of the resulting configuration j is calculated.

If the change in energy $E'' = E_j - E_i$ d" 0 the configuration j is accepted with probability 1 and becomes the current configuration of the next iteration.

If $E'' > 0$, then configuration j is accepted with probability exp(- E''/kT), with the aim of obtaining a Boltzman distribution. If configuration j is rejected the current configuration$i$ remains unchanged. After a large number of iterations the accepted configurations approximate a Boltzman distribution at a particular temperature.

At present this Programme exists only in a demonstration version. (A version allowing input of site locations, names, etc., so as to produce useful results would require further work, which, due to lack of demand, is unlikely to happen.)

This demo version, TS3DEMO.EXE (Version 3.10 — 37,919 bytes), can be downloaded from this site for personal, non-commercial, use (it is also contained in TS3DEMO.ZIP — 37,132 bytes).

The Programme is run from the DOS prompt. If no command line parameters are given then upon startup *The Travelling Salesman* Programme displays the following notice:

The Travelling Salesman, Version 3.10This is the demonstration version (and at present the only version) of"The Travelling Salesman" Programme, written by Peter Meyer.

This Programme uses the Simulated Annealing Algorithm to solve a form of thetravelling salesman problem, which is to find the shortest (or a nearlyshortest) path connecting a set of sites, such as cities or delivery points.

Two input values can be specified on the DOS command line:Use: "TS3DEMO N:num_sites L:layout"The number of sites ("num_sites") must be in the range 9 through 240.

There are two types of layout available:"L:G" produces a rectangular grid. "L:R" produces a random layout.Default values are N:81 and L:RFor example, to specify 120 locations situated randomly use "TS3DEMO N:120".To specify 169 locations on an 13×13 grid use "TS3DEMO N:169 L:G".

Here are three results obtained using a Pentium II running at 300 MHz. Firstly the initial and final states for 100 sites in a random layout:

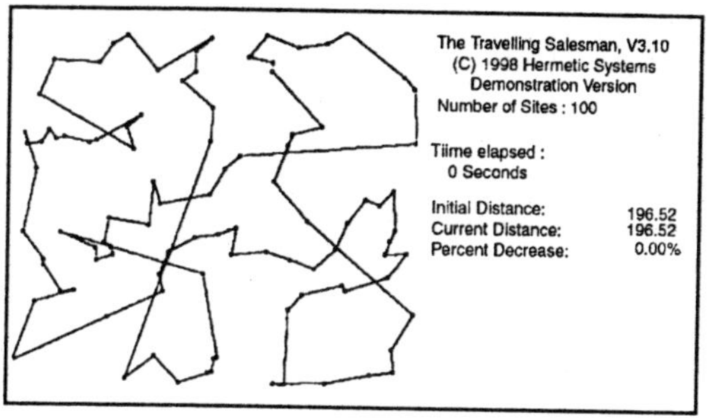

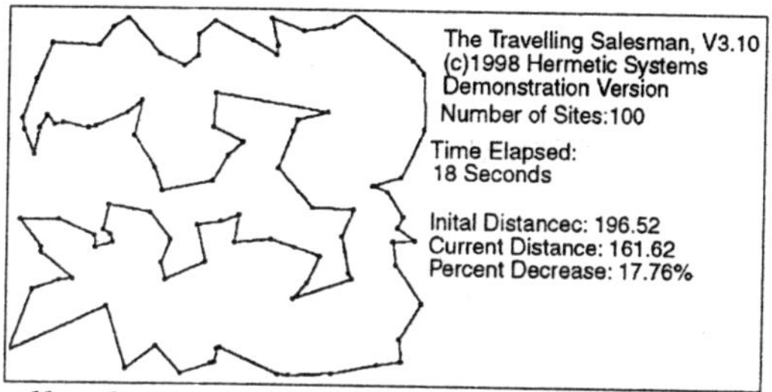

Secondly the initial and final states for 225 sites in a random layout:

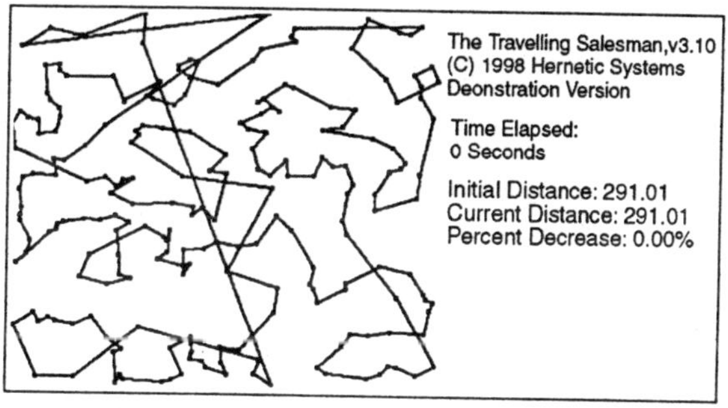

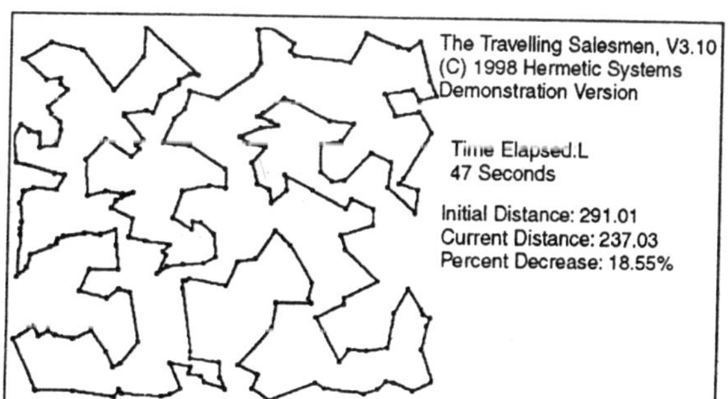

Thirdly the initial and final states for 100 sites in a grid layout:

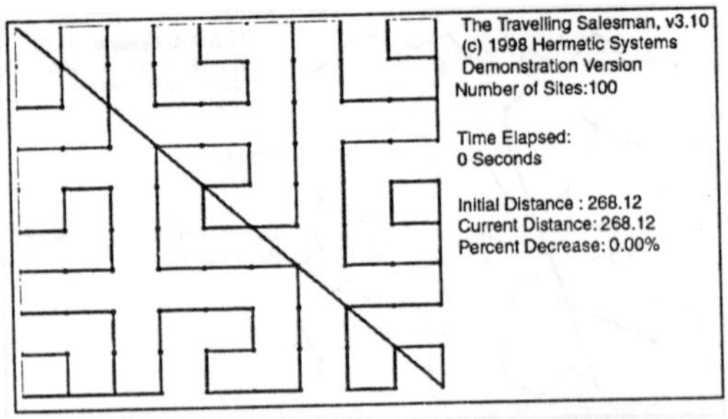

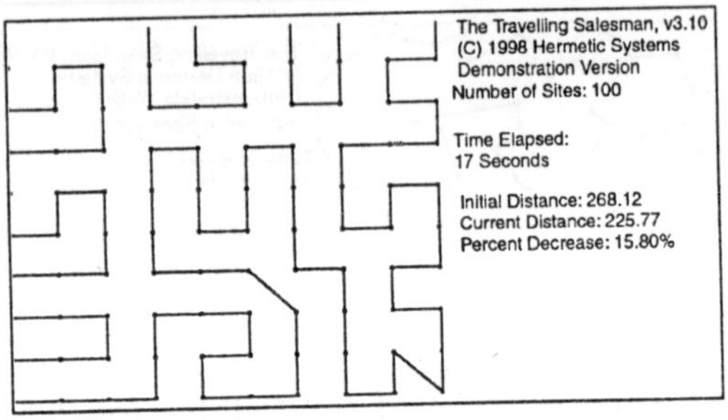

USING GENETIC ALGORITHMS

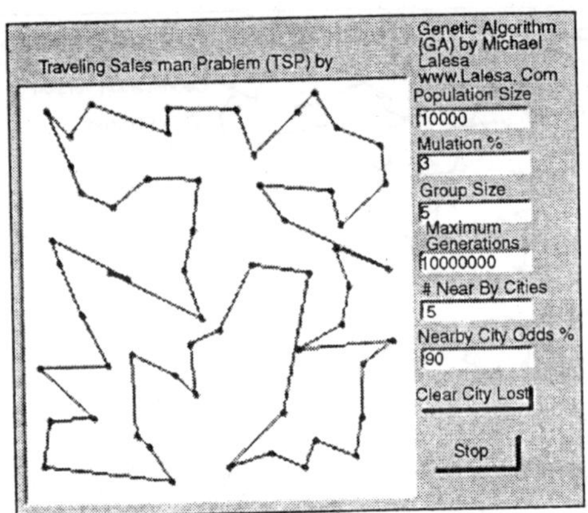

Developed a solution to the Traveling Salesman Problem (TSP) using a Genetic Algorithm (GA). In the Traveling Salesman Problem, the goal is to find the shortest distance between N different cities. The path that the salesman takes is called a tour.

Testing every possibility for an N city tour would be N! math additions. A 30 city tour would have to measure the total distance of be 2.65×10^{32} different tours. Assuming a trillion additions per second, this would take 252,333,390,232,297 years. Adding one more city would cause the time to increase by a factor of 31. Obviously, this is an impossible solution.

A genetic algorithm can be used to find a solution is much less time. Although it might not find the best solution, it can find a near perfect solution for a 100 city tour in less than a minute. There are a couple of basic steps to solving the traveling salesman problem using a GA.

- First, create a group of many random tours in what is called a population. This algorithm uses a greedy initial propulation that gives preference to linking cities that are close to each other.
- Second, pick 2 of the better (shorter) tours parents in the population and combine them to make 2 new child tours. Hopefully, these children tour will be better than either parent.
- A small Per centage of the time, the child tours are mutated. This is done to prevent all tours in the population from looking identical.
- The new child tours are inserted into the population replacing two of the longer tours. The size of the population remains the same.
- New children tours are repeatedly created until the desired goal is reached.

As the name implies, Genetic Algorithms mimic nature and evolution using the principles of Survival of the Fittest.

The two complex issues with using a Genetic Algorithm to solve the Traveling Salesman Problem are the encoding of the tour and the crossoveralgorithm that is used to combine the two parent tours to make the child tours.

In a standard Genetic Algorithm, the encoding is a simple sequence of numbers and Crossover is performed by picking a random point in the parent's sequences and switching every number in the sequence after that point. In this example, the crossover point is between the 3rd and 4th item in the list. To create the children, every item in the parent's sequence after the crossover point is swapped.

Parent 1	F A B I E C G D
Parent 2	D E A I C G B F
Child 1	F A B I C G B F
Child 1	D E A I E C G D

The difficulty with the Traveling Salesman Problem is that every city can only be used once in a tour. If the letters in the above example represented cities, this child tours created by this crossover operation would be invalid. Child 1 goes to city F & B twice, and never goes to cities D or E.

The encoding cannot simply be the list of cities in the order they are traveled. Other encoding methods have been created that solve the crossover problem. Although these methods will not create invalid tours, they do not take into account the fact that the tour "A B C D E F G" is the same as "G F E D C B A". To solve the problem properly the crossover algorithm will have to get much more complicated.

My solution stores the links in both directions for each tour. In the above tour example, Parent 1 would be stored as:

City	First Connection	Second Connection
A	F	B
B	A	E
C	E	G
D	G	F
E	B	C
F	D	A
G	C	D

The crossover operation is more complicated than combining 2 strings. The crossover will take every link that exists in both parents and place those links in both children. Then, for Child 1 it alternates between taking links that appear in Parent 2 and then Parent 1.

For Child 2, it alternates between Parent 2 and Parent 1 taking a different set of links. For either child, there is a chance that a link could create an invalid tour where instead of a single path in the tour there are several disconnected paths.

These links must be rejected. To fill in the remaining missing links, cities are chosen at random. Since the crossover is not completely random, this is considered a greedy crossover.

Eventually, this GA would make every solution look identical. This is not ideal. Once every tour in the population is identical, the GA will not be able to find a better solution. There are two ways around this. The first is to use a very large initial population so that it takes the GA longer to make all of the solutions the same. The second method is mutation, where some child tours are randomly altered to produce a new unique tour.

This Genetic Algorithm also uses a greedy initial population. The city links in the initial tours are not completely random. The GA will prefer to make links between cities that are close to each other. This is not done 100% of the time, becuase that would cause every tour in the initial population to be very similar.

There are 6 parameters to control the operation of the Genetic Algorithm:

- *Population Size*: The population size is the initial number of random tours that are created when the algorithm starts. A large population takes longer to find a result. A smaller population increases the chance that every tour in the population will eventually look the same. This increases the chance that the best solution will not be found.
- *Neighbourhood/ Group Size*: Each generation, this number of tours are randomly chosen from the population. The best 2 tours are the parents. The worst 2 tours get replaced by the children. For group size, a high number will increase the likelyhood that the really good tours will be selected as parents, but it will also cause many tours to never be used as parents. A large group size will cause the algorithm to run faster, but it might not find the best solution.
- *Mutation%*: The Per centage that each child after crossover will undergo mutation When a tour is mutated, one of the cities is randomly moved from one point in the tour to another.

- *# Nearby Cities*: As part of a greedy initial population, the GA will prefer to link cities that are close to each other to make the initial tours. When creating the initial population this is the number of cities that are considered to be close.
- *Nearby City Odds%*: This is the Per cent chance that any one link in a random tour in the initial population will prefer to use a nearby city instead of a completely random city. If the GA chooses to use a nearby city, then there is an equally random chance that it will be any one of the cities from the previous parameter.
- *Maximum Generations*: How many crossovers are run before the algorithm is terminated.

The other options that can be configured are (note: these are only available in the downloadable version):

- *Random Seed*: This is the seed for the random number generator. By having a fixed instead of a random seed, you can duplicate previous results as long as all other parameters are the same. This is very helpful when looking for errors in the algorithm.
- *City List*: The downloadable version allows you to import city lists from XML files. Again, when debugging problems it is useful to be able to run the algorithm with the same exact parameters.

The starting parameter values are:

Parameter	**Initial Value**
Population Size	10,000
Group Size	5
Mutation	3%
# Nearby Cities	5
Nearby City Odds	90%

Note: I originally wrote this Programme in 1995 in straight C. The tours in the population were stored as an array of 32 bit int's, where each bit indicated a connection. Ex: If tour[0] = 00000000000010000000100000000000 in binary, then city 0 connected to city 11 and 19. That implementation was much faster than the current C# version. The greedy part of crossover could be performed by doing a binary AND on the two tours. While that code was very fast, it had a lot of binary operations, was limited in the number of cities it could support, and the code wasn't readable. Hopefully, this new version will allow for more re-use.

Chapter 5

Randomization of Algorithms

APPROACH

Randomization has become a standard approach in algorithm design and it can be applied in a wide range of problems.

Often it leads to more efficient, simpler and shorter solutions than their deterministic counterparts. As opposed to a deterministic algorithm, a randomized algorithm takes a source of random numbers and makes random choices during execution. Hence, the Behaviour of the algorithm can change even on a fixed input and is likely to be good on *every* input.

The first class of randomized algorithms are Las Vegas algorithms, which always give *correct* results, the only variation from one run to another being its running time. The running time is a random variable whose expectation is bounded, for example by a polynomial.

The second class are Monte Carlo algorithms, whose running time is deterministic, but whose results are only correct with a probability of ≥ 1/3. A widely known example of a Monte Carlo algorithm is the Miller-Rabin primality test.

One of the most widely used randomized algorithms is the randomized Quicksort, which I will talk about. I picked it because it is very practical, easily comprehendible and the implementation is trivial. It is an example of a Las Vegas algorithm.

Also, many of you are probably already familiar with either the *normal* (deterministic) or the randomized version, or both.

QUICKSORT

Quicksort is a divide and conquer sorting algorithm developed by Tony Hoare, who published the first version in the *Communications of the ACM*, Volume 4, Issue 7, in July 1961. (Oh, just in case any Slashdotters happen to read this: No, the fact he is a senior researcher at *Microsoft* Research does *not* make him an evil person.)

The algorithm works by first partitioning (dividing/ rearranging) an input array containing the elements to be sorted into 2 sub-arrays around an element called the pivot x such that all the elements in the lower (left) sub-array are ≥, the pivot x≤ all the elements in the upper (right) sub-array. Following the division is the conquer step, which recursively sorts both sub-arrays. Eventually, there is no work required to combine the sub-arrays since they are sorted in place. A lot of people actually see the recursiveness of Quicksort as one of its weaknesses. I appreciate the compactness and elegance it introduces.

Anyhow, we all know that code says more than a thousand words, so here we go. The following code is one of the simpler implementations of Quicksort, without any optimizations, as it appeared in Steven Skiena's The Algorithm Design Manual.

```
void quicksort(int s[], int l, int h)
{
   int p;/* index of partition */
   if ((h - l) > 0) {
        p = partition(s, l, h);
        quicksort(s, l, p - 1);
        quicksort(s, p + 1, h);
     }
}
int partition(int s[], int l, int h)
{
   int i;
   int p;/* pivot element index */
   int firsthigh;/* divider position for pivot
   element */
```

```
    p= h;
    firsthigh = l;
    for (i = l; i < h; i++)
         if(s[i] < s[p]) {
              swap(&s[i], &s[firsthigh]);
              firsthigh++;
    }
   swap(&s[p], &s[firsthigh]);
   return(firsthigh);
 }
 void    swap(int    *a,    int    *b)
 {
            int x;
            x = *a;
            *a = *b;
            *b = x;
 }
```

I will skip an eLabourate analysis of the deterministic Quicksort, as we want to emphasize on the randomized version. Most of you are likely to know that Quicksort has an expected running time of θ(n log n) on an input array of *n*elements, which is remarkably efficient. If we are unlucky though, it has worst case running time of $\theta(n^2)$ - which is worse than Heapsort and Mergesort. This Behaviour occurs when the partitioning routine produces one sub-array with n–1 elements and another one with 0 elements. That happens when the input array n is already sorted, no matter if forward or backwards. In this situation, even insertion sort would run in the shorter time of O(n). So what can we do about that? What is an easy way to improve the performance of Quicksort? There are actually two ways. One would be to randomize the input array. Another one, the one we will talk about now, is to pick the pivot randomly.

RANDOMIZED QUICKSORT

The above implementation automatically selects the last element in each sub-array as the pivot. We will now look at a technique called *random sampling*. So instead of always taking the last element in each sub-array, we will select a random element as the pivot during the partitioning. One possible implementation based on our previous code looks like this:

```
int partition(int s[], int l, int h)
{
        int i;
        int p;/* pivot element index */
        int firsthigh;/* divider position for
        pivot element */
        p = l + (random()% (h - l + 1);
        swap(&s[p], &s);
        firsthigh = l;
        for (i = l; i < h; i++)
            if(s[i] < s) {
                swap(&s[i], &s[firsthigh]);
                firsthigh++;
        }
    swap(&s, &s[firsthigh]);
    return(firsthigh);
}
```

Well, so what are the advantages of the randomized version?

The running time is independent of input ordering:

- The algorithms does not makes any assumptions about the distribution of the elements in the input array. Already sorted arrays will work as well as random ones.
- No specific input that can produce the worst case Behaviour, which is determined only by the random number generator.

As we can see, by introducing some randomness the worst case running time of $\theta(n^2)$ becomes increasingly unlikely and leaves us with the property that the algorithm has a worst-case expected running time of $\theta(n \log n)$.So how to we proof the correctness of this assumption? This is where some probabilistic analysis comes in handy. The following proof is taken from Manuel Blum's lecture notes from his class *CMU 15-451* on algorithms.

ANALYSIS OF RANDOMIZED QUICKSORT

First of all, let's assume that no two elements in the in put array are equal. We will be writing will be the quantity we care about (the total number of comparisons) as a sum of simpler random variables, and then just Analyse the simpler ones. Define a random variable X_{ij} to be 1 if the algorithm *does* compare the *i*th smallest and *j*th smallest elements during the sort and 0 if it does not. This is called an expectation variable. X denotes the total number of comparisons made by the algorithm. Since we never compare the same pair of elements twice, we have,

$$X = \sum_{i=1}^{n} \sum_{j=i+1}^{n} Xij$$

and therefore,

$$E[X] = \sum_{i=1}^{n} \sum_{j=i+1}^{n} E[Xij]$$

Let's consider one of these X_{ij} for $i < j$. Denote the *i*th smallest element by in the array by e_i and the *j*th smallest element by e_j, and conceptually imagine lining up the elements in sorted order. If the pivot we choose happens to be either e_i or e_j then we compare them. If our pivot is less than e_i or greater than e_j then both end up in the same bucket and we have to choose another pivot. So, we can think of this like a dart game: we throw a dart at random into the array: if we hit e_i or e_j then X_{ij} becomes 1, if we hit between them X_{ij} becomes 0, and otherwise we throw another dart. At each step, the probability that X_{ij} equals 1 conditioned on the event that the game ends in that step is exactly $2/(j - i + 1)$. So now we can say that the overall probability that X_{ij} equals 1 is $2/(j - i + 1)$.

In other words, for a given element *i*, it is compared to element i+1 with probability 1, to element i+2 with probability 2/3, to element i+3 with probability 2/4, to element..., yes, and so on. That gives us

$$E[X] = \sum_{i=1}^{n} 2\left(\frac{1}{2} + \frac{1}{3} + \frac{1}{4} + \frac{1}{5} + \ldots + \frac{1}{n-i-+1}\right)$$

The quantity 1+1/2+1/3+...+1/n, denoted H_n, is called the *n*th harmonic number and is in the range [Inn,1 + Inn] (this can be seen by considering the integral of f(x) = 1/x)). Therefore,

$$E[x] < 2n(H_n - 1)K \le 2n \ln n.$$

SUMMONING THE EVIL

In 1999 Doug McIlroy from *Dartmouth College* published a paper called A Killer Adversary for Quicksort which describes a simple way to find the inputs that even force the randomized Quicksort into the worst case running time of $\theta(n^2)$. It also provides a simple C Programme illustrating the technique.

Quicksort can be made to go quadratic by constructing input on the fly in response to the sequence of items compared. The technique is illustrated by a specific adversary for the standard C qsort function. The general method works against any implementation of quicksort–even a randomizing one–that satisfies certain very mild and realistic assumptions. Russ Cox wrote a post about this paper, too.

CONCLUSION AND ONE MORE THING

This is just a very trivial example of randomized algorithms and many of you are likely to be already familiar with it. Though, if this post happens to attract some interest in this topic, I might write up some more posts about randomized algorithms. If you want to learn more about Quicksort and the analysis of both, the randomized and the deterministic version, there is a good video lecture available at MIT OpenCourseWare here.

I chose to post source code in C, as I think that it is one of the languages most of you know, that it is more practical than pseudocode and that at the same time it is rather easy to read. If you happen to not be happy with my decision, feel free to post an implementation in your Favourite Programmeming language as a comment.

Also, as this is my first rather *deep* post, if you happen to find an error in this post, please leave a comment and I will correct the mistake. Unfortunately, though, I won't be able to reward you with a hexadecimal dollar as Donald Knuthdoes.

STRING MATCHING

"You will Always have my Love,
My Love, for the love I love is
Lovely as Loves It Self."

[Love] ?

Input

"You will Always have my [Love]
my [Love] , for the [Love] I [Love]
is [Love] ly as [Love] Itself."

Output

Description: A text string t of length n. A patterns string p of length m.

Problem: Find the first (or all) instances of the pattern in the text.

Excerpt from The Algorithm Design Manual: String matching is fundamental to database and text processing applications. Every text editor must contain a mechanism to search the current document for arbitrary strings. Pattern matching Programmeming languages such as Perl and Awk derive much of their power from their built-in string matching primitives, making it easy to fashion Programmes that filter and modify text. Spelling checkers scan an input text for words in the dictionary and reject any strings that do not match.

REGULAR EXPRESSIONS

A regular expression is contained in slashes, and matching occurs with the =~ operator. The following expression is true if the string *the* appears in variable $sentence.

```
$sentence =~/the/
```

The RE is case sensitive, so if

```
$sentence = "The quick brown fox";
```

then the above match will be false. The operator !~ is used for spotting a non-match. In the above example

```
$sentence !~/the/
```

is true because the string *the* does not appear in $sentence.

THE $_ SPECIAL VARIABLE

We could use a conditional as

```
if ($sentence =~/under/)
{
        print "We're talking about rugby\n";
}
```

which would print out a message if we had either of the following

```
$sentence = "Up and under";
$sentence = "Best winkles in Sunderland";
```

But it's often much easier if we assign the sentence to the special variable $_ which is of course a scalar. If we do this then we can avoid using the match and non-match operators and the above can be written simply as

```
if (/under/)
{
     print "We're talking about rugby\n";
}
```

The $_ variable is the default for many Perl operations and tends to be used very heavily.

MORE ON RES

In an RE there are plenty of special characters, and it is these that both give them their power and make them appear very complicated. It's best to build up your use of REs slowly; their creation can be something of an art form.

Here are some special RE characters and their meaning:

```
.     # Any single character except a newline
^     # The beginning of the line or string
$     # The end of the line or string
*     # Zero or more of the last character
+     # One or more of the last character
```

```
?    # Zero or one of the last character
```

and here are some example matches. Remember that should be enclosed in/.../ slashes to be used.

```
t.e    # t followed by anthing followed by e
       # This will match the
       # tre
       # tle
       # but not te
       # tale
^f     # f at the beginning of a line
^ftp   # ftp at the beginning of a line
e$     # e at the end of a line
tle$   # tle at the end of a line
und*   # un followed by zero or more d characters
       # This will match un
       # und
       # undd
       # unddd (etc)
 *     # Any string without a newline. This is
        because
       #the. matches anything except a newline
        and
       # the * means zero or more of these.
^$     # A line with nothing in it.
```

There are even more options. Square brackets are used to match any one of the characters inside them. Inside square brackets a - indicates "between" and a ^ at the beginning means "not":

```
[qjk]       # Either q or j or k
[^qjk]     # Neither q nor j nor k
[a-z]       # Anything from a to z inclusive
[^a-z]     # No lower case letters
[a-zA-Z]   # Any letter
[a-z]+     # Any non-zero sequence of lower
             case letters
```

At this point you can probably skip to the end and do at least most of the exercise. The rest is mostly just for reference.

A vertical bar | represents an "or" and parentheses (...) can be used to group things together:

```
jelly|cream    # Either jelly or cream
(eg|le)gs       # Either eggs or legs
(da)+           # Either da or dada or dadada
                      or...
```

Here are some more special characters:

```
\n     # A newline
\t     # A tab
\w     # Any alphanumeric (word) character.
        # The same as [a-zA-Z0-9_]
\W     # Any non-word character.
        # The same as [^a-zA-Z0-9_]
\d     # Any digit. The same as [0-9]
\D     # Any non-digit. The same as [^0-9]
\s     # Any whitespace character: space,
        # tab, newline, etc
\S     # Any non-whitespace character
\b     # A word boundary, outside [] only
\B     # No word boundary
```

Clearly characters like $, |, [,), \,/ and so on are peculiar cases in regular expressions. If you want to match for one of those then you have to preceed it by a backslash.

So:

```
\|     # Vertical bar
\[     # An open square bracket
\)     # A closing parenthesis
\*     # An asterisk
\^     # A carat symbol
\/     # A slash
\\     # A backslash
```

and so on.

SOME EXAMPLE

As was mentioned earlier, it's probably best to build up your use of regular expressions slowly. Here are a few examples. Remember that to use them for matching they should be put in/.../ slashes

```
  [01]      # Either "0" or "1"
  \/0       # A division by zero: "/0"
  \/ 0      # A division by zero with a space:
              "/ 0"
  \/\s0   # A division by zero with a
              whitespace:
              # "/ 0" where the space may be a
              tab  etc.
              \/ *0 # A division by zero with
              possibly some
              # spaces: "/0" or "/ 0" or "/ 0"
              etc.
   \/\s*0# A division by zero with possibly
              some
              # whitespace.
\/\s*0\.0* # As the previous one, but with
              decimal
              # point and maybe some 0s after it.
              Accepts
             # "/0." and "/0.0" and "/0.00" etc
             and
             # "/ 0." and "/ 0.0" and "/ 0.00"
           etc.
```

Exercise

Previously your Programme counted non-empty lines. Alter it so that instead of counting non-empty lines it counts only lines with

- The letter *x*
- The string *the*
- The string *the* which may or may not have a capital *t*
- The word *the* with or without a capital. Use \b to detect word boundaries.

In each case the Programme should print out every line, but it should only number those specified. Try to use the $_ variable to avoid using the =~ match operator explicitly.

NP-COMPLETENESS

So far we've seen a lot of good news: such-and-such a problem can be solved quickly (in close to linear time, or at least a time that is some small polynomial function of the input size). NP-completeness is a form of bad news: evidence that many important problems can't be solved quickly.

CARING

These NP-complete problems really come up all the time. Knowing they're hard lets you stop beating your head against a wall trying to solve them, and do something better:

- *Use a heuristic*: If you can't quickly solve the problem with a good worst case time, maybe you can come up with a method for solving a reasonable fraction of the common cases.
- *Solve the problem approximately instead of exactly*: A lot of the time it is possible to come up with a provably fast algorithm, that doesn't solve the problem exactly but comes up with a solution you can prove is close to right.
- *Use an exponential time solution anyway*: If you really have to solve the problem exactly, you can settle down to writing an exponential time algorithm and stop worrying about finding a better solution.
- *Choose a better abstraction*: The NP-complete abstract problem you're trying to solve presumably comes from ignoring some of the seemingly unimportant details of a more complicated real world problem. Perhaps some of those details shouldn't have been ignored, and make the difference between what you can and can't solve.

CLASSIFICATION OF PROBLEMS

The subject of *computational complexity theory* is dedicated to classifying problems by how hard they are. There are many different classifications; some of the most common and useful are the following. (One technical point: these are all really defined in terms of yes-or-no problems — does a certain structure exist rather than how do I find the structure.)

- *P*: Problems that can be solved in polynomial time. ("P" stands for polynomial.) These problems have formed the main material of this course.
- *NP*: This stands for "nondeterministic polynomial time" where nondeterministic is just a fancy way of talking about guessing a solution. A problem is in NP if you can quickly (in polynomial time) test whether a solution is correct (without worrying about how hard it might be to find the solution). Problems in NP are still relatively easy: if only we could guess the right solution, we could then quickly test it.

NP does not stand for "non-polynomial". There are many complexity classes that are much harder than NP.

- *Pspace*: Problems that can be solved using a reasonable amount of memory (again defined formally as a polynomial in the input size) without regard to how much time the solution takes.
- *Exptime*: Problems that can be solved in exponential time. This class contains most problems you are likely to run into, including everything in the previous three classes. It may be surprising that this class is not all-inclusive: there are problems for which the best algorithms take even more than exponential time.
- *Undecidable*: For some problems, we can prove that there is no algorithm that always solves them, no matter how much time or space is allowed. One very uninformative proof of this is based on the fact that there are as many problems as there real numbers, and only as many Programmes as there are integers, so there are not enough Programmes to solve all the problems. But we can also define explicit and useful problems which can't be solved.

Although defined theoretically, many of these classes have practical implications. For instance P is a very good approximation to the class of problems which can be solved quickly in practice — usually if this is true, we can prove a polynomial worst case time bound, and conversely the polynomial time bounds we can prove are usually small enough that the corresponding algorithms really are practical. NP-completeness theory is concerned with the distinction between the first two classes, P and NP.

EXAMPLES

Example 1: Long Simple Paths

A *simple path* in a graph is just one without any repeated edges or vertices. To describe the problem of finding long paths in terms of complexity theory, we need to formalize it as a yes-or-no question: given a graph G, vertices s and t, and a number k, does there exist a simple path from s to t with at least k edges? A solution to this problem would then consist of such a path.

Why is this in NP? If you're given a path, you can quickly look at it and add up the length, double-checking that it really is a path with length at least k. This can all be done in linear time, so certainly it can be done in polynomial time.

However we don't know whether this problem is in P; I haven't told you a good way for finding such a path (with time polynomial in m,n, and K). And in fact this problem is NP-complete, so we believe that no such algorithm exists.

There are algorithms that solve the problem; for instance, list all 2^m subsets of edges and check whether any of them solves the problem. But as far as we know there is no algorithm that runs in polynomial time.

Example 2: Cryptography

Suppose we have an encryption function e.g.

```
code=RSA(key,text)
```

The "RSA" encryption works by performing some simple integer arithmetic on the code and the key, which consists of a pair (p,q) of large prime numbers. One can perform the encryption only knowing the product pq; but to decrypt the code you instead need to know a different product, (p–1)(q–1).

A standard assumption in cryptography is the "known plaintext attack": we have the code for some message, and we know (or can guess) the text of that message. We want to use that information to discover the key, so we can decrypt other messages sent using the same key.

Formalized as an NP problem, we simply want to find a key for which code=RSA(key,text). If you're given a key, you can test it by doing the encryption yourself, so this is in NP.

The hard question is, how do you find the key? For the code to be strong we hope it isn't possible to do much better than a brute force search.

Another common use of RSA involves "public key cryptography": a user of the system publishes the product pq, but doesn't publish p, q, or (p-1)(q-1). That way anyone can send a message to that user by using the RSA encryption, but only the user can decrypt it. Breaking this scheme can also be thought of as a different NP problem: given a composite number pq, find a factorization into smaller numbers.

One can test a factorization quickly (just multiply the factors back together again), so the problem is in NP. Finding a factorization seems to be difficult, and we think it may not be in P. However there is some strong evidence that it is not NP-complete either; it seems to be one of the (very rare) examples of problems between P and NP-complete in difficulty.

Example 3: Chess

We've seen in the news recently a match between the world chess champion, Gary Kasparov, and a very fast chess computer, Deep Blue. The computer lost the match, but won one game and tied others.

What is involved in chess Programmeming? Essentially the sequences of possible moves form a tree: The first player has a choice of 20 different moves (most of which are not very good), after each of which the second player has a choice of many responses, and so on. Chess playing Programmes work by traversing this tree finding what the possible consequences would be of each different move.

The tree of moves is not very deep — a typical chess game might last 40 moves, and it is rare for one to reach 200 moves.

Since each move involves a step by each player, there are at most 400 positions involved in most games. If we traversed the tree of chess positions only to that depth, we would only need enough memory to store the 400 positions on a single path at a time. This much memory is easily available on the smallest computers you are likely to use.

So perfect chess playing is a problem in PSPACE. (Actually one must be more careful in definitions. There is only a finite number of positions in chess, so in principle you could write down the solution in constant time. But that constant would be very large. Generalized versions of chess on larger boards are in PSPACE.)

The reason this deep game-tree search method can't be used in practice is that the tree of moves is very bushy, so that even though it is not deep it has an enormous number of vertices. We won't run out of space if we try to traverse it, but we will run out of time before we get even a small fraction of the way through. Some pruning methods, notably"alpha-beta search" can help reduce the portion of the tree that needs to be examined, but not enough to solve this difficulty. For this reason, actual chess Programmes instead only search a much smaller depth (such as up to 7 moves), at which point they don't have enough information to evaluate the true consequences of the moves and are forced to guess by using heuristic"evaluation functions" that measure simple quantities such as the total number of pieces left.

Example 4: Knots

If I give you a three-dimensional polygon (e.g. as a sequence of vertex coordinate triples), is there some way of twisting and bending the polygon around until it becomes flat? Or is it knotted?

There is an algorithm for solving this problem, which is very complicated and has not really been adequately Analysed. However it runs in at least exponential time.

One way of proving that certain polygons are not knots is to find a collection of triangles forming a surface with the polygon as its boundary. However this is not always possible (without adding exponentially many new vertices) and even when possible it's NP-complete to find these triangles.

There are also some heuristics based on finding a non-Euclidean geometry for the space outside of a knot that work very well for many knots, but are not known to work for all knots. So this is one of the rare examples of a problem that can often be solved efficiently in practice even though it is theoretically not known to be in P.

Certain related problems in higher dimensions (is this four-dimensional surface equivalent to a four-dimensional sphere) are provably undecidable.

Example 5: Halting problem

Suppose you're working on a lab for a Programmeming class, have written your Programme, and start to run it. After five minutes, it is still going. Does this mean it's in an infinite loop, or is it just slow?

It would be convenient if your compiler could tell you that your Programme has an infinite loop. However this is an undecidable problem: there is no Programme that will always correctly detect infinite loops.

Some people have used this idea as evidence that people are inherently smarter than computers, since it shows that there are problems computers can't solve. However it's not clear to me that people can solve them either. Here's an example:

```
main()
{
int x = 3;
for (;;) {
for (int a = 1; a Ü x; a++)
      for (int b = 1; b Ü x; b++)
      for (int c = 1; c Ü x; c++)
            for (int i = 3; i Ü x; i++)
            if(pow(a,i) + pow(b,i) == pow(c,i))
            exit;
     ++;
```

```
}
}
```

This Programme searches for solutions to Fermat's last theorem. Does it halt? (You can assume I'm using a multiple-precision integer package instead of built in integers, so don't worry about arithmetic overflow complications.) To be able to answer this, you have to understand the recent proof of Fermat's last theorem. There are many similar problems for which no proof is known, so we are clueless whether the corresponding Programmes halt.

PROBLEMS OF COMPLEXITY THEORY

The most famous open problem in theoretical science is whether P = NP. In other words, if it's always easy to check a solution, should it also be easy to find the solution?

We have no reason to believe it should be true, so the expectation among most theoreticians is that it's false. But we also don't have a proof...

So we have this nice construction of complexity classes P and NP but we can't even say that there's one problem in NP and not in P. So what good is the theory if it can't tell us how hard any particular problem is to solve?

NP-COMPLETENESS

The theory of NP-completeness is a solution to the practical problem of applying complexity theory to individual problems. NP-complete problems are defined in a precise sense as the hardest problems in P. Even though we don't know whether there is any problem in NP that is not in P, we can point to an NP-complete problem and say that if there are any hard problems in NP, that problems is one of the hard ones.

Conversely if everything in NP is easy, those problems are easy. So NP-completeness can be thought of as a way of making the big P=NP question equivalent to smaller questions about the hardness of individual problems.

So if we believe that P and NP are unequal, and we prove that some problem is NP-complete, we should believe that it doesn't have a fast algorithm.

For unknown reasons, most problems we've looked at in NP turn out either to be in P or NP-complete. So the theory of NP-completeness turns out to be a good way of showing that a problem is likely to be hard, because it applies to a lot of problems. But there are problems that are in NP, not known to be in P, and not likely to be NP-complete; for instance the code-breaking example I gave earlier.

REDUCTION

Formally, NP-completeness is defined in terms of "reduction" which is just a complicated way of saying one problem is easier than another.

We say that A is easier than B, and write A < B, if we can write down an algorithm for solving A that uses a small number of calls to a subroutine for B (with everything outside the subroutine calls being fast, polynomial time).

There are several minor variations of this definition depending on the detailed meaning of "small" — it may be a polynomial number of calls, a fixed constant number, or just one call.

Then if A < B, and B is in P, so is A: we can write down a polynomial algorithm for A by expanding the subroutine calls to use the fast algorithm for B.

So "easier" in this context means that if one problem can be solved in polynomial time, so can the other. It is possible for the algorithms for A to be slower than those for B, even though A < B.

As an example, consider the Hamiltonian cycle problem. Does a given graph have a cycle visiting each vertex exactly once? Here's a solution, using longest path as a subroutine:

```
for each edge (u,v) of G
if there is a simple path of length n-1 from
u to v
    return yes// path + edge form a cycle
return no
```

This algorithm makes m calls to a longest path subroutine, and does O(m) work outside those subroutine calls, so it shows that Hamiltonian cycle < longest path. (It doesn't show that

Hamiltonian cycle is in P, because we don't know how to solve the longest path subproblems quickly.)

As a second example, consider a polynomial time problem such as the minimum spanning tree. Then for every other problem B, B < minimum spanning tree, since there is a fast algorithm for minimum spanning trees using a subroutine for B.

COOK'S THEOREM

We are now ready to formally define NP-completeness. We say that a problem A in NP is NP-complete when, for every other problem B in NP, B < A.

This seems like a very strong definition. After all, the notion of reduction we've defined above seems to imply that if B < A, then the two problems are very closely related; for instance Hamiltonian cycle and longest path are both about finding very similar structures in graphs. Why should there be a problem that closely related to all the different problems in NP?

Theorem: An NP-complete problem exists.

We prove this by example. One NP-complete problem can be found by modifying the halting problem (which without modification is undecidable).

Index